QUADRANGLE
CONSIDERATIONS

by

William J. Byron, S.J.

Loyola University Press
Chicago 60657

© 1989 William J. Byron, S.J.

Printed and bound in the United States of America

ISBN 0-8294-0630-1

Dedication

*For the Faculties
at Loyola/Baltimore, Loyola/New Orleans,
Scranton, and CUA*

Table of Contents

QUADRANGLE
CONSIDERATIONS

Introduction

These reflections relate to my own experience in the world of higher education. I have experienced that world as student, professor, dean, president, trustee, consultant, and as a member of a variety of committees, commissions, and task forces. Most of my experience is in the independent sector, although I did doctoral studies in a state university and taught there while writing my dissertation. I am, however, more familiar with and most at home in the Catholic college or university.

In collecting and presenting these thoughts as "Quadrangle Considerations," I may be surfacing an unconscious admission of my preference for the "square," the traditional back-to-basics, core-content, value-oriented education. I do indeed confess to that tendency; I would not attempt to disown that preference.

"Quadrangle," of course, conjures up the image of a college campus. That is where these reflections are rooted, although some look to the schooling preparatory to college, and others reach beyond the campus into areas of public policy.

I have in mind an audience not exclusively, but primarily, of faculty friends who benefit occasionally from an administrator's perspective on the world in which they work. More to the point, I write for faculty, because I hope for better of the higher education enterprise. This will not happen unless faculty members make it happen. I like to remind faculty that one need not be ill in order to get better. The effort to improve is certainly no admission of present inadequacy. In fact, improvement is most likely to happen where strength is already firmly positioned.

I also have trustees, regents, benefactors, and public policy makers in mind as I present the considerations contained in the following chapters. Trustees and regents are a good audience for a book like this, not simply because they can afford to buy it but because higher education in general, and independent higher education in particular, cannot afford not to have them well-informed and properly motivated for their indispensable role as partners in the enterprise. The importance of benefactors to the independent sector has long been evident; now it is commonly agreed that the public sector of higher education must look to private philanthropy for assistance on the road to excellence. Without wise public policy, both sectors of education at all levels will face frustration and dilution of potential for service to the community. I am hopeful that these reflections will prove helpful to policy makers as they work to meet their responsibilities toward education.

The reader will find relatedness but not tightly-reasoned continuity, chapter by chapter, throughout this book. That fact in itself speaks volumes about the range of tasks that fall to the academic administrator; it also illustrates the diversity of claims on the attention of the administrative mind. These reflections emerge from 20 years of on-the-job experience. That aside, most of what follows has appeared before in essay or lecture form. Most of that has been rewritten for the present purpose; several chapters appear here for the first time.

These essays are offered under five headings: Purpose, Values, Curriculum, Management, and Policy. Those blocks build the house in which the educational enterprise lives. And just as the road to success is usually found to be still under construction, it should surprise no one to find a need for some tucks and pointing on the walls of the house of intellect. The structures we have in place are, in the main, quite strong. I hope the reflections in this book will serve to stimulate other reflections in other minds, all intent on strengthening structured learning in the diverse schools, high and higher, in America.

I am grateful to Avery Dulles for reading portions of the manuscript, and to Rosemary Donley and Terrence Toland for reading it all. Sister Paul Gabriel, S.C., contributed valuable copy-editing. My executive assistant at The Catholic University of America, Margaret Proctor, and my secretary, Jane Gallagher, prepared the manuscript with characteristic generosity, efficiency, and cheerful competence. The help of all is much appreciated.

I am also grateful to the editors and lecture hosts whose invitations and cooperation encouraged me to transfer ideas from back-of-the-envelope outlines to manuscript, and eventually onto the printed page. I hope this book will prove useful to people who care about the future of education in America.

W. J. B.

Washington, D.C., Autumn, 1989
The centenary of the first roll call at
The Catholic University of America

Part I
Purpose and Identity

1 Maintaining Diversity

No one can think about the future of Catholic colleges and universities in the United States without considering the future of higher education's independent sector as a whole in this country. That sector is an American treasure. It could become an endangered species in the groves of academe if independent educators lose heart and citizens at large lose interest. At issue is a question of freedom.

Freedom is the fragile foundation of independent higher education. Freedom is also the firm footing of the academic enterprise. Fragile and firm, foundation and footing — freedom is the ultimate explanation of independent higher education's very reason for existence.

Students freely choose to enroll in independent colleges and universities. If all students chose state-supported schools, the independents would still have a reason for existence but no opportunity to pursue their purpose.

Benefactors freely choose to support independent higher education. If contributors chose not to give, the colleges and universities would shrivel and die. Freedom is their fragile foundation.

Structural support for independent higher education stretches quite simply from freedom to freedom — free choices to enroll, free choices to contribute.

Freedom is, moreover, the atmosphere within which professors teach, do research, and communicate the results of their free inquiry. In an environment of free inquiry, both investigation and instruction are ultimately limited only by the bounds of truth itself, although other limits, discussed later in this book, can come into play.

It is in the interest of a nation that values freedom, and finds its own identity in a declaration of independence, to foster the growth of independent higher education.

Similarly, it is in the interest of the nation's independent businesses and professions to promote the vitality of independent higher education, without which the vitality of business and the professions would be correspondingly diminished.

Every American and all areas of American life, including government and government-supported education, benefit from the work of America's institutions of independent higher learning. The case for pluralism, creativity, and progress in America cannot be made without reference to independent higher education.

But now it is time in American history to make the case for independent higher education itself. It is a case I intend to make in four statements that would speak, in turn, of the research university, the liberal arts college, the church-related institution, and the urban university or "university college" — the student-oriented, career-focused independent institution that meets both city and citizen where they are, in hopes of improving the quality of life for both. And it is a case that speaks simultaneously to the potential student, the potential supporter, and to the men and women of government. All who cherish freedom will be sympathetic to this argument, I hope; I also hope that those who are convinced by this case will do what they can to convince others in the policy debates that nourish political will in America.

This four-sided case would amount, in these days of a "flattening out" in American ideas, values, and culture, to a case for pluralism itself. There is no better place for the preservation of pluralism in America than in its higher education community. Without strong independent research universities, liberal arts colleges, church-related institutions, and independent urban universities, America would suffer a diminution of quality,

2

innovation, and freedom. It would also witness an abandonment of tradition. The nation would experience a loss of memory. The people would be less free because they would be less different in those deep-down values which make national unity possible while safeguarding it from uniformity. It is only out of significant differences that real unity can be achieved; it is only out of lost differences that uniformity can be produced. Uniformity is not an environment conducive to creativity. Such an environment permits, even encourages, one mind to do all the thinking.

The quality of American life is enriched by the cultural pluralism which is not simply tolerated but encouraged by freedom of worship, freedom of speech, freedom of assembly, and the other freedoms whose exercise produces the cultural diversity which makes America unique. Pluralism within the higher education community protects pluralism within the national culture.

The fact of the matter is simply this: without independent higher education, diversity would diminish and cultural impoverishment would ensue. Hence this "quadrangle case" for the preservation of freedom and pluralism through independent higher education.

Side One: The Case for the Independent Research University.

The academy is virtually the only place in America where free inquiry goes on without regard to political advantage or to commercial-financial reward. Research is really not the purpose of government, nor is it the purpose of business. It is, however, along with teaching and the preparation of scholars, the purpose of the research university. Formal, persistent, professional pursuit of new and better understandings of all things real is the reason for existence of the research university.

What is special, and thus worth preserving, about the independent research university? Free inquiry is central to the research enterprise. Free communication of research results is essential, if the common good is to be served by the research enterprise. The university that stands free of state, political, corporate, or commercial control is, to that extent, more likely to

3

guarantee to its scholarly investigators freedom of inquiry and freedom of communication of their research results.

Since freedom is the most precious and fragile element in all the values that constitute the American heritage, the preservation of the independent research university relates directly to the preservation of the American heritage.

Any research project begins with a question. If certain valid human questions are politically inopportune or constitutionally inappropriate, they will not be asked in government-supported research universities. If questions of human value are unrelated to corporate profit, it is unlikely that they will be researched in corporate settings.

Questions of interest to business and government, however, are researched in independent universities. Such questions receive there a fuller exploration than would be possible in settings where ethical, political, historical, and the broadest possible cultural consideration is impossible because of the absence of some of the disciplines and, in some cases, the interests that are typically present in the independent research university. The independent, church-related research universities are not without their problems in protecting freedom of inquiry. The question of ecclesial limits on academic freedom will be discussed in chapter 4. The point to be made here at the outset is that a balanced mix of universities of different sponsorship guarantees that all valid research questions will be pursued.

The case for the independent research university must, of course, attend to the issue of competence — a question of quality. This is not to suggest the absence of quality and competence in the state-supported research universities. Evidence to the contrary is abundant and clear. The point, however, must be made that a longer tradition of quality and competence in research resides in the independent sector of higher education. Moreover, a greater concentration of high-quality research results, on a wider range of research interests, can be found in independent research universities than can be found elsewhere.

No nation can afford to permit its values to go unexamined for an undue length of time. A reaffirmation of the value of research, and of independent research universities, is long overdue in America. It is in the setting of the independent research university that the core value in American life — freedom — is most likely to receive the attention and respect it deserves.

Side Two: The Case for the Independent Liberal Arts College.

Human life is a precious gift, wonderful in all its dimensions and, by almost any measure, all too short in length. The human mind is marvelous, but all too limited in the face of all there is to know, to experience, to discover. What is best in human thought, experience, and discovery is the content of a liberal arts education.

The liberal arts college, with regard for the relative brevity of our learning time and respect for the limits of the mind's capacity to absorb the best of human thought, experience, and discovery, presents a program of study which spells out the meaning of the word "significant."

Knowledge of great events and discoveries in human history, along with reflection on the best ideas, and exposure to the best images and forms to emerge from human creativity, will have the good educational result of cultivating in the student an appreciation of the significant. One liberal arts educator was fond of reminding his students that "the fool collects, the wise person chooses." Good liberal arts education is an antidote to foolishness, a preparation for the practice of discernment and choice. It is much more than mere training. It prepares people for the exercise of principled judgment for the rest of their lives.

In a time of bewildering change, of accelerated advances in knowledge, and of enormous technological possibilities for both service and assault to the human person, wise choices must be made at all levels of human existence. Insignificant gadgets, diversions, and issues can displace deeper values and distract the American mind from choosing wisely. It is the unreflective person who leads the unexamined life and, as a consequence, almost always chooses unwisely. The liberal arts college fosters reflection. Considering the destructive consequences of unwise

5

choices at all levels of human existence, it is difficult to think of anything more practical than reflection on ideas, images, and experiences promoted by the liberal arts college.

But liberal arts colleges today are concerned that there will be a withdrawal of support from either or both sides of the dual structure that upholds them — students choosing to enroll, benefactors choosing to provide financial assistance; not to mention diminishing federal support for student aid. Growing numbers in a declining pool of college-bound students focus exclusively on career outcomes, while ignoring the formative value of the liberal arts. Contributors to higher education look more to the support of technical, scientific, and technological education where the return on investment is anticipated to take the immediate form of a stronger national economy or a stronger national defense. They tend not to notice that our best line of defense, more important by far, is a wise population. They also fail to notice that a technologically superior economy can become a dangerous tool when used as a means to pursue carelessly chosen ends.

If we look at our nation and our young and agree that "a mind is a terrible thing to waste," we will surely also agree on the terrible national loss incurred when we deprive the mind of the full stretch of the liberal arts.

With few exceptions, women's colleges are in the liberal arts tradition and in the independent sector. For several generations many women have found greater opportunity for personal development and the exercise of leadership in single-sex colleges. As opportunities for female students open up in previously all-male academic preserves, there will remain a national need for the college that defines itself in service to women and locates itself in the great liberal arts tradition.

The courageous colleges that stake their sole reason for existence, as well as their identity, on the liberal arts are, inevitably, independent. Within larger state-supported academic communities there are offerings in the liberal arts of high quality and great value. But only in the independent sector will one find the free-standing liberal arts college where the scale, style, values,

6

and identity of the academic community itself attest to the significance of the liberal arts. Without such centers of learning, the nation would quite literally lose its memory, the higher education community would be inexcusably incomplete, and the people and their leaders would be seriously impaired in their capacity to choose wisely.

Side Three: The Case for the Independent Church-Related Institution.

In the United States, it is redundant to speak of the independent, church-related institution. Under our Constitution, the state may not "establish" a church or a church-related college. Any church-related college or university in the United States is, by definition and by law, independent of state sponsorship. But the same First Amendment that provides the "non-establishment" clause in our Constitution also includes the "free exercise" clause, which attaches a Constitutional guarantee to every citizen's right to religious freedom. Without church-related colleges and universities, there would be no sure place in American higher education for academic reflection, research, and communication of revealed truth; there would be no place for the integration of religious practice into the rest of the life of an academic community. There would thus be no academic protection of another core value in the American heritage.

Religious centers like Hillel and Newman are indeed present but peripheral to the state and secular institutions of higher learning. Presence on the periphery makes a statement about the relative importance of religion and revelation to the life of the mind. Only the church-related college or university makes an affirmative institutional statement about the centrality of revealed religion to the full human life and then translates that statement into all areas of institutional life. Church-related higher education provides a conscious opening to the transcendent in all its research, instruction, and community life. On Catholic campuses, "campus ministry" is the usual designation given to the office which attends to serving the pastoral needs of the campus

7

community. Chapter 9 will outline in some detail my thoughts on campus ministry.

The non-establishment clause places a burden on church-related colleges and universities by limiting somewhat their access to state and federal funds. These colleges and universities, however, return a benefit to the nation by providing, among other things, an academic preserve for religion in America.

The typical denominational college is really more faith-committed than church-related. Central to all it does is a respect for faith as it daily demonstrates in classroom, laboratory, and library the compatibility of faith and reason. Faith-commitment in no way requires an abandonment of intellect. On the contrary, intellectual investigations without an opening to the transcendent and without a provision for a faith dimension fall short of realizing the full potential of the human mind. To put it another way, the completely secular education is an incomplete education.

It is probably more accurate to say "faith-committed" than "church-related" in describing the religiously-oriented college or university, because academic freedom is a controlling principle in virtually all of them. Ecclesiastical, hierarchical, denominational influence is present; but influence is not equal to control. Church bodies provide some financial support, in some cases significant financial support. But most church-related colleges and universities are juridically independent of ecclesiastical, hierarchical, and denominational control. Most are chartered by the state, controlled by independent, self-perpetuating boards of trustees, and conducted in harmony with the principles of institutional autonomy and academic freedom. They embody within themselves and communicate to their students the wealth of religious tradition handed on in theology, history, literature, and ritual by faith communities from antiquity to the present day. And their students are challenged to discover ways of applying that tradition to present-day problems while constructing a vision that will help them cope with the problems of tomorrow.

The very existence of church-related colleges and universities in our day constitutes a strong case for their continued existence through all the tomorrows of American higher education.

Side Four: The Case for the Urban University.

Difficult to define, but occupying an important place on the spectrum between the liberal arts college and the research-intensive university, is the "urban university." Sometimes called "university college" or "metroversity," this type of independent institution defines itself in terms of educational service to the city and its citizens. It offers higher education, of course; but the education it offers is often quite practical and unapologetically career-oriented. Its research interests are typically focused on urban problems. Its community service sometimes crosses educational boundaries to include social and other human services. Its campus is hospitable to the non-traditional student. Its services reach out to the poor and disadvantaged.

Just as education in general is a condition for the national welfare, so higher education in service to the city is a precondition of urban progress.

Words like policy, polite, politics, and police all derive from the Greek "polis," the city. They help to outline the range of reality that constitutes the education-and-training agenda of the urban university.

Urban economics, urban sociology, urban mass transportation, urban planning — all find a congenial setting in a university dedicated to service of the city. Examples of courses and concentrations could be multiplied, but the point is already plain. There is a natural partnership — a relationship of reciprocal influence and mutual dependency — between the urban community and the urban university, between the city and the university college in service to its citizens.

To the extent that we are a "nation of cities," our strength as a nation depends on the strength of our urban universities.

It is beyond dispute that the urban environment has the potential to enlarge or diminish the human person. The urban university can foster the life-enlarging and spirit-expanding impact of good education while equipping the student with practical skills that provide access to productive positions in the urban economy. Both city and citizen are, as a result, better off. The urban university encourages and enables both to "choose life." Like all institutions of independent higher education, the urban university walks a taut high-wire that stretches from freedom to freedom. Unlike some of the research universities and liberal arts colleges, however, the urban university ordinarily has no safety net, no deep endowment to provide supplemental operating income. Free decisions to enroll and pay tuition, free decisions to contribute financial support — decisions made individually, annually, and often unpredictably — are the fragile foundation upon which the security of the independent urban university rests.

Federal and state grants and loans to students are indispensable. The case for the urban university is in itself a special case for the maintenance of student financial aid.

City and county grants of property-tax exemption to the urban university are not only important but totally justifiable in terms of more-than-offsetting returns to the civic community and local economy. In many urban areas, higher education has become a dominant industry. But it is also a non-profit industry and thus incapable of meeting the levies that local governments seem daily more anxious to impose.

Federal, state, and local governments' purchases of research and educational services at full cost (i.e., at prices that cover actual expenses including overhead) are necessary and useful sources of income for urban universities; sources, it should be noted, that are perfectly consistent with this kind of institution's reason for existence.

The case for the urban university is inextricably part of the case for the city in America. Hence the case for the university must be made anew in this period of crisis for the American city. Some will ask whether the universities are at fault for permitting the decay of urban infrastructure and the decline of urban life. No university would deny responsibility although none could, in truth, hold itself guilty. All, however, would, with full faith in their ability to enhance the quality of urban life, plead for a place in the present effort to meet the challenge of the city. Gaining that place is not difficult. The universities are already there. Holding that place is another matter.

Money alone, important as a secure flow of operating income is, will not guarantee the survival of the urban university. With the dollars, there must also come the reinforcement of prestige. Only persons can provide prestige — persons like alumni who have benefitted directly from what the urban university offered in the past, persons like civic leaders who recognize the worth of the enterprise to the city and its citizens, persons with an eye for value who can identify the elements of quality that are present and help the institution to fashion an image that accurately reflects those elements of quality. The case for the urban university, no less than the case for the small college or the research-intensive university, is, at bottom, a case for quality. Because they do not possess the "right name" or own sufficient acres of greenspace and brickwalk, urban universities are often overlooked by those who measure quality by breadth of campus and height of gothic tower.

The case for the independent urban university is particularly dependent on those people whose lives and communities are better because the school was there to serve them. These beneficiaries are best able to reflect credit on their institution. Their loyalty and gratitude are best expressed when they encourage someone else to enroll there (best of all, their own sons and daughters), when they donate dollars, and when they speak well of the place in the broader community. If enough people in the urban community do these things, the entire community, and others not nearby, will notice. The institution will enjoy prestige — the recognition it deserves for the excellence it has achieved.

The quality is there. And so is the best hope for the future of the city.

And so it is with independent higher education in general. The quality is there. Not at the expense of the quality that is also present in the public sector. Nor is quality among the independents at some absolute level which cannot be improved upon. But the quality already there and the human scale of the typical independent operation invite support from all who care about the life of the American mind and the preservation of America's core values.

When I attended an independent college on the G.I. Bill of Rights after World War II, enrollment in higher education in America was evenly divided between the two sectors. Today the publicly supported colleges and universities enroll 80 percent of the students while the independents enroll only 20 percent. That just about puts the independent sector in the category of an endangered species. It is time for private citizens who care, and for elected officials — and their appointees — who are sworn to preserve the values independent colleges and universities live on, to make absolutely sure that the sector does not die. Private gifts and public subsidies are indispensable. Federal student aid must show sufficient tuition sensitivity so that an independent college is a real option for a low-income student. Indeed Federal student aid should be radically restructured if the choice of an independent college is to remain a viable option. My proposal for the needed restructuring is offered in chapter 23.

Public policy measures that trim the Federal deficit at the expense of independent higher education will not, of themselves, balance the Federal budget. They will, however, further threaten the already fragile foundations upon which the independent sector rests. That, in my judgment, cannot be anything but bad for the land of the free and the home of the largest and most vibrant set of independent colleges and universities to be found anywhere in the world.

2 Teaching and Research

It would be a serious mistake to leave research to the research universities. Liberal arts colleges, urban universities, and most other colleges support research and expect scholarly productivity of their faculty, just as research universities expect excellent teaching of theirs. In fact, the two belong together. The higher education enterprise is enhanced to the extent that its professors connect themselves to research activity.

The songwriter who reminded a generation of Americans that "love and marriage" go together "like a horse and carriage" could make a great cultural contribution today by coming up with a persuasive musical argument about the connection between teaching and research. "Research and Teaching" — repeat — "Research and Teaching" — belong together. If rhyme or reason, or both, could produce a musical couplet capable of convincing all educators and policy makers of the connectedness, the reciprocal influence, the working partnership between research and teaching, the higher education enterprise would be all the stronger as a result.

On campuses across the country it is evident that not every good teacher is an able researcher; not every effective researcher is also a stimulating teacher. Yet basic teaching and research abilities should be resident in every professional who is a classroom professor or an in-laboratory or in-library investigator anywhere in higher education. It is important to keep teaching and research in the same harness. Most faculties have the "horses" but most of them carry excessively heavy teaching loads while enjoying insufficient research support — funding, facilities, and student (particularly graduate student) assistance. Most libraries need improvement and most computer centers are not yet strong enough to satisfy all research needs of all the faculty. But that is no excuse for any faculty member to abandon research.

Division of labor between discovery and the communication of research-results can be encouraged in research universities but never permitted to become absolute. The two functions should never be separated completely one from the other. There are levels of intensity in research which tend to correlate negatively with the time the investigator has available to devote to classroom teaching. But no one belongs in a college classroom as professor on a full-time basis, even with an exclusively undergraduate instructional responsibility, who is not also an active researcher. Full-time undergraduate teachers have research time available to them, just less of it. The question is: What importance do they attach to the use of that time?

Similarly, full time researchers on any university campus have time for teaching, if only in small seminars or occasional lectures. University researchers are expected, like all academic professionals, to be able oral and written communicators. The best academic researchers should also stand out for their ability to organize and clarify their findings and communicate them effectively, even persuasively, in a stimulating style to an academic audience. That is one of the best ways we have to attract and motivate the next generation of academic researchers.

Teachers, anywhere, as part of their professional responsibility, should always be exploring new questions, opening new lines of disciplined and interdisciplinary inquiry, and maintaining, through the reading of professional journals and attendance at professional meetings, contact with research developments. The classroom professor, as Alfred North Whitehead remarked with no desire at all to demean the profession, "is an ignorant man thinking." If he were around today to repeat the remark,

14

Whitehead would surely say that the professor "is an ignorant man or woman thinking," and he would regard the comment as an admiring portrayal of the central figure in a noble occupation who attends to that ignorance by thinking, by life-long learning, by self-propelled intellectual inquiry — now in original research, now assimilating the results of the research of others — always attentive to a personal and professional responsibility to never stop learning.

Here, as I see them, are the levels of research observable today in American higher education.

I like to think of research as the discovery of new understandings. If the discovery is absolutely new, in the sense that no one has grasped that understanding before, I would call it *original* research. If the discovery is new for a given researcher and nuanced by that person to broaden or update an older understanding, I would call it *derivative* research. Finally, if a discovery in one's sphere of knowledge, say, chemistry, can be joined to a discovery in another sphere, say, economics, and then in combination the two generate a new understanding of an old problem, I would call that *conjunctive* research.

The traditional categories of "basic" and "applied" research are, of course, both valid and useful for any discussion of this topic. The problem that I have with those categories, however, is that "basic research" tends to be associated in the popular mind with high-powered, generously funded centers in government, isolated institutes, or research-oriented universities. And "applied research" is sometimes thought of as the exclusive province of off-campus industrial laboratories or overseas field experiment stations. Neither basic nor applied research should, in my view, be defined so narrowly as to foreclose participation on the part of the academic professional whose primary identity is associated with the classroom. Such a person will, however, be more likely to participate in what I have called derivative or conjunctive research. The point is that some ongoing research activity is part of any faculty member's professional responsibility.

There are, by contrast, also observable in the academy, levels of teaching that differ in terms of time expended and extent of direct student contact. Most noticeable is the large undergraduate lecture class. The professor there exercises a performing art.

Organization of the teaching-learning transaction in classes of any size and courses of any description is primarily the professor's responsibility. So, too, is the selection of course materials. Clear and stimulating presentation is expected in any instructional setting, but especially in the large lecture hall which calls, quite literally, for a platform performance by the teaching professional. These professors also become blue-book "weight-lifters" at semester's end. Only they can describe the joys of correcting the large volume of exam papers and term papers that are part of the classroom professor's life.

Smaller classes and roundtable seminar-style presentations require a vital professional presence, but the mode is more conversational than oratorical. More is expected by way of student participation in such settings. In order to elicit that participation, the professor must possess enabling skills — the ability to question without intimidating, to facilitate and not manipulate student responses. No student anywhere in American higher education should be a stranger to lively seminars.

At the smallest scale, the teaching-learning transaction embodies the spirit of what United States president James A. Garfield is reputed to have said about one of his former professors: "The ideal college is Mark Hopkins on one end of a log and a student on the other." In the 1960's, some college professors would have revised that remark to have the mentor sitting on the student and talking to the log. But times have changed.

The one-on-one exchanges are precious moments in the learning experience. Colleges typically try to guarantee that such exchanges will happen by requiring posted office hours of all faculty and hoping that students will pass frequently through those open office doors. Most faculty take office hours seriously. Most are within reach when students need them. And most give solid academic advice. The problem, however, is convincing

16

students to pass through that open office door early and often every semester.

Thesis and dissertation direction relies on the person-to-person instructural mode which offers, better than any other, the opportunity to encourage the learner. Learners at all levels need constant encouragement; curiously, our grading systems at all levels are designed to "mark them down." The professor has to be resourceful and persistent in building them up. This is more easily done in smaller interpersonal instructional settings.

In any teaching situation, the professor will be livelier and, by definition, have more to say, if he or she is an active researcher. Familiarity with the research of others will serve the same energizing purpose for the educational process. Publication by the classroom teacher of his or her own research results, even in more popular magazines and newspaper opinion pieces, will enhance the professor's authority in the student eye, if not in the judgment of the rank-and-tenure committee. But student opinion is important and rank-and-tenure requirements can be met through sabbatical research and other scholarly efforts.

Technology now permits teaching by cassette — audio or video — as well as interactive televised instruction. Always possible, to both teacher and researcher, is employment of the printed word to communicate ideas to absent audiences. Professors are often in print. But one need not be professionally committed to life within the academy to produce books, journal- or magazine-articles capable of helping others learn. Publication often takes place beyond the borders of academe in other places of intellectual activity where there may or may not exist the community of scholars, both teachers and learners, that the university is uniquely designed to attract and hold. Hence the importance of interaction between teachers and researchers within the academy, on a given campus. Hence the desirability of pervasive research and extended instruction throughout a university. Otherwise, the university will see activity once regarded as its exclusive domain drift away. That activity will migrate toward government and commercial laboratories; to independent institutes more focused on policy, more driven by ideology, and less concerned perhaps with history than the university would be.

Catholic universities are, of course, concerned with history, committed to values, and working hard to represent the Church in the front ranks of American higher education. Pope John Paul II has remarked that Catholic colleges and universities should help "to make the Church's presence felt in the world of culture and science." Any college or university intent upon meeting that challenge must keep research and teaching in harness.

Keeping research and teaching together on any campus is a faculty responsibility which can be met with remarkable results despite heavy teaching loads and slim research support. It is also an administrative responsibility. Administrators have to find the funds to support faculty research more generously. Administrators and faculty both are responsible for intensifying the institutional commitment to research while maintaining the vitality and quality of classroom instruction. Research and teaching belong together for the benefit of all who are attracted to the campus, as well as for the well-being of all the off-campus constituencies the institution exists to serve.

3 Catholic Identity

There is no avoiding the alliterative accent of the words "Catholic College." Further alliteration is unavoidable in any effort to unpack that phrase and identify the central elements of a college that is Catholic. Two such elements would be commitment and community.

Commitment can and does create a Catholic college. A Catholic college is a learning community, a climate of inquiry which acknowledges without apology the compatibility of faith and reason. Such an academic community locates itself in relation to the transcendental — not simply to a transcendental idea but to Someone who transcends the limits of time and space, to Someone who created us and our material universe, to Someone who stepped decisively into our human history and opened, for all who believe, a way to become more fully free, human, and eternally secure.

To be Catholic means, first of all, that the college is committed to the person and gospel of Jesus Christ as the primary source of values and attitudes that are reflected in the campus culture and thus characteristic of the campus community. Chief among these values is faith. Hence, a Catholic college is faith-committed. In any college, faith is a value to be respected. In a Catholic college, faith is a value to be freely accepted and lived. Quite literally, a Catholic community is a *con-fident* community, not arrogant but humbly confident, entrusting itself individually and collectively to the triune God who is the all-powerful source of everything good, true, and beautiful.

A minimal expectation of any collegiate community, Catholic or not, is a common commitment to truth. Hence, open inquiry in the Catholic collegiate community is not unusual and certainly not a threat. In any Catholic college, special care must be taken not to substitute authority for thought. The college would violate its trust if it failed to foster in its students a critical sense. An authoritarian college quenches the wick in the lamp of learning.

Truth itself is both norm and goal of the continuing quest which is the Catholic college. There is no truth which can be labeled inappropriate or inadmissible in a Catholic college, where the search for truth is conducted within the structured disciplines and forms of creativity that belong in any authentic academic setting.

We who inhabit the various Catholic academic communities are part of a larger worldwide community that appears to be moving, by God's will, toward a religious lifestyle that prefers to be more quietly Catholic on the way to becoming more completely Christian. This historical process has generated problems of uncertainty, ambiguity, and misunderstanding in the Catholic world. These problems are particularly troublesome to the Catholic college which, by its very nature, guides a quest for certainty and cultivates both clarity and understanding as the very atmosphere of the learning environment.

The commitment that creates a Catholic college is a commitment to the person and gospel of Jesus Christ and to truth in every form. That college-creating commitment must, moreover, extend to the community which is the Church; thus, the college is Church-related. This does not mean "owned and operated" by the Church through a diocesan structure or in the person of the bishop. But there is a special relationship to the local bishop of the area where those who inhabit a particular Catholic academic community gather to teach and learn. The bishop, ordained to be teacher and pastor of his people, is not a member of the college faculty nor an administrator of the academic enterprise. Ideally, the relationship between the bishop and the Catholic college located within his area of ecclesiastical jurisdiction is one of mutual affection and respect, of mutual service and support, and of reciprocity in the roles of teacher and learner. Both college and bishop must learn in order to teach. The college has much to learn from the bishop; the bishop has much to learn from the college. In this reciprocal relationship, each must retain an appropriate freedom, each must recognize the other's responsibilities in fidelity to the gospel mandate to "teach all nations" (Mt. 28:19) a "truth (which) shall make you free" (Jn. 8:32).

The modern Catholic college in America is typically chartered by the state and "owned and operated" by an independent board of trustees. In some cases a religious community like the Christian Brothers, the Sisters of Mercy, the Congregation of the Holy Cross, or the Jesuits, or Benedictines, or Franciscans will provide an identifiable tradition and a core group of religious faculty and administrators to give the enterprise a distinctive character. The particular religious spirit, different in the case of each religious community, is present in the college only to the extent that it is embodied in the members of the religious community who work there and who share their spirit with willing lay colleagues. Hence, the importance of religious-lay colleagueship. Hence, the importance of attracting and retaining an effective religious community-presence in the academic enterprise. And hence, the importance of selecting for leadership in the enterprise a person who embodies the tradition of the community as well as the experience and credentials normally associated with positions of academic leadership. The Catholic style of academic leadership should be patterned, not surprisingly, on the mission of the founder of Christianity who came "not to be served, but to serve, and to give his life as a ransom for many" (Mk. 10:45). According to this pattern, authority resides in a leader, not a ruler, in one who makes himself or herself in Dennis Goulet's words "available, accountable, and vulnerable" in imitation of the Person upon whom the identity of the enterprise ultimately rests.

I know that I offend no honest academician when I say that these reflections must move now from rhetoric (although there is nothing wrong with rhetoric) to plainer speech more directly descriptive of reality. It is helpful, indeed necessary from time to time, to rehearse the rhetoric of Catholic collegiality in a community of faith-committed teachers and learners. But the reality often mirrors a divided community. The reality often reflects deep misunderstandings and distrust. It is not surprising to find evidence of ignorance of the religious tradition which launched the college in members of the present-day college community. On many Catholic college campuses there are indications that materialism is gaining ground at the expense of the fundamental faith-commitment. There is evidence that essential gospel values remain distant and counter-cultural and are not, in fact, widely shared. One wonders at times in the midst of a faith-committed academic community whether there is anything fully and freely shared.

This is not at all to suggest that uniformity makes a college Catholic. It would not be a good thing to have an all-Catholic board, an all-Catholic administration, faculty, staff and student body. Diversity makes good boards, good faculties, good collegiate communities. Diversity in an atmosphere of free inquiry is essential for a good Catholic college. And the unity, not the uniformity but the unity, that can emerge from such diversity is a sign, an ecumenically hopeful sign, that free and thinking human beings can become one people under God. The good Catholic college can bear witness to this promise, to this hope. But even the very best Catholic college falls short of this great goal.

In all of this I am stating nothing beyond the obvious fact that there is no completely Catholic college; there is no perfect academic community. Why then do so many of us think that the enterprise is still worth our while? Why do we stay in there?

We stay in there because we agree, I suspect, with Henri DeLubac's view that "To differ, even deeply, one from another, is not to be enemies: it is simply to be. To recognize and accept one's own difference is not pride. To recognize and accept the difference of others is not weakness. If union has to be, if union offers any meaning at all, it must be union between different people. And it is above all in the recognition and acceptance of difference that difference is overcome and union achieved" (*Further Paradoxes*, Longmans, Green, 1958). We stay in there, because we believe that human unity is possible and that what we do will help to bring it about.

We remain committed to the Catholic collegiate enterprise because we believe that Jesus Christ was and is true God and true man. We are convinced that education without Him is incomplete. We are further convinced that because God freely chose to become human, all things human are, as a result, infinitely more special and more meaningful. When God took on our flesh, the human became the locus of divine activity in an altogether new and unique way. If the academic enterprise ignores this reality, if inquiry into the arts and sciences, the humanities and technologies, prescinds from this pivotal truth — not denies it, just prescinds from it — then, we maintain, truth itself will be less fully comprehended and human potential less fully realized.

We state our position humbly, because we recognize that there are not many truly great Catholic colleges and universities in this country. But we stay in there because we — those of us who work in our Catholic institutions of higher education — we have seen wonders worked on our campuses, wonders in the development of human potential, wonders in the discovery of self, wonders in the discovery of truth, wonders in the discovery of God. And we see solid evidence of qualitative progress continuing on all these fronts.

It is all God's work, we believe, just as we believe that what we do is most authentically human, reasonable, and respectful of human freedom.

Without Catholic colleges, and without other faith-committed institutions of higher learning in the other religious traditions, those of us who treasure the gift of faith, and the vocation to teach and search out the truth in all things human, would be prevented from the full exercise of our freedom and the full development of our potential. And those who choose to come to us for an education would be similarly prevented. That is why we stay in there.

Others stay in there too. Lutherans, Baptists, Mennonites, Methodists, and many others sponsor their faith-committed and church-related educational enterprises. In all of these institutions there is a discernible identity and purpose.

The university movement owes its very origins to the Church. In this country, the rich diversity of Church-college relationships is one of the glories and strengths of our higher education system. Despite episodes of anti-intellectualism in some periods of various denominational histories, the Church has found that it needs the university as the safeguard and the proof of the compatibility of faith and reason. Moreover, the university needs the Church for its own integrity.

Like so many others who have committed themselves to Church-related higher education, I find myself wondering, from time to time, about my personal mission and purpose within the larger mission and purpose of a university whose reason for existence rests on a foundation of faith.

There are many ways to live out a personal faith commitment. There are many styles of service to the community of faith which is the Church. Church-related higher education is just one of many ways. And even when that one way is chosen, the service of faith can find expression in teaching, or scholarship, or trusteeship, or the ministry we refer to as administration. Whatever the mode of expression, the ministry exercised in higher education is a vocation within a vocation. It liberates us who choose it to lead the life of the mind. It puts us not in control of but in contact with the sources of truth. It puts us not in charge of but in touch with the young. They, as everyone agrees, are our hope for the future. With them, we are on the growing edge of the Church in the world. For them, we work in the development of their own human potential. And we pray that God may shape them into men and women of lasting faith. Prayer is an integral part of the work we do.

I am convinced that the Church-related college or university is the place where the Church should do a substantial amount of its thinking. I said "thinking," not "training." There is a difference. Even if you agree on a theoretical level that the Church should do its thinking in the university, you will be hard pressed to produce much evidence that this in fact happens with great frequency or effectiveness in the United States.

I also think that the university is the best if not the only place the Church has to meet its young in a spirit of open inquiry on solid intellectual grounds bordered only by a full range of academic disciplines designed to guide the development of. human understanding. In such a setting faith has nothing to fear.

The young are such a precious resource to the Church, too precious to risk losing through disinterest or detachment of the Church from the university. When that detachment occurs, it almost inevitably follows that the full range of academic disciplines is diminished by the loss of theology done in a clear ecclesial tradition. The ecclesial accent is lost along other avenues of inquiry also — history, to name but one. And both the identity and vitality that should characterize campus ministry fade a bit and are sometimes lost.

The university-related Church (to borrow the delightful turn of phrase the Methodists have used) should, in my view, take more seriously the opportunity it has not just to think but to celebrate in campus settings. The students have something to teach us on this point. The most sure- and light-footed among them will not attempt new dance steps in the center of the ballroom floor or the disco deck. They try them first at home. Why should not the Church feel sufficiently "at home" in the campus chapel to explore with the young, and those who serve them pastorally, new modes of celebrating their redemption or, more precisely, new integrations of word, music, art, and ritual to surround their earthbound (and therefore time-conditioned) celebration of the "new and eternal covenant" God has made with them?

We who spend our working lives in universities and colleges related to the Church should pause on occasion to remind ourselves that the Church we serve exists for no other purpose than to bring people to God. Hence, exploration into God and into every dimension of His creation is what is expected of Church-related higher education. This God, who creates and draws us to

25

Himself, is infinite in all His attributes. And since we attribute to Him power, truth, love, beauty, justice, mercy, wisdom, and so much more, we should permit ourselves occasionally to be astounded by the scale and sweep of our educational agenda. We view ourselves, moreover, as related to the Church of Christ, and thereby consciously include on our educational agenda a special interest in understanding all things human because the human became, in Christ, the locus of divine activity.

It is, therefore, not surprising that human and societal issues will be under examination in our Church-related colleges and universities. I'll list a few. Hunger, racism, global awareness — all of these belong on our agenda, as does the special pedagogical problem of integrating value considerations into the curriculum of the Church-related college. We must also be concerned with peace studies (even if the denomination to which the college relates is not a so-called "peace church"), family studies, unemployment, inflation, and energy, with problems of the cities and of the less developed countries. Social issues belong on our educational agenda. Why? Because we are related to a Church which is incarnational at its very foundation. It is neither boastful nor blind to assert, as we must when we are honest with ourselves, that society's future depends on what we do and how well we do it.

In these days Church-related educators have to address the questions of our practical viability in the face of complicated legal issues, vexing financial issues, and the challenges ahead in the area of public policy. We also have work to do on the "vision" questions of purpose and identity as well as future forms of Church-relatedness. In all of these categories I have deep personal concerns, as does every other president in Church-related higher education.

It should neither surprise nor scandalize any of us, particularly those of us charged with the administration of Church-related higher education, to recognize that discouragement afflicts us from time to time. We know our failures; we are aware of our weaknesses. In our pessimistic or even cynical moments, we come close to convincing ourselves that most of Thoreau's men live their "lives of quiet desperation" on our faculties. There they lodge their life-long discontent with themselves, their lot, their failures to be or become reflections of the greatness that remains within, struggling to be born as the very days for borning fade away. Or so it sometimes seems to harried administrators who appear, in turn, to the faculty eye as bottom-line bureaucrats whose least concern is quality education.

But we all know in our better moments that our faculties are populated and dominated by free persons of integrity and intelligence, great men and women whose lives witness to eternal truths. Their way of life, moreover, often witnesses to a detached simplicity, in some cases freely chosen though in all cases virtually dictated by the economics of an undervalued service profession. And the faculty perception of administrators is, much more often than not, a sympathetic one which sees dedicated people working under pressure for the improvement of a place and the advancement of a cause in which they believe.

Many of us administrators find ourselves saying "I love this place" when we speak of our respective campuses. We mean, of course, that we love the people assembled there in the community that *is* the University. We are a people related to a Church, most of us related by a faith-commitment, all of us related by a desire to serve.

Central to any religious work is the development of human potential. The positive side of human potential stretches into eternity, toward union with the Creator of that human potential. The negative side points to the possibility of eternal alienation.

Formal education's interests are coextensive with the entire range of positive possibilities for human development. The Church recognizes this and often chooses formal education as an extraordinarily valuable instrument for its work in the development of human potential.

Higher education touches that range of positive possibilities in a privileged way. Skills and maturity acquired in earlier stages of educational growth make possible the conscious pursuit of wisdom. Not information only, nor technique, nor accumulated experience, but wisdom is a real possibility at the stage of human development associated with higher education. At this level it is the privilege of educators to group themselves into communities of inquiry which may in fact become or beget wisdom communities. At the level of higher education it is the responsibility of educators to work for the formation of wise and reflective human beings.

Higher education is a medium. It is not just a means. It has intrinsic value. Involving, as it does, the pursuit of wisdom, higher education is worth much in purely human terms and thus worthy of dedicated human effort. But the worth of higher education, as both means and medium, transcends the human and touches the divine.

The religious purpose in higher education is to move the minds and hearts of developing human persons. The direction of this movement is Godward. The norm is truth. The outcome, it is to be hoped, is wisdom. And wisdom is a gift from God.

If, as faith directs, everything depends on God, then wisdom would suggest that everything must be entrusted to God. Such wisdom lies at the beginning and end of religiously-grounded education.

4 Academic Freedom

The notion of academic freedom applies to those conditions or circumstances wherein a structured teaching-learning transaction can take place. Academic freedom resides in persons — teachers and learners — who meet in a setting designed to foster disciplined inquiry. What happens there is the exploration and communication of knowledge.

Sometimes no one is there but the investigator, the lone researcher seeking further understanding of an identifiable dimension of truth. Academic freedom protects the isolated investigator.

Sometimes many people are present, often as students receiving instruction, frequently as co-investigators searching for new understandings. Academic freedom protects all participants in any given teaching-learning transaction.

Why have academic freedom? To protect the disciplined inquirer from the unwelcome whims or reprisals of powerful others who may disagree with his or her views. That is quite different, of course, from the welcome outcome of having one's views displaced by better evidence or sounder reasoning. Academic freedom provides a needed measure of employment security to professionals whose ideas might displease their academic employers. It also is intended to assure students access to all legitimate fonts of knowledge. Intellectual discovery and growth in understanding prosper in non-coercive environments. Academic freedom guarantees such an environment to teachers and learners.

In any academic context there are limits on academic freedom. First is the limit of truth itself. Teachers are not free to profess falsehood. Next is the limit imposed by the canons and associated competencies the community of scholars expects to find in a given academic discipline. Disciplined inquiry implies, first of all, responsible inquiry and then competent communication of the results of inquiry. Another limit on academic freedom is human prudence, especially with respect to the communication of truths that would not be appropriately communicated in certain circumstances or to members of certain age groups. These limits apply and are acknowledged to belong wherever the academy functions.

The question facing Catholic colleges and universities today looks to freedom of inquiry and communication of theological knowledge on a Catholic campus in light of the institution's relationship, however indirect, to a hierarchical, authoritarian Church. Is there an ecclesial limit on academic freedom? Can there be an acceptable constraint on investigation, but, more importantly, on communication of truth on a Catholic campus because of the Church-relationship? Moreover, what happens to academic freedom when a question of truth or error is decided outside the academy?

I think there can be and is an ecclesial limit on academic freedom. And I think this ecclesial limit need not violate academic freedom so long as a church-related institution, whether Catholic or not, understands itself to be also faith-related and faith, on that campus, is shared by many and respected by all. "Ecclesial" is a word distinct from, but not unrelated to, "ecclesiastical"; it is, however, a broader term. "Ecclesial" refers to an assembly, a community of believers, the Church understood as a people of God, the faith community. "Ecclesiastical" refers to structure and governance within the faith community.

Faith, of course, is a gift of God freely accepted by the believing person. Acceptance of limits associated with religious faith suggests to me not a denial of freedom but the exercise of freedom, the freedom of religious commitment.

If faith is first, last, and always a gift — and Catholic theology is unambiguous in so describing it — language regarding the communication of an understanding of faith must be used with care lest "teaching the faith" be thought of in images of transfusion or injection. Faith, the ineffable gift that draws one into contact with a God of mystery, can nonetheless, and up to a point, be explained. At least the "tenets" of a faith community — those formulations of religious truth which are "held" by members of a faith community — can be articulated in their present stage of development, located in their scriptural foundations, and analyzed at different stages of historical controversy perhaps, of philosophical expression, and of official ecclesiastical formulation.

Reflection on past understandings is only part of the work of a theologian. Development of new and deeper understandings is a special responsibility. This is the professional and scientific expression of *fides quaerens intellectum* for theologians in the Church. The ecclesial limit on this exercise of human understanding in the Church is continuity with the tradition of the Church. The tradition, however, is a living and growing reality. Hence the ecclesial limit on a theologian's academic freedom is more viaduct than retaining wall. It is, in any case and by whatever metaphor, a limiting factor.

Discontinuity would mean, by definition, a break of greater or lesser proportions from the tradition, a separation from the faith community. Hence the development of new, better, and deeper understandings can always expect to confront an ecclesial limit, a protective layer or buffer zone intended to prevent breaks. This need not be an insurmountable barrier to inquiry nor a clamp on communication. Instead it can serve to remind the communicator that the teaching of Catholic theology is not communication only, but communion with the community of faith his or her theology is intended to serve. That faith community, in the case of Roman Catholicism, is organized hierarchically with clear lines of authority.

It is consistent with Catholic principles to have ecclesiastical authority exercised in a way that "authors" — in the sense of encouraging, enabling, and drawing out — the creative potential of theologians in the Church, encouraging the exploration of ideas, and fostering the development of what will eventually become official Catholic doctrine. Such "authorship" on the part of the Church authorities would always look to continuity with the tradition. Continuity will function as the ecclesial limit on the academic freedom of theologians in the Church. Another way of stating this limit is to describe it as fidelity to, and respect for, the teaching authority of the Church.

Who is to decide whether a given development represents a continuous advance of tradition or a discontinuous break? Who is to determine whether a Catholic theologian is in or out of communion with the teaching Church in his or her efforts to advance the tradition? And how are these judgments to find their proper place within the Catholic college or university, thus protecting the institution's autonomy and the professor's integrity as a free academic working within appropriate limits? The answer to this last question presupposes an answer to the question of Catholic identity: what, in fact, makes a university or college Catholic?

I think theologians and bishops should examine together questions of continuity or break; then the bishops should decide. I think theologians and bishops should examine together whether or not a theologian is in or out of communion with the teaching Church when the theologian offers theories or theses intended to advance the tradition. The formal determination remains the province of the bishop. If the final determination is, in fact, the province of the bishop, how can the institution where that theologian works be said to be autonomous? By virtue of the identity it has chosen for itself. It has a freely chosen Catholic character expressed in its mission statement and subscribed to by the campus community. The internalization of the Catholic identity includes institutional acceptance of all things Catholic as congenial to the range of inquiry on campus, and nothing

Catholic is viewed as foreign to the enterprise. The range of interest goes far beyond the Catholic, of course, but the point to note is that nothing Catholic is excluded. The assertion of institutional autonomy in the face of an ecclesial limit on academic freedom is, therefore, no denial of academic freedom. It simply points to an identity — internal, freely chosen, and accepted by all in the campus community (as distinguished from the broader faith community) — which acknowledges a role for Church authority in doctrinal matters. Those who choose not to accept, or no longer subscribe to, the Catholic identity of the institution do not disqualify themselves from the faith community, but they do separate themselves from identification with the campus community. To identify with an institution without accepting that institution's self-proclaimed identity makes no sense. To proclaim a Catholic identity without accepting an ecclesial limit on theological exploration and communication is to misunderstand not only the nature of church-relatedness, but also the idea of a university and the meaning of academic freedom. Academic freedom can be limited without being violated.

In his preface to *The Idea of a University*, John Henry Newman noted that "when the Church founds a University, she is not cherishing talent, genius, or knowledge for their own sake, but for the sake of her children, with a view to their spiritual welfare and their religious influence and usefulness, with the object of training them to fill their respective posts in life better, and of making them more intelligent, capable, active members of society" (all citations will be from the Loyola University Press edition, 1927, re-issued in 1987).

In the first of his nine "Discourses" on "University Teaching" (for all practical purposes, chapter one in Part One of *The Idea of a University*), Newman comments on the role of ecclesiastical authority in the establishment of a Catholic university. "Ecclesiastical authority, not argument, is the supreme rule and the appropriate guide for Catholics in matters of religion. It has always the right to interpose, and sometimes, in the conflict of parties and opinions, it is called on to exercise that right. It has lately exercised it in our own instance: it has interposed in favor of a pure University system for Catholic youth, forbidding compromise or accommodation of any kind. Of course its decision must be heartily accepted and obeyed, and that the more, because the decision proceeds, not simply from the Bishops of Ireland, great as their authority is, but the highest authority on earth, from the Chair of St. Peter." To that, Newman adds: "Moreover, such a decision not only demands our submission, but has a claim upon our trust." And the basis for this trust? "It is the decision of the Holy See; St. Peter has spoken, it is he who has enjoined that which seems to us so unpromising. He has spoken, and has a claim on us to trust him. He is no recluse, no solitary student, no dreamer about the past, no doter upon the dead and gone, no projector of the visionary. He for eighteen hundred years has lived in the world; he has seen all fortunes, he has encountered all adversaries, he has shaped himself for all emergencies. If ever there was a power on earth who had an eye for the times, who has confined himself to the practicable, and has been happy in his anticipations, whose words have been facts, and whose commands prophecies, such is he in the history of ages, who sits from generation to generation in the Chair of the Apostles, as the Vicar of Christ, and the Doctor of His Church."

These views may seem quaint, even naive, to the present-day reader who turns to Newman with a wide open mind and the best of will. But they help to explain why Newman had no hesitation in stating that "ecclesiastical authority, not argument, is the supreme rule and the appropriate guide for Catholics in matters of religion." Nor does Newman claim here that the Pope is always right, just that the Catholic will never go wrong by trusting him.

It would be safe to presume that Newman's evident respect and trust of the Church's influence relative to the founding of a university would extend to a special role for the Church in the theological life of the university. Much later in his book, in a chapter on "Duties of the Church Towards Knowledge," he writes: "(T)he Church has no call to watch over and protect

34

Science; but towards Theology she has a distinct duty: it is one of the special trusts committed to her keeping. Where Theology is, there she must be; and if a University cannot fulfill its name and office without the recognition of Revealed Truth [a point argued earlier in the book], she must be there to see that it is a *bona fide* recognition, sincerely made and consistently acted on."

Those who dismiss the notion of a Catholic university as a contradiction in terms will be relieved perhaps to note that the great theoretician of Catholic higher education assigns a "watch over" function—quite literally, an *epi-scopus* or "episcopal" role — to the Church only in the area of theology. They might wonder how that episcopal role can be implemented without impinging on the autonomy of the university, and that question raises again the issue of identity. Being open to all things Catholic (one way of expressing Catholic identity) means being open to episcopal oversight in the area of theology.

Without appearing to be excessively defensive, and certainly without adopting an offensive attack as the best defensive measure, the "contradiction-in-terms" Catholic university might fairly ask its secular counterparts how they can claim university status — *Studium Generale,* or "School of Universal Learning" would be Newman's designation — if their disciplined inquiry makes no systematic pursuit of revealed truth. Some would reply that they are simply not interested in theology. Others would point to ongoing teaching and research in religious studies taking place on their campuses. For a variety of reasons — legal on the part of state universities, preference in the independent sector — many universities will not conduct disciplined inquiry and communication of religious truth with fidelity to any particular faith tradition. There, of course, is the opening the church-related college or university wants to fill.

Since no one thinks it strange to have state universities with identities drawn from geographic boundaries, with special service relationships to the citizens of their respective states, with openness to state influence, dependence on state funding, and daily challenges to their autonomy from outside pressures that threaten to translate influence into control, why should it be regarded as unusual to have private universities with church-related identities and relationships to a faith-community that parallel the public institutions' relationships to the civic community? It is, of course, not unusual, as the widespread presence of church-related higher education in the U.S., with its constitutional guarantee of the free exercise of religious commitment, attests. Both state-related and church-related universities will always need the protection of academic freedom against undue external influences. Both types of institution will first, by virtue of their respective charters, have internalized control and vested it in a governing board. And both types can welcome or withstand external influence by exercising, as they wish, their chartered autonomy. Autonomy simply means that the governing board makes its own decisions, under its charter, in pursuit of its educational mission. And finally, all types of institutions of higher learning, not just those interested in theology, would be expected to provide the protection of academic freedom against undue internal influence, including undue influence from the governing board.

Why should those who think theology is integral to university life appear to be on the defensive in our day? Probably because of the dogmatism of science in contemporary higher education. "Scientists believe in science in the same way that the majority of Catholics believe in the Church, namely as Truth crystallized in an infallible collective opinion," wrote Simone Weil; "they contrive to believe this in spite of the continual changes in theory. In both cases it is through lack of faith in God." This biting comment is recorded by Robert Coles in *Simone Weil: A Modern Pilgrimage* (Addison-Wesley, 1987). "A Catholic directs his thought secondarily towards the truth, but primarily towards conformity with the Church's doctrine," argued Weil; she then added: "A scientist does the same, only in this case there is no established doctrine but a collective opinion in the process of formation." And Robert Coles comments: "That collective opinion can be not only helpful and instructive to those anxious to learn more, but also an instrument of control, a means by which compliance is exacted and disagreement punished." Sad to say, science has become the most emphatic expression of the extraordinarily secular tone of contemporary society.

I am not lamenting the existence of authorities — persons of superior intellect — in the scientific community; I wish we had more of them. Nor am I suggesting that there should be no authorities by virtue of intellect alone in the theological community. I wish we had more of them. I am lamenting the attitude, the kind of peer pressure that has emerged from the environment of physical and life sciences, that displays a bias against, or at least an indifference toward, the spiritual, the immaterial, the religious and theological realities of life.

Neither physical science nor theology can presume to be free of pressures, influences, limits, and controls within the academy. Both science and theology belong in the academy. Each depends on the other if it is to realize its full potential. Neither should underestimate the other's concern for objectivity and freedom from inappropriate control. And in considering the critique of Simone Weil, Catholics should note their companionship with scientists in her sweeping charge that both suffer from a lack of faith in God. Those who feel the impulse for control of Catholic theology should "walk humbly" as they attempt to see, in specific matters theological, just how God's authority is to be ascertained.

Secular academics might fairly invite religious educators, in the interest of preservation of the idea of a university, to keep a watchful eye on the line between influence and control, as all universities must. And the church-related institutions, grateful for the opportunity to exist freely here in America, are quite willing to write control along with religious identity into their civil charters. Under their charters, control is exercised by a duly constituted board of trustees, which in all cases must respect both due process and academic freedom. Outside the charter, and from a variety of off-campus command posts, the impulse for control will probably always find the college or university campus a desirable target. That says a great deal about the importance of the idea which has evolved over the centuries into what we call a university. It is so important an idea that the church, the state, and various other entities sacrifice to make it their own and vie with one another to make their embodiment of the idea the best.

In Catholic circles, the impulse for control by ecclesiastical authorities focuses on theology, the central element of the institution's Catholic identity. Here again, Newman can be helpful. In fact, his entire chapter on "Christianity and Scientific Investigation" could well serve as a preamble to discussion between bishops and theologians once they find the right structure for joint participation in theological dialogue. "(T)here must be great care taken to avoid scandal," writes Newman, "or shocking the popular mind, or unsettling the weak; the association between truth and error being so strong in particular minds that it is impossible to weed them of the error without rooting up the wheat with it."

> I am not, then, supposing the scientific investigator (1) to be *coming into collision with dogma*; nor (2) venturing, by means of his investigations, upon any interpretation of *Scripture*, or upon other conclusion *in the matter of religion*; nor (3) of his *teaching*, even in his own science, religious paradoxes, when he should be investigating and proposing; nor (4) of his recklessly *scandalizing the weak*; but, these explanations being made, I still say that a scientific speculator or inquirer is not bound, in conducting his researches, to be every moment adjusting his course by the maxims of the schools or by popular traditions, or by those of any other science distinct from his own, or to be ever narrowly watching what those external sciences have to say to him, or to be determined to be edifying, or to be ever answering heretics and unbelievers; being confident, from the impulse of a generous faith, that, however his line of investigation may swerve now and then, and vary to and fro in its course, or threaten momentary collision or embarrassment with any other department of knowledge, theological or not, yet, if he lets it alone, it will be sure to come home, because truth never can really be contrary to truth, and because often what at first sight is an "exceptio," in the event most emphatically "probat regulam" (emphasis in the original).

Newman quite literally underlines the importance of what I referred to earlier as prudence and respect for the canons of a scientific discipline when I identified limits on academic freedom. Truth also is a limit, as I noted above. What, then, can be said about error in this regard? "[I]n scientific researches error may be said, without a paradox, to be in some instances the way to truth, and the only way. Moreover, it is not often the fortune of any one man to live through an investigation; the process is one of not only many stages, but of many minds. What one begins, another finishes; and a true conclusion is at length worked out by the co-operation of independent schools and the perseverance of successive generations. This being the case, we are obliged, under the circumstances, to bear for awhile with what we feel to be error, in consideration of the truth in which it is eventually to issue."

In perhaps his strongest expression of feeling on this point, Newman exclaims, "Let us eschew secular history, and science, and philosophy for good and all, if we are not allowed to be sure that Revelation is so true that the altercations and perplexities of human opinion cannot really or eventually injure its authority." The question then, of course, becomes: what, in fact, is included in divine revelation; what form must a theological declaration take to indicate that a given doctrine is proposed for belief as belonging to the body of divine revelation?

"Great minds need elbow-room," writes Newman, "not indeed in the domain of faith, but of thought. And so indeed do lesser minds, and all minds."

The theologian, like a scientific investigator, operates within constraints. His or her "elbow-room" will have an ecclesial limit, namely, continuity with the tradition, especially at what John Courtney Murray used to call its "growing edge." Newman has a final word directed specifically to theologians:

> [W]hat I would venture to recommend to theologians, ...is a great and firm belief in the sovereignty of Truth. Error may flourish for a time, but Truth will prevail in the end. The only effect of error ultimately is to promote Truth..... On the other

39

hand, it must be of course remembered, Gentlemen, that I am supposing all along good faith, honest intentions, a loyal Catholic spirit, and a deep sense of responsibility. I am supposing, in the scientific inquirer, a due fear of giving scandal, of seeming to countenance views which he does not really countenance, and of siding with parties with whom he heartily differs. I am supposing that he is fully alive to the existence and the power of the infidelity of the age; that he keeps in mind the moral weakness and the intellectual confusion of the majority of men; and that he has no wish at all that any one soul should get harm from certain speculations today, though he may have the satisfaction of being sure that those speculations will, as far as they are erroneous or misunderstood, be corrected in the course of the next half-century. "

With those words, Newman ends his essay on "Christianity and Scientific Investigation." Those same words, it seems to me, would be a useful keynote to open regional and even local exchanges between bishops and theologians as they attempt to come to a common understanding of the ecclesial limits on the disciplined theological inquiry the bishops and the rest of the Church urgently need, and which Catholic theologians, from their positions within the academy, are ready to provide.

Pope John Paul II addressed an assembly of U.S. Catholic college and university administrators in New Orleans at Xavier University on September 12, 1987. He spoke to the issue of what makes a Catholic college or university Catholic. In his view, Catholic identity "depends upon the explicit profession of Catholicity on the part of the university as an institution, and also upon the personal conviction and sense of mission on the part of its professors and administrators." The Pope looks to these institutions to help "to make the Church's presence felt in the world of culture and science." Meeting this challenge requires "the personal conviction and sense of mission" of professors and administrators, those mainly responsible for the articulation and implementation of the Catholic identity.

And later in his New Orleans address, with the simple assertion that "religious faith itself calls for intellectual inquiry," the

Pope assumes that there should be theological inquiry — faith seeking understanding — on a Catholic campus. "[T]hat there can be no contradiction between faith and reason is a distinctive feature of the Catholic humanistic tradition." Since the Catholic university" is dedicated to the service of truth,

> ...there is an intimate relationship between the Catholic university and the teaching office of the Church. The bishops of the Church, as *Doctores et Magistri Fidei*, should be seen not as external agents but as participants in the life of the Catholic university in its privileged role as protagonist in the encounter between faith and science, and between revealed truth and culture."

Bishops and theologians alike must enable the Gospel always to "challenge the accomplishments and assumptions of the age" (cf. Rom. 12: 2), so that the Gospel can "purify the culture, uplift it, and orient it to the service of what is authentically human. Humanity's very survival may depend on it." Required of both bishop and theologian is "fidelity to the word of God, to ensure that human progress takes into account the entire revealed truth of the external act of love in which the universe and especially the human person acquire ultimate meaning."

But how is this relationship between bishop and theologian to work out in practice? The Pope sees it this way:

> Theology is at the service of the whole ecclesial community. The work of theology involves an interaction among the various members of the community of faith. The bishops, united with the Pope, have the mission of authentically teaching the message of Christ; as pastors they are called to sustain the unity in faith and Christian living of the entire People of God. In this they need the assistance of Catholic theologians, who perform an inestimable service to the Church. But theologians also need the charism entrusted by Christ to the bishops and, in the first place, to enrich the life-stream of the ecclesial community, must ultimately be tested and validated by the Magisterium. In effect, therefore, the ecclesial context of Catholic theology gives it a special character and value, even when theology exists in an academic setting.

41

A structure is needed in every Catholic college to facilitate participation by the local bishop in the theological dialogue of the college, not in the governance of the college but in the theological discussion and debate which are part of the life of the college or university. This should be reciprocal influence of theologian on bishop and bishop on theologian, as faith continues its quest for understanding. An appropriate teaching-learning structure, respectful of this desired reciprocity, is needed. Perhaps the seminar room, as opposed to the lecture hall, is an appropriate model that will foster the kind of exchange that is desirable. A roundtable, "horizontal" model is natural to a campus. It is properly collegial and certainly preferable to a one-way, "vertical" delivery system of judgments and conclusions from bishop to theologians, or vice versa. Any on-campus collegial model is superior to the distant and detached exchange characteristic of correspondence schools. The Post Office is no substitute for direct dialogue. Theologians and bishops have to get together for the exploration of all theological questions. If they do, they will surely grow in love and respect for one another, and in their understanding of the revelation God has entrusted to His Church. In this way bishops can, as the Holy Father suggests, be "participants in the life of the Catholic university in its privileged role as protagonist in the encounter between faith and science and between revealed truth and culture." Such participation would do no violence to institutional autonomy. Outsiders from the fields of law, medicine, business, the arts and countless other fields of knowledge are routinely invited to participate in intellectual exchanges on campus.

Nor, in my view, would the fact that the outcome of this fully participatory theological reflection "must ultimately be tested and validated by the Magisterium" necessarily imply an infringement on academic freedom. Outside courts validate legal theories debated on campuses. Outside agencies license drugs tested in university laboratories. Patents and copyrights are granted to professors by outside authorities. That Catholic theology should be "tested and validated" by off-campus ecclesiastical authorities is, of course, a special case involving only Catholic theologians and Catholic campuses, but not so special as to disqualify the Catholic campus from membership in the larger set of special cases that make up the world of American higher education.

A question that cannot be avoided on the side of ecclesiastical authorities relates to the preparedness and willingness of bishops to participate in dialogue with academic theologians. Not all bishops are theologians. Nor have all bishops who hold academic degrees in theology "kept up" with developments sufficiently to qualify them for participation in academic dialogue. Another way of posing the problem raised by the Pope's New Orleans proposal is to suggest that bishops will now have to be attentive to their personal bibliographies.

In order to participate in theological dialogue, one must be a contributor to theological reflection. One's own reflection, one's understanding of the tradition, one's insights relative to clarifying or advancing the tradition — all these must be articulated and communicated to the other participants in the dialogue. The traditional way of communicating these insights is through the delivery of papers and the publication of manuscripts. Bishops who are not academics would not, of course, be expected to have bibliographies that would rival those of the professors. (Some bishops might quip that they are where they are because of the way they chose, at an earlier career stage, to handle the publish or parish option!) But bishop-participants in theological dialogue should be willing to put their thoughts on paper. That paper would be shared before the dialogue begins with the theologian-participants, just as the writings of the theologians would be in the hands of the bishops by way of preparation for the structured dialogue. If a bishop is incapable of articulating and presenting his theological reflection in this way, it seems to me that he therefore disqualifies himself from participation in the theological life of the Catholic university and, more importantly, he recuses himself from judging the quality of the theological reflection of others.

43

He can, of course, make his own the judgments about quality and even orthodoxy rendered by others; bishops are, after all, to be judges of orthodoxy, not of theology as such. But then what would be the intellectual grounds he could claim for inclusion in that key sentence in the Holy Father's speech in New Orleans? "The bishops of the Church, as *Doctores et Magistri Fidei*, should be seen not as external agents but as participants in the life of the Catholic university in its privileged role as protagonist in the encounter between faith and science and between revealed truth and culture." Typically and quite properly the concern of the bishop will be centered on the pastoral implications of what emerges from theological reflection. There is no better place to register that concern than in the process of theological reflection within the university.

To invite the participation of a bishop in theological discussion on campus is not to presume that differences between a local bishop and a given theologian over what constitutes sound Catholic doctrine would immediately become grounds for action against the theologian. The whole point of putting a structure for discussion in place is to create common ground for fuller understanding on both sides, for heightened sensitivities to values like academic freedom, pastoral concern, and many more. Indeed the structure itself should become a barrier against arbitrary dismissal to the extent that it guides the work of understanding theology is intended to do, namely, reflection on the data of revelation and the application of these understandings to the practice of life. Moreover, the presence of structured dialogue will help to shape the understanding of academic freedom on a given campus relative to theology. Internal to the discipline of Catholic theology is respect for, and fidelity to, the teaching authority of the Church. In some way, Catholic theology finds its base in the teaching of the magisterium. To make this relationship between Catholic bishops and Catholic theologians more visible, even at the micro level of a given campus in a given diocese, will, I think, tend to increase the probability of theologians becoming more influential and more secure in their service to the Church.

5 A Case in Point

Those who choose to serve the Catholic Church as professors on "ecclesiastical" (once called "pontifical") faculties must be credentialed, commissioned, and free.

The necessary academic credential — doctorate, licentiate, or other appropriate degree — is earned in the usual way at an accredited institution. But for those who would occupy positions on ecclesiastical faculties, more than the appropriate credential is needed. They must also have permission to teach in the name of the Church. This permission comes by way of a special commission.

In the case of The Catholic University of America, the commissioning of appropriately credentialed professors is done by the Chancellor of the University, the Archbishop of Washington, as representative of the Holy See. The commission means, quite literally, a formal participation in the teaching mission of the Church as that mission is advanced through properly constituted ecclesiastical faculties which, at CUA, are found only in the disciplines of theology, philosophy, and canon law. Other faculties of instruction at all levels of Catholic education participate in some way in the teaching mission of the Church, and most Catholic theologians and philosophers, including most of those at work in Catholic institutions, teach without any formal tie to an ecclesiastical faculty. Typically, the theologians among them are teaching Catholic theology (although they could teach any

45

theological tradition that falls within their academic competence); they are not, however, commissioned officially to teach in the name of the Church. It is noteworthy that the only university in the United States where ecclesiastical faculties are found is The Catholic University of America, although such faculties exist in other universities in other parts of the world.

Once they take faculty positions in a university, those who are both credentialed and commissioned to teach in the name of the Church must also be free. The university must guarantee them freedom of inquiry — what we would regard here in the United States as full academic freedom. Disciplined theological investigation and instruction (i.e., research and teaching conducted within the generally accepted norms of the particular academic discipline) must be protected. Both inquiry and communication of discovery should have no limits except those limits required by prudence, or by truth itself, or, as I argued in Chapter 4, there can be ecclesial limits.

Is there an appropriate limiting role for the Church in the case of Catholic theological inquiry and instruction conducted in the name of the Church? There is. But the limits the Church might choose to set on theological research or teaching can be imposed without violence to academic freedom only if the limits are themselves expressions of prudence or truth, as I indicated in the preceding chapter.

Catholic theology is an exercise of intellect; it is an intellectual exercise conducted, however, in the light of faith. One of the objects of that faith is the Church itself. The Catholic Church, whose existence depends on faith, comes to a better understanding of itself through the work of theology, which is one of the chief means whereby the Church itself learns what it will teach. The Catholic theological enterprise must acknowledge not only the limiting force of prudence, applicable to any academic discipline, but the limit of those truths which faith knows with certainty, a certainty which may indeed lie beyond the reach of reason. Where no such certainty is found, the theological investigation not only may but must continue to probe and search.

46

And even where such certainty is found, the theological mind should continue its exploration for a deeper understanding.

The Church, through its formal teaching authority, the magisterium, defines its points of certainty. It does this rarely, when it teaches infallibly. It also teaches authoritatively, although not definitively, day in and day out as an essential part of its mission. The problem for the competent, prudent theologian fully respectful of both Church and truth, is to discern how best to serve the interests of both — Church and truth — in those areas where the Church has not declared itself to be completely, unambiguously, and irreversibly certain, even though it has declared a position authoritatively. Similarly, the theologian must decide how best to proceed in examining those questions on which the Church does not hesitate to speak, but concerning which the truth is not yet completely and compellingly clear.

The problem for the teaching-learning Church is compounded by its pastoral regard for the faithful who could become confused or misled by theological debates. This is not, however, sufficient reason to eliminate the debates. Through its pastoral experience, the Church most readily discovers, particulary in the moral area, those questions most in need of further reflection and additional clarification. This is the work that professional theologians are best qualified to do. It cannot, therefore, be said as easily in the case of theology, as it might be said with reference to other academic disciplines, that there should be no limits on teaching and research except the limits of prudence and truth. But with due allowance for the fact that Catholic theology searches for understanding in the light of the Catholic faith and thus in an ecclesial context which can itself become a limiting factor, that is exactly what must be said if officially commissioned theologians are to serve the Church effectively and if theology is to be respected as a discipline in a university setting.

For any professor anywhere, violations of the established canons of a discipline in the work of research or teaching amount to violations of the integrity of the discipline and of the person who exceeds the bounds of the discipline. Assuming integrity on both fronts, the university, as an institution, stakes its own integrity on the guarantee of freedom to the professors it hires, houses, tenures, and rewards.

What is the university to do when a commissioned professor loses his or her commission? At CUA, the loss would come as a result of action initiated by the Chancellor but affirmed by the Board of Trustees. It would thus be a decision taken by an independent governing board which is self-perpetuating and which operates under a civil charter distinct from the Vatican charter required for the establishment of the ecclesiastical faculties. The original appointment to an ecclesiastical faculty at CUA would follow consultation by the Chancellor with the bishop-members of the Board of Trustees (which, by the University's by-laws, is made up of 40 persons — half clergy, half lay — in addition to two ex-officio members, the Chancellor and the President) and also with the Holy See. Specifically, the Chancellor would consult with the Roman Congregation for Catholic Education before granting a "nihil obstat" for the original appointment.

For its part, the University must do all it can to assure due process to its professors, according to its own well-defined and previously approved internal procedures. Due process, granted to any professor faced with the possible loss of commission, will place the reasons for removal under public review. If the outcome of the review is not a restoration of the commission, the University can provide an alternate faculty position to a professor whose competence and integrity have been reaffirmed by due process, but whose commission to teach in the name of the Church no longer obtains.

Do Church authorities have the right to invite and expect commissioned professional theologians to teach in their name? They do. And Church authorities also have the right to withdraw or urge the withdrawal of a commission when they no longer desire to have a particular theologian teaching in the name of the Church. The professor also has rights, and thus a tension is bound to arise when these respective rights are caught in conflict — a conflict between freedom and authority.

A university which is chartered by the Church, as is The Catholic University of America, will respect the right of Church authorities to express approval or disapproval of the work of theologians who make themselves available for such service to the Church in a Church-related university setting. The Catholic University of America also operates under a civil charter and within the American tradition of academic freedom. The University will therefore respect the academic freedom of those at work on any and all of its faculties. That freedom is not without limits; but the limits are drawn by widely-shared professional agreement and protected by peer-regulated due process. If, after all due process, and after reaffirmation by peers of a professor's integrity and competence, the Chancellor and the other members of the CUA Board of Trustees withdraw from a professor permission to teach in the name of the Church, the unresolved conflict between professor and episcopal authorities will surely be seen as a conflict touching upon academic freedom precisely because some of those authorities sit on the University's governing board and operate under its civil as well as pontifical charter. But a broader freedom is at issue. The conflicted relationship is between personal freedom and authority in a hierarchical Church.

This question was not touched by the Second Vatican Council's famous Declaration on Religious Freedom. The question stands, in fact, as the most prominent portion of the unsolved remainder of Vatican II. As the Church works its way through this question, assisted indeed by the tensions which will inevitably arise between its theologians and its doctrinal overseers, a university which stands in a special relationship to the Church, as does The Catholic University of America, can provide academic freedom only to those who are credentialed and, in the case of ecclesiastical faculties, also commissioned to teach.

All of this is more or less directly applicable to the case of Father Charles E. Curran. His well-publicized disagreement with ecclesiastical authorities resulted in the removal, by the University's Board of Trustees, of his commission to teach in the name of the Church. The decision of the Chancellor and other

49

members of the CUA Board of Trustees to remove the commission is consistent with institutional autonomy, quite obviously respectful of Roman authority, and no more intrusive on academic freedom than the limiting factors of truth and prudence so long as the Church is acknowledged to have a right to decide who may or may not teach in its name. That corporate decision did not remove Father Curran's tenure. Moreover, that corporate decision was taken with care to respect the recommendation of an ad-hoc committee of Father Curran's peers, appointed by the University's Academic Senate, in accordance with provisions for due process laid out in the CUA Faculty Handbook. The committee communicated to the Board of Trustees a willingness to accept removal of the canonical mission, if their faculty colleague were offered an alternate teaching assignment within "his area of professional competence, namely moral theology and/or ethics."

The finding of the Vatican Congregation for the Doctrine of the Faith (July 25, 1986) that Father Curran will "no longer be considered suitable nor eligible to exercise the function of a Professor of Catholic Theology" led the University's Board of Trustees to remove his canonical mission. The finding of the Academic Senate's specially-constituted review committee led the Board to instruct the Administration to offer him the opportunity to teach social ethics in the University's School of Arts and Sciences. In both instances, the Board responded to influence, but retained control.

The conflict of Father Curran's freedom and ecclesiastical authority centered on the issue of continued public dissent from authoritative but not infallible Church teaching in the area of sexual morality and human life issues. Underlying the conflict is not only the unresolved problem of freedom and authority in the Church, but also a theological debate concerning the changeability of long-standing, official teaching which does not bear the stamp of infallibility. Virtually all of the Church's teaching in the area of morals, as opposed to questions of faith, is authoritatively but not infallibly taught. This is not to say that it is wrong, or will be changed, or should be changed. It is simply to say that the potential for dispute is there.

Church authorities tend to favor order over freedom. As the Church works its way through the unresolved question of freedom and authority, an emphasis on order would put pressure on Christian freedom, just as surely as an emphasis on freedom would release the ever-present impulse for order. Theology, meanwhile, cannot stand still. It must continue to serve the faith community.

Without freedom of theological inquiry, Catholic theologians will not be able to serve to the full extent of their competence the Church that commands their love and loyalty. Without theology, the Church, including its dedicated Vatican authorities, will not grow in its understanding of the full implications of the gospel of Christ.

Catholic theological energy — commissioned or not, but properly credentialed for the task — will help the Church work out this problem of freedom and authority only to the degree that theology itself enjoys responsible freedom. It is precisely there, in the guarantee of responsible freedom to the theologians on its faculty, that the Church-related university, as university, makes its proper contribution to theological progress.

Meanwhile, issues of great interest to the Church — questions of war and peace, economic justice, poverty, hunger, and related matters of social concern — remain ready to be researched and taught at The Catholic University of America under the rubric of social ethics. This could be done by Father Curran if he were to accept both the declarative judgment of the Vatican and the University's offer of alternative employment in the area of ethics. He has chosen not to take this option even after the Superior Court of the District of Columbia decided against him on February 28, 1989, in his breach-of-contract suit against CUA. His presence at a conflicted intersection of freedom and authority in a particular moment of history will serve, I hope, to strengthen both Church and University in their search for answers to the questions of our times.

Part II
Values and the University

6 Principled Judgment

> I think we should support, or if necessary create, a group of men and women whose business it is to think far ahead of their contemporaries, whose business is not to represent their own country, their own class, their own times, men and women who should be excused from many of the pressures and passions of their own day and permitted to imagine a different kind of world, to anticipate problems and propose solutions to them....Needless to say, we have, at least in embryo, just such a class. I refer to the university.
>
> — Henry Steele Commager

In the era and mood associated with the famous word "Watergate," university people began anew to think ahead of their contemporaries, imagining a different kind of world. The need for values in the post-Watergate world was evident. That need re-emerges in consciousness with appalling regularity as violations of trust and new national scandals point to the erosion of integrity in America. What might be done in colleges and universities to assist young men and women to prepare themselves for life in a world where integrity seems always to be under assault?

Educational institutions tend to favor the hypothesis that one is better off thinking his or her way into new ways of acting than acting one's way into new ways of thinking. "Think before you act," is, after all, solid and perennial advice. But I tend to think that one is much more likely to act his or her way into new (and better) ways of thinking. Reflection on experience is the thought-before-action required of a prudent person. But experience,

55

direct and personal, is, in this dynamic sense, father to the thought.

It is not enough to provide libraries and lecture halls where students can tap the experience of the past, where they can review, for instance, the presence or absence of principles in the judgments and decisions of others. The educational environment should encourage students to reflect on their own experience, to discover the presence or absence of principles in themselves. The need for such reflective discovery has been with us for centuries. Hollow men and moral nomads have dominated public life in the past. I take it to be the responsibility of the universities to provide future publics with integral persons of principled judgment, prepared and available for the service of leadership.

Playwright Robert Bolt has his imprisoned hero, Sir Thomas More, use a striking simile to explain to his daughter why he will not swear to the Act of Succession and thus gain his freedom at the price of violating his conscience:

> When a man takes an oath, Meg, he's holding his own self in his own hands. Like water. (He cups his hands.) And if he opens his fingers *then* — he needn't hope to find himself again. Some aren't capable of this, but I'd be loathe to think your father one of them. (*A Man for All Seasons*, Act II.)

In a preface to his play, Bolt explains his mood and his social perceptions as he wrote *A Man for All Seasons*. He was troubled by the thin fabric of contemporary human character, by modern man's tendency to think of himself in the Third Person, to describe himself "in terms more appropriate to somebody seen through a window." Bolt then provides a penetrating insight amounting to a one-sentence summary of the cultural ills that prepared the way for Watergate: "Both socially and individually it is with us as it is with our cities — an accelerating flight to the periphery, leaving a center which is empty when the hours of business are over." (*A Man for All Seasons*, Vintage Books, 1960.) A full decade before Watergate, Robert Bolt asked: "[W]hy do I take as my hero a man who brings about his own death because he can't put his hand on an old black book and tell an ordinary lie?"

> For this reason: A man takes an oath only when he wants to commit himself quite exceptionally to the statement, when he wants to make an identity between the truth of it and his own virtue; he offers himself as a guarantee. And it works. There is a special kind of shrug for a perjurer; we feel that the man has no self to commit, no guarantee to offer.

An educational enterprise, a learning community, a climate of inquiry called a university, should at the very least provide an environment designed to assist the student in acquiring a properly developed sense of selfhood. I believe that a clear sense of self can emerge only if the student locates himself or herself in reference to the transcendental. I would specify: Someone transcendental. Others would settle for something transcendental. In either case, value enters the picture. This in no way conflicts with the university's commitment to the rational. Since Watergate, there have been fewer voices protesting that an interest in transcendental values is unreasonable. In certain universities, as we have seen, faith is a value to be consciously fostered. In any university, faith is a value to be respected.

Another mininal expectation in any university community is a common commitment to truth. Hence open inquiry in the university community is not a threat. In a faith-committed Roman Catholic university, as I have indicated, special care must be taken not to substitute authority for thought. We violate our trust if we fail to foster in our students a critical sense. To think critically, one must have a place to stand. One must be able to locate himself or herself, to have some fixed reference points. A Catholic university stands on its Catholic commitment, without apology; but it does so with care.

Our care is to avoid absolutizing incidentals and accidentals. Our care, moreover, is to guarantee freedom of faith commitment to all our students, to all our faculty. In matters of morality, we take care to avoid a multiplication of absolutes. Catholics

QUADRANGLE CONSIDERATIONS

anywhere — in or outside universities — must take great care to avoid giving the false impression that their Church wants to translate its moral precepts into the criminal code of the nation. Such is not and should not be the case, unenlightened efforts to the contrary notwithstanding. Catholic morality should not be public law. Law, however, should in every case be moral. Those who make, execute, and enforce laws must in all cases be moral. And those who break the law may do so, we believe, only when the law itself is unjust (in which case the violater must accept the consequences of his act under the law), or a higher law intervenes (in which case one's moral integrity could cost his or her life).

Graduates of Loyola University of New Orleans, where I once served as dean of arts and sciences, should, in the language of the university's Goals Statement, "be capable of principled judgment in the face of complexity and ambiguity...."

What are the ingredients of a "principled judgment"? There can, and I suppose there should be, a value-free answer to that question. But the content of any concrete "principled judgment" cannot, it seems to me, be value-free. It is precisely the ignorance or abandonment of principles that permits the emergence in national affairs of statesmen and their political associates who appear to be moral nomads, unencumbered by conscience, by familiarity with any ethical tradition, and free of the wisdom that comes from making moral choices. Such freedom is really slavery to the whims of impulse, instinct, and opportunism.

In my view, a university should work through its curriculum and every other available means, including appropriate off-campus experience with on-campus reflective follow-up, to educe from its environment men and women capable of making principled judgments. Not just informed judgments, because information all too often falls short of wisdom, a point worth emphasizing in a so-called "Information Society."

When educators speak of assisting students to locate themselves, to establish a sense of selfhood, to become familiar with where they begin and where they leave off, there is always the danger of slipping into an excessive individualism, even a narcissistic withdrawal from societal awareness. This of course would be the result of bad education. Any university is capable of giving bad education. To admit it is more wisdom than weakness. To admit it is to recognize that no one discipline, no one course, no one religious tradition, no one book or project or professor is the conduit of all wisdom. If such were the case, once a student was properly plugged into the unique source, principled judgments would be guaranteed. Such will never be the case. Students need creative combinations in appropriate amounts of all the resources a university can offer. From the past, from the present; from science, from the arts; from the faculty and from each other, the students will themselves draw many of the ingredients of principled judgments.

We all know that moral issues arise in any area covered by any intellectual discipline. To settle the issue definitively is not the job of a classroom professor. To ignore the issue is often inept or dishonest pedagogy. To discuss it may or may not be appropriate, depending on the nature and purpose of the course as well as the availability of another, possibly more suitable, forum within the university where the moral issue might be explored. But somewhere in their university experience, students should disclose, at least to themselves, where they stand on these issues and just what the principles are upon which any given stance is grounded.

To repeat, the university is an atmosphere of open inquiry and a free quest for truth. In such a setting, enlightened pedagogy may fairly insist that a student's moral judgments be (1) his or her own; and (2) part of an identifiable (though incomplete), coherent (though riddled with doubt), and consistent (though self-made and embryonic instead of traditional and finished) system of moral choice. Eclecticism and hybrid systems have a proper place in the university and also in the individual. So do unresolved questions and tentative positions. But contradictory positions, lopsided social-over-personal or personal-over-social ethics, and thinly veiled "moral" positions which are obtusely oppositional if not mindlessly anarchic, should be identified for what they are. Moral skepticism and moral dogmatism should be equally open to challenge.

That said, let me suggest that the university should always be doing something to keep the ethical side of the life issue alive. The legal decision in Roe v. Wade did not end the ethical debate. Now the question is how *ought* the freedom made possible by the Court's decision be used? What ethically should be going on in a woman's mind as she makes up her mind? What ethically is required of the father by way of participation in this decision? What ethically should be going on in the medical mind? It is quite possible that little if anything of an ethical nature will be going on when the situation arises. This will certainly be the case if nowhere in the university experience can a student face the issue unless she (and a companion he) finds herself personally and directly confronted with the problem.

Similarly, in politics and the military, in business and the professions, ethical sensitivities will be dull or absent if curricular or co-curricular attention was not given to ethical principles and their application in the university experience.

Not every ethical dilemma, obviously, can be experienced and reflected upon in the student years. Vicarious experience through case studies, role-playing, films and literature is, however, not to be overlooked by anyone responsible for providing a liberal and liberating education. Otherwise, hollow men and women, of thin and soft commitments, will continue to populate our alumni rolls.

Robert Bolt spoke of man offering himself as a guarantee when he takes an oath. And Bolt sees in the perjurer one who "has no self to commit, no guarantee to offer."

University educators may find that the curriculum they are offering is ethically hollow and thus ill-equipped to produce a man or woman capable of being his or her own guarantee. Somehow, through a creative, catalytic curriculum, the student should meet in professors, peers, books, and projects — but most especially in himself or herself — the values which, in developed and personalized form, will eventually guarantee that his or her judgments will be principled. A university should want to produce such men and women for all circumstances, for all seasons. An education to this end is an education to be human. No need to apologize for that.

Watergate occurred a full generation after Hiroshima and Nagasaki. On the moral map, the events are not unrelated. To demonstrate this, I borrow from the brilliantly perceptive James Agee who wrote the lead story in *Time* magazine's issue that marked the end of World War II. Agee's untimely death in 1955 deprived the world of letters of a developing talent; his piece for *Time*, on the implications of the atomic destruction visited upon the Japanese, delivered a warning we have yet to receive.

> The greatest and most terrible of wars ended, this week, in the echoes of an enormous event—an event so much more enormous that, relative to it, the war itself shrank to minor significance....
>
> With the controlled splitting of the atom, humanity, already profoundly perplexed and disunified, was brought inescapably into a new age in which all thoughts and things were split—and far from controlled....
>
> All thoughts and things were split....The race had been won... but the demonstration of power against living creatures instead of dead matter created a bottomless wound in the living conscience of the race. The rational mind had won the most Promethean of its conquests over nature, and had put into the hands of common man the fire and force of the sun itself.
>
> The promise of good and evil bordered alike on the infinite — with this further, terrible split in the fact: that upon a people already so nearly drowned in materialism even in peacetime, the good uses of this power might easily bring disaster as prodigious as the evil.... When the bomb split open the universe and revealed the prospect of the infinitely extraordinary, it also revealed the oldest, simplest, commonest, most neglected and most important of facts: that each man is eternally and above all else responsible for his own soul, and, in the terrible words of the Psalmist, that no man may deliver his brother, nor make agreement unto God for him.

Man's fate has forever been shaped between the hands of reason and spirit, now in collaboration, again in conflict. Now reason and spirit meet on final ground. If either or anything is to survive, they must find a way to create an indissoluble partnership.

When will all the universities get the message? When will they recognize that values provide the necessary bridge between reason and spirit?

7 Critical Issues

The word "crisis" is overworked in contemporary discourse, on campus or off. There is a widespread tendency to confuse periods of societal transition (which are always taking place) with points of social crisis (which occur far less frequently). Crisis, in popular and personal usage, inevitably raises a question of survival.

Before considering critical issues in contemporary society, I want first to locate the word in its appropriate etymological surroundings.

"Crisis" is a Latin transliteration of the Greek noun *krisis*, which means "a sifting, a separation, a judgment or discernment." It relates to the verb *krinein*, "to sift." The adjective *kritikos* means "able to discern, to judge." Critic, criticism, criterion, and crisis all belong to the same family of meaning.

Perhaps our popular penchant for pessimism has succeeded in freighting the word crisis with negative presuppositions concerning the outcomes of medical, legal, financial, or moral crises in personal experience. Perhaps we project that pessimism onto a larger social canvas. In any case, the word crisis implies a point of judgment. It invites action, preventative or remedial; and it permits inaction, the hapless state of fatalism. Fatalism is unworthy of the Christian; so, the first point to be made in examining critical issues in the light of Christian values is this: our values provide us with principles of action, and our actions, following our best judgments, should be directed to the right resolution of those issues we discern to be, in fact, critical. Not every crisis is preventable or resolvable by human effort, although many are. And no crisis, in the Christian perspective, is beyond the reach of prayer. "Thy will be done," is hardly a fatalistic lament. That it is His will for us to get on with the necessary "doing" (corrective or preventative) is a likely theological reflection on most crisis situations.

I was asked recently by a group of college students what I considered to be the "most pressing" issue their generation would have to face over the course of their collective lifetime.

My reaction to the question began with an acknowledgment that "most pressing" could mean "most immediate" or "quite urgent," but that it should not be taken in so short-term a context as to lose sight of that which is truly significant. Immediacy, urgency, and significance are not always the same thing. So I chose to take "most pressing" to mean simply "most important" in a time-frame that would be coextensive with the average life expectancy of today's college student. This time-frame pushes the perspective out by at least 50 or 60 years, assuming that life on the planet can extend its lease that long. In a very real sense, the students were asking for an estimate of just how long their lease on life would be. They are concerned about survival.

I was being asked to identify an issue of deepest significance and greatest importance to be dealt with by this collegiate generation over its allotted span of life. Consider the candidates for inclusion on this list of most pressing issues.

Foremost in the minds of the young is the question of war — nuclear war with no winners. We will trip over ourselves into war, they fear, if we continue the nuclear weapons buildup in a senseless arms race with other nuclear powers. No one doubts the importance of the issue of war and peace in our time. But is *it* the "most pressing"?

Another very pressing issue on the minds of the young is the AIDS epidemic. But again, does that dreadful disease constitute the *most* pressing issue?

64

Another candidate for that title is poverty — around the world and around the corner. Poverty is sustained deprivation. We have to ask: deprived of what? sustained by what or by whom? We can measure deprivation of food, shelter, employment, education and health care over against the levels of these necessities which basic human dignity requires for every human person. We know poverty when we see it. We do not so readily recognize its causes. Do systems — economic, political, cultural, and social — sustain the poverty we see? Or, is it sustained by persons; persons other than the poor themselves? Or, is poverty sustained by a combination of systems and persons? How do we get at the problem? How do the poor gain necessary participation in the economic system? How do deprived persons get out from under the oppressive restraints on their human potential? Is this complex problem of poverty the "most pressing" one with which our graduating collegians will have to deal in the decades allotted to them?

Perhaps hunger is the most important problem. Surely for millions it is at this moment the most urgent. Hunger is the most urgent form of poverty. Chronic malnutrition and severe deprivation of food spell ultimate physical deprivation and denial of life itself. Will hunger be the "most pressing" issue confronting us in the next half century? By the very debilitating nature of the hunger problem, it is obvious that those who must rise to the challenge of eliminating hunger are not those who are afflicted by the scourge of hunger. The same can be said of poverty.

Maybe ecological deterioration is the issue most deserving of attention. If we continue to pollute our streams, abuse our soil, poison our air, and lose our croplands to erosion on the one hand and asphalt on the other, we will be without the physical base we need to sustain life. Sustainability may be the issue for the next half century.

Is population growth the most pressing problem? How about the problem of economic development, without which problems like overpopulation and undernutrition will never be brought under control?

Should the memory of the Holocaust in Germany serve to remind us that an ever present problem is our capacity to hate, to murder, to disregard and destroy human life and dignity? The contemporary "life" issues like abortion, euthanasia, and capital punishment offer additional nominations for the top spot on our list of "most pressing" issues.

There are other pressing problems, of course. I think of family instability, the break-up of marriages, the loss of a sense of commitment in our lives and relationships. One of the most difficult words for today's youth to utter is "forever." I see a widespread problem of purposelessness in America's young. The nation offers them no central project; the economy tells many of them they really aren't needed. The nuclear cloud and the survival syndrome contribute ambiguity rather than clarity of purpose to their lives.

Other problems — all pressing, none open to simple solutions — deserve a place on our list. This final set of problems falls into what I like to call the "isms" category. The suffix "ism" throws a noun into boldface or italics. It signifies a bias, an emphasis, and almost always a disproportion. Racism, sexism, militarism, and terrorism would be good contemporary examples. Are the problems they connote high or low on the "most pressing" list for our times?

Atheism is surely a pressing and significant problem for this or any age. If the problem of atheism were attended to, would solutions to the other problems more readily fall into place?

Other "isms" will occur to anyone interested in taking inventory of the really important problems in the world in which we live. The list, then, is long. It is not the point of this exercise to collect, but to choose. The original question put to me by serious and appropriately concerned students was: "What is the most pressing issue you see for us in our generation?" My answer to them was, "materialism." This is the "ism" most to be feared.

It seems to me that the common denominator underlying the candidates for inclusion in any inventory of urgent, pressing, important, and significant problems to be dealt with by the generation now coming out of our educational system into our social, political, economic, and cultural systems is materialism. The word reminds us of the present and constant danger of overemphasizing the material side of our existence to the exclusion of the spiritual. To have becomes more important than to be. To possess is better than to share. To do for self takes precedence over doing for others. Property takes on more importance than people — other people, that is. And things, rather than ideas, assume a controlling influence in the lives of the materialistic majority in a materialistic society.

As the problem becomes all-pervasive, it touches virtually everyone. This, of course, means that virtually anyone can make a direct contribution toward a solution. Anyone can assess the extent to which the material has displaced the spiritual in his or her life, and decide to take corrective action to restore the balance. Anyone can take a self-administered test to estimate the relative importance of things and ideas in his or her life, the relative importance of library cards over credit cards, the eagerness to acquire over the willingness to share. Anyone can notice neglect of the soul and obsession with the body. Soul and body belong together, but they belong in balance. We are for the most part a quite unbalanced people in contemporary America. An unbalanced materialism has produced an unbalanced commercialism which permeates our recreation — our re-creative activities — and is now stifling our spirit.

We are a people drowning in a sea of materialism, as James Agee put it, and we are not really aware that something deadly serious is afflicting us. So we bemoan our fate, buy better locks, withdraw from the needy, and escape these suffocating realities by freely permitting ourselves to become addicted to dependency devices of one kind or another, some more harmful physically and psychologically than others, all, however, taking their toll at that pay-station which is me — the individual, unique human person. And it is precisely there, with the person — the unique, free individual who has the power to choose — that the solution must begin.

The forward perspective I have been suggesting here ranges over five or six decades. I want now to go back six decades to a statement of the question which still faces college students today; it was phrased in the 1920s by Willa Cather in an essay written to mark the end of the pioneer era in her beloved state of Nebraska.

> We must face the fact that the splendid story of the pioneers is finished, and that no new story worthy to take its place has yet begun.... The generation now in the driver's seat hates to make anything, wants to live and die in an automobile, scudding past those acres where the old men used to follow the corn rows up and down. They want to buy everything ready-made: clothes, food, education, music, pleasure. Will the third generation — the full-blooded joyous ones just coming over the hill — be fooled? Will it believe that to live easily is to live happily?

That's a question with the potential to rescue us from materialism. The "full-blooded joyous ones" who came up in the 1920s had an inadequate answer to that question. Their counterparts who are coming up today will have to take that question much more seriously if the pressing problems of their life span are not to do them in. Materialism is not the answer. We seem to be incapable of recognizing that fact. Materialism is, in fact, the question — the most pressing, significant, urgent, and important question with which the present generation has to deal.

I have presented, up to this point, a fairly generous array of critical issues and my selection of materialism as the one to top the list, as well as my presentation of all the others, implies a point of judgment, a crisis point, a criterion, grounded in Christian values. The ultimate Christian value is love; love's minimum requirement is justice. Those two values, love and justice, must inform the actions one chooses to take — corrective or preventative — in the face of those issues judged to be critical.

When we come to the point of action we also find ourselves at the portal of prudence. Not every action is wise and prudent. Not every wise and prudent action for others is appropriate for me in my particular circumstances. I must judge; I must choose. I may not, however, choose to do absolutely nothing. Recall that no crisis, in the Christian perspective, is beyond the reach of prayer which, in some cases, will be the only thing you can do.

One of your first choices with respect to most, if not all, critical social issues will relate to the question of alliances, joining others in a search for a solution. Inevitably, this search will raise the complicated question of the appropriateness of translating shared values into public policy. "There oughta be a law!" Should we legislate morality?

I'm indebted to Richard McCormick for recalling in an *America* article (12/7/85) what John Courtney Murray stated with characteristic clarity in *We Hold These Truths* (Sheed and Ward, 1960): "A moral condemnation regards only the evil itself, in itself. A legal ban on an evil must consider what St. Thomas calls its own 'possiblity.' That is, will the ban be obeyed, at least by the generality? Is it enforceable against the disobedient? Is it prudent to undertake the enforcement of this or that ban, in view of the possibility of harmful effects in other areas of social life? Is the instrumentality of coercive law a good means for the eradication of this or that social vice? And since a means is not a good means if it fails to work in most cases, what are the lessons of experience in this matter?"

When evil spawns a crisis situation, action related to the crisis should include unequivocal condemnation of that evil. Moreover, moral persuasion directed toward persons unaware of, implicated in, or hardened by the evil is appropriate when based on factual judgments and when conducted with respect for the dignity of the persons perceived to be in need of persuasion. Legal coercion may be appropriate but, in a representative democracy like our own, only when there is a consensus strong and wide enough to support it. I do not intend to lobby for laws against materialism!

One of the outcomes of effective moral education is the production of a consensus strong and wide enough to enact legal protection for shared values, when such protection is judged to be necessary. The broader outcome of good moral education is a heightened sensitivity throughtout society to the social requirements of love and justice. To demonstrate what I see as the present need for this heightened sensitivity and thus for the moral education capable of producing it, let me cite some findings from the Fall 1984 report on *The American Freshman*, the annual survey of college freshmen that was begun over 20 years ago by Alexander Astin and others at the University of California in Los Angeles — though the survey is national in scope, not limited to UCLA.

> The movement in student values toward material concerns and financial security continued this year, reaching an all-time high. Fully seven students in ten (71.2 percent) indicated that "being very well off financially" was an important personal goal. The 1984 figure is up from 69.3 percent in 1983 and only 43.5 percent in 1967. In contrast, student interest in "developing a meaningful life philosophy" was at 44.6 percent this year, up very slightly from the 1983 low of 44.1 percent but well below the peak of 82.9 percent in Fall 1967.

The trend continues to move in the same depressing direction. In 1987, a record 76 percent of freshmen said "being well off financially" was a key goal. Only 39 percent put strong emphasis on "developing a meaningful life philosophy."

There is a job to be done in moral education. I think it should begin with an examination (and condemnation) of the evil of materialism. Once an individual becomes sensitive to his or her own materalistic tendencies, he or she can begin to see a personal link to many societal problems of crisis potential. If you know yourself, you also know "where to begin." Deciding to take personal action against one's own personal portion of the problem is an indispensable first step. It must be followed by many other steps with many other persons — sometimes in social movements, sometimes through institutionalized effort, sometimes through the enactment of laws — before our pressing issues and critical problems can be satisfactorily managed or suitably contained.

As the decade of the 1980s opened, the "Congressional Clearing House on the Future" sponsored a lecture series by authors of new books dealing with critical issues facing America. The first lecturer (October 21, 1981) was Daniel Yankelovich, whose lecture title was "Critical Issues Facing America" (reprinted in the *Congressional Record*, January 26, 1982).

It is interesting to note his approach to the topic. He identifies four changes taking place in America (or more accurately, in Americ*ans*) at the beginning of the decade of the '80s.

The first change relates to the fact that, as a nation, we are growing older. In the 1930s there were nine people in the work force for every one person over 65 who was not working. The so-called dependency ratio in the 1930s was 9 to 1. As Yankelovich spoke in 1981, it was 3 to 1. By 1990 it will be 2 to 1. Of course, Social Security was unheard of as the decade of the '30s opened. But today, even with Social Security, there is a societal stress developing between the young who work and the old who do not, and there is, as I see it, a fear among the elderly that their money is going to run out and that there will be no one to care for them. The tendency is strong to cling to the money they have, to put their faith in money, and to put their hearts where their diminishing treasure lies. Understandable and regrettable as this tendency may be, it is, nonetheless, another instance of material-ism in our times.

The second change observed by Yankelovich relates to events in both the economic environment and the area of foreign affairs. As the present decade began, Americans were experiencing a new and growing vulnerability. By the end of the 1970s, inflation brought an actual decline in the nation's standard of living. The long ordeal of our hostages in Iran and the Soviet incursion into Afghanistan made Americans feel both frustrated and vulner-able, and ready to commit more resources to defense. In the opinion surveys Yankelovich and his colleagues conducted in 1980, 72 percent of the public were found to believe that "this land of plenty is becoming a land of want." Moreover, the majority of Americans surveyed were expressing the opinion then that "ten years from now" they would be unable to buy a new home or to own a home of their own.

The third change is described by Yankelovich as the absence of an "interpretative framework." People have a desperate need to understand why reversals are happening, particularly why they are happening to them. Before we began feeling these new vulnerabilities, most of us thought we could enjoy our affluence. When reversals related to inflation, the energy crisis, the success of foreign economic competition, and similar happenings came upon us, the people were shocked and unprepared for changes they did not understand. They found themselves off-balance and disoriented. They had no interpretative framework. In the view of Yankelovich:

> We are living through a change that many observers have characterized as a shift to the right. I see it less as an ideological shift than an emotional one. Let me explain what I mean. There is some evidence from surveys of a growth in conservative attitudes, but there is much confusion and contradiction in the evidence. I interpret the surveys as showing that the public is suffering from temporary disequilibrium by virtue of being thrown off balance. In seeking to regain their sense of control, some new attitudes are conservative; others are not. This is quite a different matter than an enduring swing to the right. Americans are confronted with a novel situation that no one has explained and they are filling in that void with whatever explanation lies at hand. Now, the most popular explanatory framework that people have embraced is "get government off our backs." Swollen government bureaucracies and budgets explain some of our problems and contain some element of truth. But any single explanation is limited. What happens when you blame government and things don't improve? I believe that in the 1980's we will see much wild experimentation with explanatory frame works, of which blame-the-government is only the first. It's going to be a very confusing period; politically, it will be wide open to political leaders who meet people's need for a credible explanation of what is happening, why it is happening and what we should do about it.

The fourth change factor relates to social morality. In the 1950s and into the decade of the '60s, Yankelovich points out, Americans could be divided into two groups — those who put their families first, and those who put their jobs first. We didn't really see ourselves thus divided until the late 1960s produced a third type of person — "people who put their own self-fulfillment ahead of family or work." This new value of self-fulfillment was related to affluence, to materialism. Many in the nation fell into the trap of consumerism. Again Yankelovich:

> We were lulled into believing that we could afford to neglect the problems of keeping the economy vital. Many Americans assumed that we had enough affluence so that the problem, say, of making a living was "a piece of cake" — you lost your job, so what, get another one. This attitude became prevalent in the 1960's and 1970's, rooted in the conviction that there was no need to make the kinds of sacrifice one's parents had to make. It wasn't so much that people were unwilling to make the sacrifices as a feeling that there's no need for sacrifice. Why not live a little? Let us shake ourselves free of attitudes rooted in the past. We can have more of everything, and in fact we're entitled to more of everything.

This was a rejection of older values. It was a rejection reinforced by materialism. "We have challenged," says Yankelovich, "the values of traditional duty, sacrifice for others, and self-denial, experimenting instead with a new ethic based on duty-to-self. That new ethic simply isn't working."

Now in the decade of the 1980s we are putting together a new social morality. We are reclaiming some of the old values and combining them with some new ones. In the opinion of Yankelovich we are rediscovering the future, admitting to ourselves that there is a future. Hence we are becoming concerned about the future once again and, consequently, we are rediscovering quality, and excellence, and skills. Interest in the future generates interest in quality. Rediscovery of skills will enhance our chances for economic survival over against foreign competition.

We are also taking another look at technology. It is becoming more acceptable as our recent passion for nature and the natural begins to recede. We are beginning to believe that technology can pull us out of our economic slump.

We are also rediscovering moral and religious values. Americans are beginning to see that many of our troubles including crime, violence and economic weakness "have their roots in a flabby social morality."

"What, then, is new?" asks Yankelovich. "If these are some of the older values that are now re-emerging, what are the new values that will combine with them?"

The first new value he identifies is "an intense desire to retain freedom of choice in one's lifestyle. Seventy-three percent of Americans say that greater choice is what differentiates their own lives from their parents' lives."

Another "new value" is a desire to reach beyond the self and become part of a larger community; people are showing signs of a greater readiness to cooperate in pursuit of common goals.

It is interesting to note that Yankelovich has confined his "critical issues" to those that have thrown the American people off balance, into a disequilibrium they cannot, without an interpretative framework, understand. I would call that disequilibrium unbalanced materialism.

It is also interesting to note that the "new values" of freedom of choice and a readiness to cooperate open up opportunities for religion in America. Religion depends on uncoerced choice; religion provides the context of community, a community of faith, for those who want to cooperate in works related to faith. (True faith can never be content not to do justice.) And religion, I would argue, can provide the interpretative framework Americans are struggling without today. Religion must speak to materialism. In speaking to materialism, religion will be addressing the root cause of most, if not all, of our most pressing issues.

Materialism will inevitably guarantee unwise choices. Materialism will turn cooperation into collusion intent on selfish purposes. Choosing (sifting?) wisely has always been the way through crisis; nothing impedes wise choice so effectively as a selfishness grounded in materialism.

A concluding story will illustrate this point while serving as a reminder that the "Christian values" that underlie my entire

74

argument have Judaic roots. The story comes from rabbinical literature. The moral of the story provides the intepretative framework needed in America today. Under the title of "The Window and the Looking Glass," this story comes from the Hassadim, pious Jews who lived in Polish ghettos at the beginning of the eighteenth century.

> A man whose heart was hardened by wealth and who was discontent and unhappy, went to the rabbi Eisig. The rabbi took him across the room and said to the man, "Look out the window, and tell me what you see." "I see people walking up and down." Then the rabbi held up a looking glass in front of him. "Look here now and tell me what you see." "I see myself." "So you don't see the others anymore? Consider that the window and the mirror are both made of glass; but, since the mirror has a coating of silver, you see only yourself in it, while you can see others through the transparent glass of the window. I am very sorry to have to compare you to these two kinds of glass. When you were poor, you saw others and had compassion on them; but, being covered with wealth, you see only yourself. It would be much the best thing for you to scrape off the silver-coating so that you can once again see other people."

By scraping away the silver of materialism, we will be less preoccupied with self, more aware of the needs of others, and more likely to reach out to meet those needs. This, I think, is what Carl Sandburg had in mind when he wrote, "Tell them too much money has killed men and left them dead years before burial."

If we take appropriate safeguards against materialism, we will find ourselves to be a good deal happier, less vulnerable, more balanced, and in possession of the tools to deal with most of the critical issues of our day. The tool kit, not empty but not yet filled, will be something a good university wants to provide for all of its students. Filling the kit and having it handy through all stages of life is the responsibility of the developing human person, the person a university is always there to serve.

8 Realistic Expectations, Great and Small, for the Catholic College Experience

Realistically, the providers of Catholic higher education should expect all those who take it to be willing to search out and seek after an ideal. It is not unrealistic to expect commitment to an ideal. It would, of course, be unrealistic to expect realization of the ideal in every student at every moment of the collegiate experience. The developmental ladder has many rungs; students can always be expected to be moving up and slipping down. But stages of growth can be mapped out for them and ideals worth seeking clearly identified.

The ideal that Catholic higher education should place before and require of its students is sacrifice. In the United States today, this is a counter-cultural idea. To call it counter-cultural means simply that it runs counter to the dominant values of this nation. But it is and will remain the central value of Catholic-Christian living.

There are many articulations of this central value in Scripture and tradition. Its most universal symbol is the sign of the cross. Countless statements of this ideal can be cited and conveyed to students. One citation worthy of recall is the exhortation used by the Church for many decades as part of the marriage ceremony.

"Let the security of your wedded life," said the priest to the bride and groom about to exchange their Catholic marriage vows, "rest on the great principle of self-sacrifice. Sacrifice is usually difficult and irksome; only love can make it easy, and perfect love can make it a joy."

Most students who enroll in Catholic higher education are on their way to Christian marriage. It will be a central reality of their lives. Within that reality, the central value is sacrifice, the underlying and indeed ultimate expression of love. Not heroic, split-second, loss of life for the other, but the ordinary, everyday, lay-down-your-life demands of courtesy and care for others in the intimacy of marriage and family. Although most students are not ready for this, this is where they are heading. Not to talk about it, not to point it out as an expectation, and not to structure it somehow into the collegiate experience, would be an educational failure of no small significance.

A readiness to sacrifice self for others is expected of all Christians, married or single, in all vocational circumstances. This value, therefore, should be integrated into both the collegiate experience and the expectations entertained for those enrolled in Catholic higher education. It should be expected in classrooms, residence halls, and in the total context of life on the Catholic campus. It is a value waiting to be factored into the Catholic collegiate experience.

The issue here is one of culture. I think of culture as a shared way of life. There are, of course, cultures within a culture, but in every instance, there is a value or set of values defining the culture. To share a way of life is to share the values underlying that way of life, to participate as well in shared meanings. It is interesting to think of a campus culture and to look for expressions of Catholic values in a Catholic campus culture.

One's thoughts, actions, and feelings are all culturally conditioned; the values that constitute the culture influence thinking, acting, and feeling within the culture. A very practical question for the Catholic collegian relates to whose values or which values dominate his or her thoughts, actions, and feelings.

Culture (and hence its dominant values) is transmitted socially, not genetically. Learning is therefore important if a shared way of life (a culture) is to be preserved. Education is part of the process of enculturation; so is entertainment, recreation, imitation, and observation. Education, of course, is not the whole of learning. The educator has to deal with other forces, some of them hostile, in the effort to preserve culture. Margaret Mead put the problem well:

> In small societies children learn by imitating their parents, relatives, and neighbors. In our huge society we use our mass entertainments to instruct our children on how they should express their emotions and what values they should have....We are showing our youngsters exactly the opposite of what we want them to imitate. We are showing them men who brutally attack others when angry. We show people who murder because of hatred and expediency. We show that love is expressed only by hunger for another's body and we show them little else. ["The Educative Environment," *The Newsletter*, Bureau of Educational Research and Service, Ohio State University, Columbus, Edgar Dale and Hazel Gibbony, eds., XXVI, No. 8 (May, 1961)]

The word "show" or "showing" is used by Margaret Mead five times in that brief scan of the educative environment. Obviously, "showtime" on stage, television, movie screen, and, by extension, on radio "shows," is an element to be examined in the question of conveying and preserving culture. Schooltime (elementary, high, and higher) should not try to compete with showtime, but neither can it ignore it. Schooltime should use its own time better to create a mindset or climate of opinion that is open to change but clear on central principles and critical of false values. Students should be encouraged to ask themselves, in the face of magazine and television advertising, not, "What does this ad invite me to buy?" but rather, "What does this ad expect me to be?" Behind the ad stands a value waiting to be confronted by the values which define one's culture, one's shared way of life.

Catholic college students should be open to change, but only for the better. Moreover, they should be perceptive enough to avoid being seduced away from their Catholic values and from the thoughts, actions, and feelings their Catholic values might reasonably be expected to foster. It is no exaggeration to say that, for all practical purposes, we leave our doors and our minds open to strangers when we permit televised advertisements to enter our consciousness. We should at least recognize the possibility of value conflict; students should be encouraged to make the consequent comparisons. In this kind of exercise, if the Catholic college student notices no value conflict, the Catholic college is not doing its job.

Let me simply say what I understand a value to be. A value is a quality — the quality attached to a person, idea, or thing so that it is prized and cherished. It therefore has worth. Association with, or possession of, that which I value is worth my while, my thought, my time, my money. In the principles that organize my life, I can find the values which define me and which disclose my ultimate concerns.

Those responsible for the provision of Catholic higher education in the United States should be asking their students, "Around what principles are you organizing your life?" In order to process the answers, educators should read or re-read Daniel Yankelovich's 1981 book, *New Rules: Searching for Self-Fulfillment in a World Turned Upside Down* (Random House). In a speech delivered around the time the contents of this book were very much on his mind, Yankelovich remarked that we used to be able to separate working adults into two categories: those who put job first and those who put family first. In the mid-1960s, he noted, a new phenomenon emerged, the person who put self ahead of both job and family. Self-denial has been virtually abandoned by seekers of self-fulfillment. Needed, says this chronicler of social and cultural change in America, is a new social ethic.

Faulty thinking about the self has led to faulty thinking about social rules, keeping us from developing a sound social ethic to replace the eroding ethic of self-denial. When millions of Americans began to forsake self-denial, they did so because our culture had encouraged them.

Yankelovich calls for an "ethic of commitment," understood as a shift in emphasis "away from the self (either self-denial or self-fulfillment) toward connectedness with the world." This, in my view, is not likely to work as well as he would hope. Nor should it, since it would mean abandonment (or concession that it has already been hopelessly abandoned) of a central Christian principle, the principle of self-denial, the idea and ideal of sacrifice. There can be no real commitment without a self to commit; the disciplined self makes the firmer commitment. Self-denial is preparation for the kind of commitments that qualify as sacrifice and express themselves as love. "Only love can make it easy, and perfect love can make it a joy," says the Catholic-Christian tradition about this heart-of-the-matter value of sacrifice. If, in the wisdom-perspective of the Church to which the Catholic college is related, this value is essential for the well-being of a person, how can that college not integrate it into its most practical expectations of its students during their collegiate experience? The Catholic campus culture has no choice but to encourage it; otherwise it would be staking its claim to be Catholic on campus ground bereft of a central Catholic value.

Yankelovich finds evidence among those he surveys of a "growing conviction that a me-first, satisfy-all-my-desires attitude leads to relationships that are superficial, transitory, and ultimately unsatisfying." He also finds some evidence of "a willingness to sacrifice those material/instrumental values that inhibit the sacred/expressive ones." This would amount to a value reversal. It should be read by the providers of Catholic higher education as encouraging news. There are signs of a new openness to what their tradition has to offer about saying no to self in order to say yes to others. It is time once more to talk about sacrifice.

In his 1987 encyclical On Social Concerns (*Sollicitudo Rei Socialis*), Pope John Paul II puts human interdependence on a moral plane. He uses solidarity — the idea of our human inter-connectedness — as a moral category. Self-denial, personal and national, is a moral obligation for all humans (our collegians not excluded) if justice is to prevail. "Today, perhaps more than in the past, people are realizing that they are linked together by a common destiny which is to be constructed together if catastrophe for all it to be avoided. From the depth of anguish, fear, and escapist phenomena like drugs, typical of the contemporary world, the idea is slowly emerging that the good to which we are all called and the happiness to which we aspire cannot be obtained without an effort and commitment on the part of all, nobody excluded, and the consequent renouncing of personal selfishness."

But what does all of this have to say to the visible realities of Catholic campus life, to the practical expectations those who provide the setting and programs for the collegiate experience might realistically have for those who live and learn there? It says, first of all, that the elders should search their own value-deposit boxes for the presence or absence of a commitment to the notion of sacrifice. It next asks how this value can be woven into the way things work on the Catholic college campus.

The elders will recall a familiar triad, rooted in Scripture and rearticulated by scholastic theologians whose propensity to divide almost any doctrine into three parts will be remembered with a smile, perhaps, but also with affection. The tradition speaks of the concupiscence of the flesh, the concupiscence of the eyes, and the pride of life. The scriptural locus is the first letter of St. John, in a portion, it should be noted, addressed to youth: "Carnal allurements, enticements for the eye, the life of empty show — all these are from the world" (1 John 2:16). The Jerusalem Bible offers this translation: "The love of the Father cannot be in any man [or woman] who loves the world, because nothing the world has to offer — the sensual body, the lustful eye, pride in possessions [explained in a footnote as "the ostentation of living"] — could ever come from the Father but only from the world; and the world, with all it craves for, is coming to an end; but anyone who does the will of God remains forever" (1 John 2:15-17).

The tradition would encourage the young to target their self-denial on the lustful desires of the flesh, the lustful desires of the eye, and the tendency to live ostentatiously — the acquisitive tendency to multiply possessions. The tradition, one might observe, surely has its work cut out for it today!

We elders tend to overreact to evidence of capitulation by the young to concupiscence of the flesh, while ignoring damage done to the young through concupiscence of the eye (recall Margaret Mead). Elders in our materialistic society have arguably yielded even more than the young to the assault on self-sacrifice implied in that third concupiscence, the pride of life. "It's gold, or glory, or God — what people worship," remarked William Carlos Williams. Most of the attention these days seems to be going to gold and glory.

C.S. Lewis still sells well in college bookstores a quarter of a century after his death. Collegians should be informed that Lewis saw himself as a defender of traditional Christian doctrine in a secular age. In a *New York Times* essay on November 22, 1988, Michael Nelson cites Lewis' own words in describing the mission he defined for himself: "Ever since I became a Christian I have thought that the best, perhaps the only, service I could do for my unbelieving neighbors was to explain and defend the belief that has been common to nearly all Christians at all times." And apropos of issues the campus elders should be discussing with students, Nelson reports C.S. Lewis as cautioning his readers to maintain a sense of balance in approaching these matters: "The sins of the flesh are bad, but they are the least bad of all sins. All the worst pleasures are purely spiritual: the pleasure of putting other people in the wrong...the pleasures of power, of hatred."

How might Catholic tradition and Catholic campus come together in common cause today if students are to be served in assimilating the tradition and indeed prepared for their role in carrying the tradition of self-sacrifice forward?

First, the central value of self-sacrifice must be identified, articulated, and discussed in class and in extra-curricular settings. It must be integrated into campus procedures, structures, codes of conduct, styles of campus life. It should have its place in anyone's set of campus expectations for students, faculty, and administration.

Consideration for the rights and needs of others should be a campus-wide expectation. This, of course, would be one affirmation, however faint, of the great ideal. It can be expressed in published rules and posted signs about litter, noise, book-return, energy conservation, parking and traffic regulation on Catholic campuses in the same language, rules, and signs that are evident on any campus. It can also be internalized, on the Catholic campus, as a common value, a shared meaning — consideration as an expression of love, a conscious even habitual response to a larger Christian ideal. A book returned on time; a stereo turned down or a light turned off; an empty soda can dropped into a trash receptacle and not tossed onto a campus lawn; all of these and countless other signs of consideration for others require self-discipline. These are surface acts, but they can reflect more than superficial values. They can express Catholic ideals.

So can attention to the arithmetic of alcohol abuse among Catholic collegians. Contemporary college students, reared on consumption patterns of superburgers, giant shakes, and 12-ounce cans of soda, have to learn that restraint is essential if alcohol is not to do them in. Eight cans of Coke in one sitting is an assault on any sensible nutritional standard. Eight cans of beer, with or without the ballast that burgers bring, will unbalance the body and unhinge behavior from standards consistent with reason and human dignity. The arithmetic of alcohol abuse should be assimilated in the Catholic mind with the help of the Catholic tradition of saying no to self in order to be better able to say yes to God and neighbor.

Drug abuse is a concern on all campuses today. Alcohol is a much more widespread problem, but drugs challenge the providers of Catholic higher education to look beyond the supply side, where they close ranks with law-enforcement officials, to the demand side. Why do young people freely choose to step into the midst of drug traffic? Why does this generation of young people choose at times to manage its dependencies in destructive ways unknown or untried by previous generations?

Has the Catholic belief in redemptive suffering, self-denial, self-realization through self-donation, been smothered by secular values that put a premium on avoidance of all pain — physical and psychological — at all times? What is so boring about home, school, and the experience or anticipation of paid employment that mind-altering drugs offer attractive exits from the borders of ordinary existence? What has happened to the potential that schooling has, with its coordinated curricular and extracurricular challenges, for displacing boredom with the prospect of achievement? Why are young people apparently less willing these days to take legitimate risks while some, at least, are reckless in their willingness to experiment with drugs? Why is failure so much to be avoided and fantasy the preferred refuge from the ordinary demands of normally manageable reality? Who knows? Well, the providers of Catholic higher education ought to have a few clues. It is surely not expecting too much of them or their campuses to give these questions some discussion and debate.

"This is not a generation that protests or complains," writes Susan Littwin of today's young people. "This is a generation that avoids." Her book, *The Postponed Generation: Why American Youth Are Growing Up Later* (Morrow, 1986), is capable of providing discussion material for use in campus settings as a gentle antidote to avoidance.

Take, for example, the notion of commitment, an indispensable element to a Catholic understanding of sexuality. What the "postponed generation" has postponed, says Littwin, who writes neither in nor of the Catholic tradition, is commitment. Providers of Catholic higher education, concerned about fostering discussion and assimilation of Catholic values related to sexuality, cannot avoid coming to terms with the notion of commitment.

I have noticed among the young a growing discomfort, over the past 25 years or so, with the idea of a permanent commitment to anyone or anything, to any person or project. The most difficult word for them to utter is "forever." Leaving to others the exploration of hypotheses about the impact of affluence, or the nuclear threat, or other variables on this hesitation to commit oneself, I prefer to let Susan Littwin be heard in her own reflections on this generation.

> "One senses that gifted young adults want what their parents have and more. They want personal gratification as part of their career bargain. They would like to achieve and have influence and recognition, but they are unwilling to take the risk. They talk a lot about freedom and adventure, which often turn out to be code words for not making a commitment. For as long as they haven't made a commitment, their illusions about life remain unchallenged. Caught between their sense of entitlement and their fear of failure, they live in a fantasy land of infinite choices."

Littwin notes that "there is, in fact, a wedding boom. But there is no marriage boom." She implies, of course, that it takes more than a wedding ceremony to make a marriage; it takes commitment. And she continues: "What is happening is that we are shifting undeniably and inexorably from a family-oriented society to a society of individuals."

> "...But today's young adults aren't just victims of social change. Their personality as a generation makes them very much part of the change. Commitment to a relationship is just as difficult for them as commitment to a career or a point of view. It is one more act that might define them and therefore limit their potential."

As I indicated earlier, most students who enroll in Catholic higher education are on their way to Christian marriage. That will be the central reality of their lives. And within that reality, I noted, the central value is sacrifice, another word for love. The suggestion now emerges that there is a link between sacrifice and commitment.

If the young are eventually going to define themselves as husband or wife, they are inevitably going to have to limit their potential for other choices, for other persons and places. In the choice of (or commitment to) another person in marriage, all the other alternatives are excluded, says the Catholic tradition. This generation tends to want to postpone that kind of commitment. But curiously, even tragically, many in the present collegiate generation do not realize that in postponing basic commitments, they are unwittingly postponing fundamental happiness.

Catholic expectations about expression and stewardship of the gift of sexuality cannot be reduced to a campus code about parietals and visitation rights. Far more profound questions concerning commitment need articulation and personal response. This is the stuff of serious discussions which one might expect to take place in structured settings on Catholic campuses. The only fully satisfying answers the Catholic campus culture can produce are all going to come down to commitment. And commitment, in the Catholic view, is always going to require sacrifice. To the extent that students may be "not quite ready for this," their Catholic tradition is also telling them they are not yet ready for the relationships parietals are designed to discourage. Students may not like the message, even reject it. But providers of Catholic higher education have a special responsibility to keep the message of sacrifice alive, whether it applies to love of persons or, as I now want to suggest, to love of learning as well.

All scholars know how crucial it is to include self-discipline in any effort to master and apply an academic discipline. Catholic people and Catholic colleges and universities are underrepresented in the front ranks of scholarly achievement in this nation. Those responsible for the provision of higher learning under Catholic auspices in America for the past 200 years have not succeeded in promoting levels of academic self-denial sufficient to produce levels of academic excellence worthy of worldwide respect. Religious prejudice cannot explain our underachievement; nor can inadequate funds. The inhibiting factor has been and remains our cultural failure to translate respect for sacrifice into a practical virtue in the academic order. Forgiveness and absolution are essential to our tradition. Without shortening the arm of forgiveness for others, we must now, as individuals, be personally unforgiving of self-indulgent avoidance of the demands of serious study.

Fostering this practical value in students is a challenge. More encouragement, recognition, and rewards from academic elders to student achievers will help. So would a cultural shift capable of converting student peer pressure from a negative or neutral influence to a positive force on Catholic campuses. Is it far-fetched to think of such a positive shift as a gesture of love, and a negative pressure as neglect (or worse) of neighbor on a Catholic campus? Not if that campus is connected to a tradition which sees sacrifice as an expression of love.

The rigorous self-discipline required for athletic excellence has a counterpart requirement in the area of academic achievement. Providers of Catholic higher education would all doubtless want their institutions recognized more for academic than athletic excellence. This will not happen, however, unless and until the Catholic campus culture, with reinforcement from the broader Catholic culture, articulates practical expectations of self-discipline in the classroom that are as plain, broadly proclaimed, widely accepted, and uniformly enforced as are training rules for varsity athletes.

It is worth noting that the best Catholic academic minds — faculty and student minds — in America are not all on Catholic campuses. It could be argued that disproportionately few are there. The reason? Other campuses are judged to provide superior academic settings. (I am prescinding from those cases where financial considerations determine choice of campus.) Another way of explaining Catholic choice of non-Catholic campuses for student or faculty careers is prestige. The places they choose are perceived to be better, academically superior. Those non-Catholic campuses, however, provide a culture which Catholics who enroll or teach there often accept without question. Some, of course, note it, mark its differences from their own Catholic values, and let it serve to tighten their grasp on their own Catholic cultural convictions. There are many examples of this. But for most, the influence of the campus culture on their attitudes and behavior is a largely unexamined reality. There is more involved in this than just a context for teaching and learning. It is a campus culture within which, among many other things, some important, life-defining choices will be made — choice of career commitment, or at least career direction; choice of friends, a spouse perhaps; assimilation of cultural values. Those values may be quite different from, even opposed to, the core values one would naturally expect to find on a Catholic college campus as expressions of an abiding Catholic culture.

No Catholic student or even faculty member should be forced to trade off academic excellence for a setting where Catholic values vivify the campus culture. Nor should they have to trade off a Catholic culture, if they would prefer it, for academic superiority. Where such trade-offs are real, the providers of Catholic higher education may not have failed, but they are not yet succeeding. The challenge before them is twofold: (1) elevate the level of academic excellence on campus, and (2) integrate core Catholic values with the curricular and extracurricular life on campus. Either one without the other will spell failure for the Catholic higher educational enterprise.

It is a realizable goal, in my view, for Catholic colleges generally to be perceived as superior for the quality of classroom teaching. This is already the case in many places and attainable in others without massive infusions of money, buildings, and equipment. Superiority in research is another question; until answered in terms of top-tier achievement, it may explain the absence of some Catholic intellectuals from Catholic faculties and some Catholic graduate students from Catholic centers of higher learning. But it is well within the reach of Catholic campuses today to become prestigious centers of quality undergraduate teaching. The risk these campuses run at the moment is that they will attract young Catholic minds on the strength of quality teaching while having nothing culturally Catholic to offer the student — mind and body — in a collegiate experience conscious of its connection to a tradition. That connection carries an obligation not only to pass the tradition on, but to engage it with the broader culture of meanings struggling to be shared in a world in need of help.

9 Campus Ministry

Campus ministry is both a relationship and a place — chapel, office, conference rooms, lounge. It is not, by any means, the exclusive province or sole preserve for values on the campus. Nor is the campus minister, or chaplain, the only conscience on the campus. But the ministers and their ministry do provide an environment for internalizing values, for discussing and debating the value dimension of an ever-changing menu of issues.

I think it more likely for positive values — religious, ethical, intellectual, and professional — to prosper in a college or university setting served by a highly competent and deeply committed campus ministry team. Such a team would be like the biblical "pearl of great price." There are not many such teams around. There are even fewer campuses willing, in the spirit of the same biblical parable, to sell all they possess in order to purchase that pearl. Fortunately for the students whose formation is served by campus ministry, those who minister are possessed by motives that lie beyond the reach of possessions.

Like ministry anywhere, campus ministry is a form of service. Catholic campus ministry can render its service on any campus, of course, wherever it is welcome. But this chapter will, with regret, ignore the secular, government-sponsored, and non-Catholic, church-related campuses — important as they are in both defining and describing the importance of Catholic campus ministry — and focus only on the Catholic college or university campus. In that context, I want to address myself to the persons, the professionals, who minister on Catholic campuses. Admittedly, all of us who work there minister in one form or another. But in offering these reflections, I have in mind those men and women whose ministry is primarily pastoral and whose base (and budget) locates them within the Office of Campus Ministry. I want also to discuss the structures that facilitate ministry, organize it, perpetuate it, and contribute to its effectiveness — assuming, all the while, the underlying presence of divine power without which any ministry, however well-structured and intended, is barren.

Structure is important. Persons are more important, but structure cannot be ignored. A structure is not necessarily a physical facility. It can be an established way of doing things. Physical space — sacred, social, working room of one kind or another — is necessary for effective campus ministry. I'm thinking of dedicated space assigned to and under the control of the Office of Campus Ministry. But Campus Ministry will often need other space, dedicated to other purposes and under the control of other offices, in order to do its work. And much of its work will be done without any special need for any particular space, as those who have engaged in pastoral ministry on campus know from personal experience. So space of one kind or another will always be important to Campus Ministry, and some dedicated space will always be included in an inventory of Campus Ministry "structures." But that inventory will also list events, transactions, intersections, and pastoral interactions all aimed at service but none pinned down to fixed points in space or time. My focus on structure, therefore, is going to have to be somewhat wide.

I think of the calendar as a structure and regard the calendar as one of the very best planning devices. In academic planning, the calendar provides the "tracks" along which the budget train runs. On Catholic campuses, that train will always have a Campus Ministry car. Some will say that the budget tracks seem always to be running uphill and the Campus Ministry car trails even the caboose, but the fact is that Campus Ministry has a rightful place in the budget on a Catholic campus and thus the office of Campus Ministry has a voice in the budget debates. The officers of Campus Ministry must therefore be planners, keying their programs to calendars and their calendars to budget cycles. Throughout the budget cycle, and thus endlessly, they are free to remind the planners that budgets have a way of embodying priorities and the appropriations for programs and facilities must always be measured against the institution's statement of mission and purpose. Spending more on the library than on Campus Ministry is not sufficient basis for charging the administration with an abandonment of religious purpose; but the adequacy of funding for the pastoral operation is a consideration not to be ignored by fiscal planners on a Catholic campus.

Campus Ministry must have its own working space — offices, conference rooms, space for counseling which is as close to soundproof as it can be (and thus no threat to confidentiality). It should have its own sacred space for daily Eucharist, a reservation chapel, a locus for quiet reflection throughout the day. Borrowed or shared space for larger community liturgies should be available and there should also be, under Campus Ministry control, all the essential equipment for liturgies held outdoors or in the fieldhouse or campus theater, whenever the need arises.

As part of its own structure, the college or university has its full-time administrators. The person in charge of Campus Ministry — director, dean, vice-president, whatever title fits best in a given situation — should have a well-defined place within that administrative table of organization. That person will have people, space, and programs to manage, as well as a leadership function to perform. The position must be visible and the person holding it clearly identifiable as the pastor of the campus community. And, as Dennis Goulet once remarked when speaking of leaders in another context, the person holding this leadership position must be "available, accountable, and vulnerable."

Part of the structure of Campus Ministry — "structured into it," so to speak — are the recurring programs of service Campus

Ministry provides for the campus community year after year. Call them elements, if you will, of the normal pastoral service the community expects from Campus Ministry, or view them as programs the institution entrusts to the leadership and management of its Campus Ministry professionals. Such programs would include: (1) sacramental ministry and all forms of public worship, (2) preaching, (3) retreats, (4) spiritual direction and counseling, (5) classes or courses of instruction, (6) lectures, (7) forums for discussion and debate, (8) training for and organization of peer ministry, (9) infirmary/hospital visitation, (10) organization and management of volunteer activities, on- or off-campus. Special events like food drives, "hand-in-hand" days with exceptional children, and vocation-awareness days could be perennial or occasional features of the Campus Ministry program. If they are to be successful, they will have to be scheduled and planned well in advance, thus part of the managerial responsibility of the person in charge of Campus Ministry. Scheduled staff meetings, reflection days, and renewal programs for the professionals are also part of the planning responsibility of the Campus Ministry manager/leader.

The way the Campus Ministry office communicates with the campus community must also be structured into its operation. The personal qualities of communicating well in speech and writing will be highlighted when I come to the question of identifying desirable professional characteristics in those who minister pastorally and professionally on campus, but the means of communication are structural elements. Signs, logos, posters, announcements, brochures, bulletins, newsletters, columns in the campus newspaper, audio- and video-cassettes, use of the campus radio or television station, where these media are available. All of these mechanisms are employed in one way or another by Campus Ministry personnel; all need not be employed at once, of course. But effective use of the printed or spoken word is indispensable in letting the campus community know about the programs Campus Ministry has to offer, attracting participation to Campus Ministry events, and in making

Campus Ministry's position known to the wider community when circumstances warrant a public statement.

Nothing I have suggested up to this point can be taken as limiting the scope of Campus Ministry activities to the pastoral care of students. Although I do regard students as the primary audience for the ministry our Campus Ministry professionals provide, I recognize a constant need for an effective outreach by Campus Ministry to faculty, staff, and others in the administration. Forgive me for putting it this way, but the highly desirable outreach to faculty is one of the chief reasons why I would put the quality of written and oral communication very close to the top of any list of skills that I would regard as indispensable to the tool-kit of the professional campus minister. Not that students do not deserve the best in speech and writing, it is just that they are less likely to notice their absence. Again, I say, forgive me! The real point to be made here, of course, is the simple truth that Campus Ministry must earn respect and acceptance from the faculty, that faculty tend to judge on the basis of the spoken and written word, and that without faculty acceptance the work of Campus Ministry will be that much more difficult and that much less effective.

Within the structures, of course, there is always room for systems. What system do we have to guarantee that any member of the campus community who is hospitalized is visited by a member of the Campus Ministry team? What system do we have to notify the community of serious illness or death among us? What systematic way does Campus Ministry have of surveying pastoral needs, of finding and filling vacancies for volunteer services, of judging the impact of the campus environment (e.g., dormitories) on student behavior, of identifying and measuring the impact of significant variables on career choice, of fostering the development of those human qualities which help the young to keep their commitments? The list of examples could run longer. Just to sketch it as I have, is to invite cooperation and communication between Campus Ministry and the social scientists on campus. What systematic contact does Campus Ministry have with the academic side of the institution? It would be natural to expect the Campus Ministry lecture programs, or discussion roundtables, to be lively locations for exploration of timely academic, particularly theological, questions. But little of this very important activity will happen if Campus Ministry fails to plan for it, budget it, and schedule it well in advance.

Nothing makes budgeting easier than the presence of an endowment. Endowed funds dedicated to the support of Campus Ministry programs yield annual operating funds. That annual yield belongs by right to Campus Ministry, reducing to that extent the competitive pressures Campus Ministry feels as it bids for its share of unrestricted general operating revenues over against all other units on campus. Endowment funds do not come easily, but when they do fall into place they provide a highly desirable financial foundation for the work of Campus Ministry.

As I turn now to the personal qualities or characteristics of those who make up the Campus Ministry team, I want to point to the obvious presence, on the Catholic campus, of many persons — some ordained, others not — who are able and willing to render pastoral service on an occasional or part-time basis as they tend to their primary responsibilities in other areas of campus life. They are waiting to be invited and willing to be scheduled, again a structural consideration.

There is no substitute for holiness in those called to minister pastorally on campus. Only men and women of deep faith can be expected to meet the needs of a faith community. Faith needs constant nourishment, and faith-committed ministers know the sources of that nourishment. They also take it as a personal and professional responsibility to bring themselves regularly to the sources.

Words like energetic, resourceful, affable, warm, friendly, and flexible immediately come to mind when compiling a list of personal qualities in the minister that will make ministry go better on campus. I mentioned earlier the importance of oral and written communication for what might easily be described as a word-based ministry. Although they work in academic settings, members of the Campus Ministry team need not be published scholars. They should, however, have a respect for scholarship and an ability to write and speak in ways that reach and draw respect from those, students and faculty alike, who place a high premium on the life of the mind.

Pastoral ministers on campus should, of course, be well versed in theology. They should be sufficiently familiar with the work of exegetes so that their homilies extend the proclamations from scripture in the right direction. Effective preachers will filter God's word through their own faith experience and attempt to match it up with the faith experience of their hearers. Busy as they inevitably will be, ministers of the word cannot, without violation of their professional responsibility, be too busy to prepare their homilies well.

Familiarity with the principles of good counseling and the psychological foundations necessary to recognize the problems that come to them should be expected of anyone on the Campus Ministry team. All should be well aware of the distinction between psychological and spiritual counseling, and more than ready to make the appropriate referrals when one's own competence does not match the client's need. And it is worth noting that an emotionally well-balanced person is not too much to hope for in any candidate for service as a campus minister.

The prophetic role cannot be ignored in any discussion of personal characteristics of campus ministers. It is not necessarily part of everyone's job description in the Campus Ministry office, but it is an important element in the Campus Ministry function. All of us benefit from occasional reminders of what the prophetic function is intended to be. We need to be refreshed on the distinction between foretelling and forthtelling, and reminded that the prophet is surely not one who predicts the future. Rather, the prophet is one who speaks up — speaks out, as we say. The prophetic person is one who is called, as all are called, to be responsive to God's word. But in the case of the prophet, God does not simply speak to the person, but through the person to the community. In response to God's prompting, the prophet points to those societal conditions which need adjustment (note the etymological link to *justice!*) so that those conditions, circumstances, or relationships may be brought into harmony with God's word, will, and plan.

In Hebrew literature, as we know, prophetic messages took the form of threats, promises, reproaches, and admonitions. If a given injustice is not attended to, such and such will befall the community. If religious neglect goes uncorrected, punishment will follow. The injustice went unattended, the neglect went uncorrected. The warning proved to be true, and the one who made the warning became known as one who could predict the future. This, of course, distorted the meaning and missed the point, to the confusion of generations up to our own. What campus ministers understand is that the prophet is the one who points to the problem. The voice must be raised; the problem must be identified. If the prophet's voice is silent, the word of God in judgment on our times (and within our communities) is not heard.

It should not surprise anyone to find the gift of prophecy associated with the campus ministry function. No one has that gift at all times and forever. And one who has the gift has a concomitant responsibility of awesome proportions.

Without evacuating all meaning from the prophetic role, it can be said that the campus minister at least echoes this function by asking questions — of the campus community, of individuals in the community. What is the purpose of the undergraduate years? What are you planning to do with your life? What is the character of this person to be hired? What are the implications of this rule of conduct? What are the values underlying this course?

Nor is it uniquely or heroically prophetic to take a stand occasionally, or even to stand for something consistently, in season and out, at the risk of being ridiculed as an "absolutist." Campus Ministry, as office and as team, should function as a reference point, a directional signal for students who are on their way. (It is interesting to note that "Journey" is the name attached at The Catholic University of America to the weekend-retreat experience our Campus Ministry team and many others provide for the students.) The campus community, or any person within it, should not come up empty if it asks itself the question: What does that member of the Campus Ministry team, or the team itself, stand for?

The prophetic role is, therefore, so natural to Campus Ministry that it should indeed be pervasive. At the same time, the gift of prophecy should properly be regarded as rare, not restricted to members of the Campus Ministry team, never contained within pre-cast structures, and always a burden to be borne with care, prayer, and the reinforcement of divine grace.

The professional committed to ministry on campus should be a perceptive and affirmative person, perceptive enough to recognize prophetic qualities in others, and generous enough to affirm those other persons in all their gifts. A saintly Jesuit of my acquaintance once remarked that the role of a superior in a religious community should be "to spray the place with praise." Not a bad description of a central element in the role of the campus minister.

Listening is another personal characteristic, skill, or ability I would regard as important for successful ministry on campus. Patience, respect for the other person, and self-denial related to one's own preference for scheduling projects and the expenditure of time, all of these are the infrastructure required for effective listening. Without listening, and listening long and carefully, the counseling-direction-advisement portions of the Campus Ministry program simply will not work. Hence the ministers must be listeners — an indispensable personal quality.

Courtesy is another important personal quality. I mention it explicitly because it can never be presumed to be present. Mentioning it also provides the opportunity to point to the positive "environmental impact" made by an office staff, especially the receptionist and secretary, who are often the points of initial contact with those seeking pastoral service from the campus ministers. If warmth and courtesy are characteristic of the office environment, the road to success for much of what Campus Ministry does is, if not perfectly paved, at least not still under construction.

Credentialing of campus ministers is an area in need of some attention. Often self-selection is the operative principle of preparation and assignment to service on a Campus Ministry team. A review of the structural considerations, program possibilities, and personal characteristics mentioned throughout this chapter would suggest elements to be included in any training program for Campus Ministry professionals. Prerequisite to a special program, however, would be solid post-baccalaureate education that would produce a "whole person" with at least one special competence — e.g., music, preaching, organizing, managing — needed for the Campus Ministry team to function well.

Given the wide and impressive range of experience, education, talent, and special skills possessed by people who present themselves (at different points in their respective stages of life) for service in campus ministry, I suspect the most practical approach to the training-and-certification issue would be a permanent institute capable of providing segmented training that would be continuing education for some and new career preparation for others. In any case, some competent professionals should be certifying persons as ready to preach, organize, counsel, direct, manage, teach, plan, and negotiate within the campus environment. It is not enough to have an academic degree and ecclesiastical faculties. We all know that, but we are slow to organize and offer the necessary training institutes.

I sometimes wonder what it would be like if we had a universally accepted credential to be submitted by anyone presenting himself or herself for full-time work as a campus ministry professional. Even if we had board- or bar-exam type sorters for entry to the profession, it is difficult to imagine unified programs of preparation analogous to law-, medicine-, or business school curricula that would "turn out" persons professionally competent for ministry. Some of the best candidates for this kind of work simply "turn up" after years of experience in other professional pursuits. Perhaps an apprenticeship model would be more appropriate as a credentialing mechanism. Maybe the ordinary driver's license is worth considering as a certification model. I would be more inclined to look to the clinical-pastoral-education model adapted to the special circumstances of campus ministry. I would set minimum standards measured by appropriate academic degrees and then require work toward special certification only when and if appropriate certification programs are available. In my view, it would be desirable to have special post-baccalaureate certification, even if the "certificate" were nothing more than the paper earned for participation in a summer institute.

Persons engaged in campus ministry are, with very few exceptions, men and women of extraordinary commitment. Their primary commitments are, quite understandably, to God, faith, Church, in some cases to family or religious community, in all cases to service. But little is done, in my observation, to foster their commitment to the profession of campus ministry, and even less to the practice of ministry on one particular campus. They have no tenure, no graded advances along a promotion path. Few have access to sabbatical opportunities. Many do not even have employment contracts. Words like "burnout," "turnover," and "experimental" occur so frequently in conversations about campus ministry that one can only wonder if application of the word "profession" to this activity is not to stretch that term beyond fair limits. This is not to say that recognition as a profession will never come to campus ministry. Its arrival will, however, be considerably hastened by the establishment of a universally accepted credential for full-time Campus Ministry practitioners.

The ideas offered for consideration here can be recapitulated in a "dry bones" line of argumentation. The structure is connected to the programs, the programs are connected to the persons, the persons provide the ministry to meet the faith needs of the campus community. I prefer to say faith needs of the campus community, instead of "faith community," because presence on campus as student, staff member, faculty, or administrator makes one a member of the campus community. Membership in a faith community, even on a Catholic campus, is more difficult to define. Campus Ministry is there to serve the faith needs of everyone on campus. Not everyone can be expected to be interested in the services Campus Ministry has to offer. Nor can Catholic campus ministry be expected to meet adequately the faith needs of all. But no one on campus should be regarded by Campus Ministry as out of reach or undeserving of attention. Hence the structure must be broadly based, the programs sufficiently diverse, and the personnel flexible enough to meet this extraordinary pastoral challenge.

10 Ideas and Images of Justice

Plato had an idea of justice. So did Aristotle, and the prophet Amos, and Augustine, Aquinas, and countless other philosophers, theologians, thinkers, and doers of all centuries. Throughout history, the exploration of the idea of justice has challenged our greatest minds. This exploration has produced some conceptual diversity. It has also uncovered differences in the way a person comes to understand the idea of justice. It is my intention to focus on two radically different approaches, in the hope of clarifying and even evaluating our ways of understanding justice. This I take to be an educational concern. In any educational, methodological inquiry, however, the question "education for what?" should be raised. So I intend to come up with some practical conclusions relating to education, specifically legal education for justice.

Both Plato and Aristotle had an idea of justice. Each of these great philosophers also had an idea of how one comes to understand the meaning of justice. I oversimplify, of course, and even magnify for purposes of illustration their difference in approach as I pose the comparison in the following terms. For Aristotle, the *experience* of justice will lead a person to an intellectual awareness of and a moral commitment to the *idea* of justice. For Plato, possession of a clear *understanding* of justice will lead to the *practice* of justice.

The educational implications are clear. In the Aristotelian approach, one will not achieve an understanding of justice apart from the practice of justice. Experience must come first. This, of course, says something that protectors of the conventional curriculum may not be prepared to hear.

The pedagogical implications of Plato's accent on understanding first, activity later, force upon us the consideration of the place of ethics in the curriculum. How well planned, how well taught is the ethics course? These are separate from the question of how effective is the ethics course in the life of the graduate out there years later in the workaday world with its economic pressures, its competition and complexity.

The Aristotelian emphasis would argue for exposure to those competitive pressures, experiencing perhaps the absence of justice or the burden of injustice as part of those pressures. This would be the best way of coming to an understanding of justice. The courses, definitions, and distinctions can come later. When they come, they will be more fully assimilated. Their effect will be longer lasting. The lesson, properly begun in activity and experience, will be fully learned. Experience is primary; reflection upon that experience is essential. A school should foster and guide reflection on experience. Schools impede and even defeat the learning process if they shield and effectively insulate the potential learner from the necessary experience.

Lest I give the false impression that it can happen only in schools, let me put on the record at this point the testimony of Nate Shaw, a former slave and tenant farmer. Theodore Rosengarten published a life of Nate Shaw in 1974. From that book, *All God's Dangers* (Knopf), I quote tape-recorded reflections taken in Tuskegee, Alabama, when Nate Shaw was 84 years along in a life that included slavery, tenant farming, and imprisonment for participating in union organizing efforts. At age 84, Nate Shaw could neither read nor write. But he could reflect on the idea of justice:

> I never tried to beat nobody out of nothin' since I've been in the world, never has, but I understands that there's a whole class of people tries to beat the other class of people out of what they

has. I've had it put on me; I've seen it put on others with these eyes. Oh, it's plain! If every man thoroughly got his rights, there wouldn't be so many rich people in the world. I spied that a long time ago. Oh, it's desperately wrong! I found out all of that because they tried to take, I don't know what all, 'way from me....

Somebody got to stand up. If I'm sworn to stand up for all the poor colored farmers and poor white farmers, if they take a notion to join, I've got to do it. If you don't like what I've done, then you are against the man I am today. I ain't going to take no backwater about it. If you won't like me for the way I have lived, go on off into the woods and bushes and shut your mouth and let me go for what I'm worth and if I come out of my scraps, all right. If I don't come out, don't let it worry you; this is me and for God's sake, don't come messin' with me. I'd fight this morning for my rights. I'd do it for other folk's rights if they'll push along.

How many people is it today, that needs and requires to carry out this movement? How many is it knows just what it's goin' to take? It's taken untold time and more time and it'll take more before it's finished....The unacknowledged ones...that's livin' here in this country, they're gonna win.

Nate Shaw witnesses to what I have labeled as an Aristotelian approach to the idea of justice.

Plato was a disciple of Socrates, who left us no writings but whose thought, chiefly in the dialogic format, has been preserved for us by the pen of his star pupil Plato. For Socrates, and for Plato after him, knowledge held the primacy. If a person has a knowledge of justice, that person will tend to act justly.

Dejected after the execution of Socrates in 399 B.C., and apparently convinced that all existing states were governed badly, Plato wrote toward the end of his life that "the only hope of finding justice for society or for the individual lay in true philosophy.... Mankind will have no respite from trouble until either real philosophers gain political power or politicians become by some miracle true philosophers."

Rather than depend on miracles to "educate" persons for justice, Plato's preference was to foster development within the individual person of a state of balance between and among three human impulses: the animal appetites, the desire to know, and the drives of human ambition. Plato has Socrates explain it to Glaucon as follows:

"Justice, therefore, we may say, is a principle of this kind; but its real concern is not with external actions, but with a man's inward self. The just man will not allow the three elements which make up his inward self to trespass on each other's functions or interfere with each other, but, by keeping all three in tune, like the notes of a scale (high, middle, and low, or whatever they be), will in the truest sense set his house in order, and be his own lord and master and at peace with himself. When he has bound these elements into a single controlled and orderly whole, and so unified himself, he will be ready for action of any kind, whether personal, financial, political or commercial; and whenever he calls any course of action just and fair, he will mean that it contributes to and helps to maintain this disposition of mind, and will call the knowledge which controls such action wisdom. Similarly, by injustice he will mean any action destructive of this disposition, and by ignorance the ideas which control such action."

"That is all absolutely true, Socrates."

"Good," I said. "So we shan't be very far wrong if we claim to have discerned what the just man and the just state are, and in what their justice consists."

"Certainly not."

"Shall we make the claim, then?"

"Yes."

"So much for that," I said. "And next, I suppose, we ought to consider injustice."

"Obviously."

"It must be some kind of internal quarrel between these same three elements, when they interfere with each other and trespass on each other's functions, or when one of them sets itself up to control the whole when it has no business to do so, because its natural role is one of subordination to the control of its superior. This sort of situation, when the elements of the mind are in confusion, is what produces injustice, indiscipline, cowardice, ignorance and vice of all kinds."

Plato identifies the three elements as (1) reason or the reflective element of the mind, (2) the irrational appetitive impulses, and (3) spirit, understood as a sense of self regard evidenced in assertiveness or, on occasion expressed in the form of indignation.

Similarly, three elements or classes make up the state: businessmen, Auxiliaries, and Guardians. When each of these three classes performs its own proper job, justice prevails, since Plato identifies justice in a state as the situation wherein all persons mind their own business. He has Socrates put the matter this way: "In fact the provision that the man naturally fitted to be a shoemaker, or carpenter, or anything else, should stick to his own trade has turned out to be a kind of image of justice — hence, its usefulness." Earlier in the dialogue, Socrates says that "justice is keeping to what belongs to one and doing one's own job."

In the state, as in the individual, justice is a matter of balance between and among the elements.

Justice, understood as a balance of appetites, is pedagogically manageable. It is also compellingly intellectual. This approach packaged, if you will, by Plato from ideas originating with Socrates, may have influenced Robinson Jeffers in his poetic celebration of the "cold passion for truth."

> ...The gang serve lies,
>   The passionate
> Man plays his part; the cold passion
>   for truth
> Hunts in no pack.
> Let boys want pleasure, and men
>   Struggle for power and women perhaps for
>   fame.
> And the servile to serve a leader and
>   the dupes to be duped.
> Yours is not theirs.

Education engages more of the human potential than just the cold passion for truth. That, of course, is fundamental, but one would hope that warm compassion as well as a thirst for justice will find their proper places atop or around that foundation of reason.

Plato's *Republic* has been called the first great book on justice. It serves as a benchmark for all subsequent probings into the meaning of justice. Professor Otto A. Bird, writing on *The Idea of Justice* (Praeger, 1967), refers to Socrates' search for justice as "the search for a definition," and goes on to list four different definitions of justice to be found in the pages of *The Republic*:

> telling the truth and rendering up what we have received;

> rendering to each his due;

> complying with the interest of the stronger, that is, of the ruling class as it is expressed in law;

> minding one's own business both in external relations with others and in the internal ordering of the soul.

My concern is more with the way we come to understand justice than with the content of that understanding. I am interested more in how we arrive at our respective ideas of justice than in the definition which matches those ideas. I think every educated person should have an idea — a coherent, personal idea — of justice. As an individual as well as a member of any larger community, the human person will have no reference points, no moorings, unless that idea of justice has been developed and internalized as a principle from which decisions and actions flow. It is in the midst of ever-changing circumstances that principled, personal decisions must be made. The unprincipled person is always off-balance. The principled person has a place to stand. Education assists the human person in finding that place and taking the appropriate stance.

I would like to draw a distinction between a rule and a principle. From an ethical perspective, rules may at times be broken. Indeed some rules at some times should be broken.

Principles, however, cannot really be broken; they can only be applied or not applied. The application is always in a context of free choice. Where an appropriate principle, sufficiently known and applicable in a particular set of circumstances, is not applied, the omission represents an ethical failure. This would not be so were the principle unintentionally applied incorrectly. If one knowingly acts contrary to one's freely held principle, the principle is not broken although its spirit is violated and the resulting choice is contrary to the decision dictated by the unbroken but also unapplied principle.

Efforts to educate for justice will be unavailing if they attempt to impose rules but fail to cultivate the personal appropriation of principles.

I would want to argue that our images of justice, our symbols, can be immensely helpful in preparing the way for personal appropriation of the principles of justice. I would also be prepared to argue that the experience of *in*justice is an excellent, at times the best, pedagogical route toward a grasp, quite literally a comprehension, of the idea of justice. One person's experience will differ perhaps from another's. Hence, there is likely to be conceptual diversity but not necessarily contradiction relating to the idea of justice. Similarly, images congenial to the eye of one observer may attract neither the attention nor interest of another. Understandings flowing from those images will understandably differ.

Images can indeed be helpful. Take, for example, the famous plumb-line image used by the prophet Amos. Shalom Spiegel has observed that a philosopher like Plato tends to deal with justice as a concept; a prophet like Amos treats justice as a command.

> This is what the lord Yahweh showed me:
>
> a man standing by a wall,
>
> plumb-line in hand.
>
> "What do you see, Amos?" Yahweh asked me.

"A plumb-line," I said.

Then the Lord said to me,

"Look, I am going to measure my people Israel

by a plumb-line; no longer will I overlook their offenses.
(Amos 7: 7-8)

The nation will be inspected. It will be measured for its up-rightness, its integrity. Just as a wall that is "out of plumb" will collapse, so a society that is unjust is going to topple. As a group or nation, we are subject to measurement for the balance of our relationships with one another. Do our dealings pass the plumb-line test? Are they on the "up and up," or "on the level," or "fair and square?" The plumb-bob falls toward the exact center of the earth. The line between hand and bob is therefore "upright," an image of justice.

Another useful image comes from the legend, if not the actual mind and words of St. Thomas More. As I mentioned in an earlier chapter, playwright Robert Bolt has his imprisoned hero, Thomas More, employ a striking simile to explain to his daughter Meg why he will not swear to the Act of Succession and thus gain his freedom at the price of violating his conscience:

"When a man takes an oath, Meg, he's holding his own self in his own hands. Like water. (He cups his hands.) And if he opens his fingers *then* — he needn't hope to find himself again. Some aren't capable of this, but I'd be loathe to think your father one of them."

I suggest that the cupped hands image the internalization of the water of justice. By opening the fingers in falsehood or infidelity, something of the self is lost. It is a matter of personal integrity.

The familiar trays in balance on a scale provide by far the best image of justice. As Barbara Ward has written, "To illustrate the degree to which philosophers have long recognized the consequences of unbalanced power, one has only to recall Thucydides', the great Greek historian's, account of Athens and Melos. 'The human spirit is so constituted that what is just is examined only if there is equal necessity on both sides. But if one is strong and the other weak, that which is possible is imposed by the first, accepted by the second.' That is why, since antiquity, the symbol of justice has been a figure holding equally balanced scales."

The scales of justice find their way onto lawyers' cuff-links, tie clips, monograms, jewelry, desk sets and coats-of-arms. In legal circles, the figure holding the scales in balance is often blindfolded, symbolizing the impartiality of the law itself. The image invites reflection.

What we experience in life as uneven is not necessarily unfair or unjust. To establish injustice, one must first establish *relatedness* between the trays. Not every imbalance is wrong. An imbalance is also an injustice when one side's advantage (the down tray) has been taken at the expense of the other side. Related to a downside gain is an upside injury (in-*jure*). Is the holder of the downside gain the active perpetrator of the injury? If so, the relatedness is quite direct. If the advantaged down-tray represents a passive benefit derived from an injury inflicted by another (even by impersonal social forces), the question of relatedness must be traced with care. The closer the relatedness, the larger the obligation to work to bring the trays into balance.

There is hardly a problem of significance to society today which cannot be examined, at least in a general fashion, through the framework of the scales of justice. One begins such an examination by locating oneself or one's group on one of the two trays. In comparative relationships between the races, between rich and poor, the well-fed and the hungry, the well-educated and the illiterate, in any comparative social or interpersonal relationship, it is possible, upon reflection, to locate oneself on the appropriate tray. That tray will be balanced equally against the other tray, or in a disadvantaged upward position, or weighted with a downside gain. If an imbalance is evident, the question to be asked is: Has one side's gain been taken at the expense of the other? Is one side up *because* the other is down? Reflection upon relatedness between the trays is not likely to happen or to be taken seriously without the prompting of an internalized principle of justice. The image without the idea is useless.

One of my lawyer friends has strong personal and professional commitments to assist the disadvantaged poor. He has done valuable work in organizing legal services for the indigent. He now trains student lawyers for service to the poor. My friend insists that the religious patron of lawyers is not St. Thomas More but St. Ives — St. Ivo Helory, a French lawyer-priest (1253-1303) whose life is summed up in the title of his biography written by A. Desjardins, *St. Yves avocat des pauvres et patron des avocats* (Paris, 1897). Already trained in canon law, Ivo Helory studied civil law at Orleans. He served as a judge in cases that came before the ecclesiastical court.

> In this capacity he protected orphans, defended the poor and administered justice with an impartiality and kindliness which gained him the goodwill even of the losing side.... His championship of the downtrodden won for him the name of "the poor man's advocate." Not content with dealing out justice to the helpless in his own court, he would personally plead for them in other courts, often paying their expenses, and visiting them when they were in prison. Never would he accept the presents or bribes which had become so customary as to be regarded as a lawyer's perquisite. He always strove, if possible, to reconcile people who were at enmity and to induce them to settle their quarrels out of court. In this manner, he prevented many of those who came to him from embarking on costly and unnecessary lawsuits.

It is generally agreed among the few who decide such things, but little known among the many whose spiritual welfare is so much the better for it, that St. Ives shares with St. Thomas More the distinction of being a spiritual advocate for those whose profession is or will be advocacy through the law.

At the Law Day Dinner of the Benjamin N. Cardozo School of Law of Yeshiva University on May 1, 1979, Congressman Peter W. Rodino, Jr., Chairman of the House Judiciary Committee, also well-remembered for his direction of that Committee during the crisis that led to the resignation of President Richard M. Nixon, had this to say to his fellow lawyers:

> Lawyers undoubtedly hold more leadership positions in America than any other group. Our influence extends through government, business and industry, education, the communications media and in every sector of our American community. Whether we like it or not, lawyers are the pacesetters, the social architects, if you will, of these United States. Because our nation is changing so rapidly and our society is becoming so amorphous, we as lawyers have greater responsibilities than ever before. Our intimate knowledge of how order is attained and our ability to define and articulate the rules for society are needed now more than ever before in our nations's history.

If St. Ives and St. Thomas More were here today, they would probably agree with Mr. Rodino's assessment of the leadership position occupied by lawyers, but disagree with his estimate of what the nation needs now from its lawyers. It would seem to me, at least, that the maintenance of order and the definition of rules are far less urgent for our nation today than the need to internalize, individually and collectively within the legal community, an idea of justice powerful enough to drive our lawyers more directly into positions of advocacy for the poor.

Those already engaged in the practice of law will need help in this regard. They will need assistance from the law schools which prepared them in measuring now the extent to which they have, in fact, internalized the principles of justice. They will need both guidance and encouragement from the law schools which produced them, if they are to evaluate the degree to which they have developed over the years their understanding of the idea of justice. This is a matter of continuing legal education. I do not intend to address it except to remark that the wealth of practical experience possessed by a body of law alumni offers a marvelous opportunity to the educator interested in taking what I characterize as an Aristotelian approach to the assimilation of a notion of justice.

For the student lawyer, however, I do have a question or two, and several practical suggestions.

What is true legal education? Will it happen that the application of student talent to the needs of the poor in clinical settings will cultivate motivation and professional capabilities for larger societal contributions later on in private or corporate practice? There is little evidence from this nation's considerable clinical experience in medical education to support this prospect. It could be otherwise in the law.

Forgetting for the moment the clinic and turning to the classroom, I would invite student lawyers and those who teach them to respond to questions Sissela Bok raises about professional schools, in her book on *Lying* (Pantheon, 1978):

> How do they cope with cheating, with plagiarism, and with fraudulent research? What pressures encourage such behavior? To what extent, and in what disciplines are deceptive techniques actually taught to students? What line do law school courses, for instance, draw with respect to courtroom tactics, or business school courses with respect to bargaining and negotiation?... What can education bring to the training of students, in order that they may be more discerning, better able to cope with the various forms of duplicity that they will encounter in working life?

This really returns us to our starting point. Should we *think* our way toward just *actions* — or *act* our way into deeper *understandings* of justice? The answer requires a balance between the two. Here again the image of the scales is helpful.

My advice to the student lawyer is to begin looking at the world through the framework of the scales of justice. Do the imbalances represent acceptable unevenness or unacceptable injustice? Whatever the student's image of justice, his or her idea of justice is likely to touch upon the notion of equity, of fair shares. There will probably be a recognition that justice does not necessarily mean prosperity, and an admission that it will always mean something related to decency and human dignity. The student's idea of justice will ordinarily apply the notion of equity first to the distribution of material goods, to the distribution of wealth and income. Only secondarily is the notion of justice likely to include considerations in the spiritual realm where equality of rights — human rights relating to freedom of speech, of religion, of conscience, and of self-determination — emerge as matters of great concern. In his speech at the United Nations on October 2, 1979, Pope John Paul II identified the two "main threats" to peace, indeed to the survival of our world, as violations of human rights in both the distribution of material goods and in the exercise of our equal rights in the spiritual realm.

A person whose professional commitment is to protect the rights of others in both these realms, to advocate equal exercise of the rights of the spirit and equal access to material necessities, is indeed a privileged person holding a sacred trust. Such is the lawyer in our society, or so the lawyer should be!

How prepare to accept this trust? I have already stressed the importance of experience — out-of-class, off-campus experience — in the development of an understanding of justice. I do not discount the importance of classroom work. Recognizing the organizational problems of managing the educational experience and how the classroom helps so much in that regard, I want to bring this discussion back to the classroom and leave it there for further discussion by those responsible for the quality of the classroom experience — administrators, professors, and students not least of all.

It is estimated that approximately 90 percent of American law schools have required courses in professional responsibility. Presumably, most such courses deal with the ethics of the profession. Daniel Callahan and Sissela Bok, co-directors of the Hastings Center's Project on the Teaching of Ethics, have examined classroom efforts in ethics education in many undergraduate and professional schools in the United States. They are persuaded that there should be at least five basic goals in the teaching of ethics:

(1) **Stimulating the moral imagination.** This means encouraging the student to develop a "moral point of view."

(2) **Recognizing ethical issues.** The point here would be to identify issues of right and wrong in their technological, psychological, sociological or political clothing.

114

(3) Developing analytical skills. This involves the cultivation of reflection, definition, and reasoned argument.

(4) Eliciting a sense of moral obligation and personal responsibility. The student must be confronted with the question, "Why ought I to be moral?"

(5) Tolerating — and resisting — disagreement and ambiguity. The issues are complex; students must be taught to handle them with respect for another person's reasoned but differing point of view.

It is difficult to imagine a better setting than a law school classroom for the vigorous pursuit of these goals. There are, however, forces of materialism at work in the profession — excessive concern with prestige, economic rewards, and personal power — which can effectively sidetrack such classroom activity. These forces can make themselves felt through students, faculty, and potential employers. A good law school will be strong enough to prevent such forces from obscuring the image or distorting the idea of justice.

11 Education for Social Justice

To put a Christian perspective on education for justice is a structural approach, not a simple adjustment in the angle of vision. To specify social justice, not justice alone, as an educational objective is also a structural specification. I shall discuss each of these points separately. First, what new reality is involved in a Christian approach to justice? Second, how does social justice differ from inter-personal justice and what, if any, are the implications for those who would attempt to educate for social justice?

In considering all that follows, the reader might consider as well an etymological suggestion. Issues of social justice are structural concerns. Would not etymology suggest that instruction, normally associated with education, might have some important relationship to the construction or reconstruction of the social order?

For the Jewish contemporaries of Jesus, the Kingdom of God connoted the realization of the ideal of a just ruler. As Walter Kasper puts it in *Jesus the Christ* (Burns & Oates, 1976), "In that ancient Middle Eastern conception, justice did not consist primarily in impartial judgments, but in help and protection for the helpless, weak, and poor. The coming of the Kingdom of God was expected to be the liberation from unjust rule and the establishment of the justice of God in the world."

In that context and to those contemporaries, Jesus proclaimed his message, "The Kingdom of God is at hand" (Mk. 1:15). He added to that proclamation the instruction to "repent" and to "believe the gospel." Hence, a response to his proclamation required both faith and an attitudinal change, a *metanoia*. Something new, some hoped-for relief from unjust and exploitative rule was, with the arrival of Jesus in human history, "at hand." Something new, some change of heart on the part of those who received the proclamation would be required to permit that which was "at hand" to be accepted, to take hold.

Those whose work is Christian education are laboring for the establishment of that same Kingdom of God, a kingdom of justice and peace, a kingdom which is still at hand but not yet grasped, not yet fully realized.

Christian education is a ministry of the Church. It is in and of the Church, a Church which is a community, a pilgrim people, on the way to Kingdom.

It is important to understand the meaning of the term "Kingdom," as Jesus used it. It is not a place. Rudolf Schnackenburg in *God's Rule and the Kingdom* (Herder and Herder, 1963) insists that it is a rule, a reign, a leadership

> ...which develops from Yahweh's absolute power and shows itself in the guidance of Israel. This original meaning, that Yahweh as king actively "rules," must be kept in mind through the whole growth of the kingdom theme. God's kingship in the Bible is not characterized by latent authority, but by the exercise of power, not by an office but a function, it is not a title, but a deed.

Jesus proclaimed himself to be the doer of that deed, the holder of that power. Kingdom is an exercise of power. The power to establish justice is the Lord's. The task to work for justice is ours. And the pity of it all is the fact that the power indeed is "at hand" and has been at hand for 2000 years, but the egalitarian characteristics of the Kingdom have not yet taken hold because the response to the proclamation has, to date, carried with it an insufficient change of heart, an insufficient attitudinal change, an

117

unwillingness on the part of those who "have" to "let go" for the benefit of those who are deprived.

Jesus' own preaching of the Kingdom destroys our own closely held preconceptions; it challenges the hearer toward value reversal. The poor, not the rich, are "blessed" he says (Mt. 5:3); the persecuted, not the comfortable, are "blessed" as well (Mt. 5:10). As John R. Donahue, S.J., has commented, there are very direct social implications in the Kingdom proclamation because Jesus shatters the social conventions of his time by making, as the sign of the arrival of the Kingdom, his fellowship with the outcasts of society. The teaching of Jesus reveals a very clear preference for the poor. He displays what might be called a compensatory bias, a characteristic impulse to use his power to empower the powerless. He tries to move, by example, by persuasion, and by threat of damnation, the heart of the unjust oppressor in order to bring relief to the victim of oppression. There is no "unrightable wrong" in face of his person and power. There are only resistant hearts and closed minds in the face of his gospel proclamation.

But what is new or different in a Christian approach to justice? What did Jesus add to earlier understandings of justice? To answer this it is necessary to consider justice as Jesus taught it. This is particularly important for Christian educators who are called, as the title of the American Bishops' 1972 Pastoral on Catholic Education puts it, "To Teach As Jesus Did."

Justice, as Jesus taught it, is something different from the justice of Plato and Aristotle.

It is my view that education for justice must be, in some recognizable form, Christian education. To the extent that this sounds outrageously arrogant, it measures with accuracy the sinfulness, the social sinfulness, of the Christian people. It also measures the distance between the contemporary Christian community and the Kingdom which was announced, 2000 years ago, to be "at hand."

There is continuity, not discontinuity, between Old Testament and New. The continuity resides in the person and teaching of Jesus. In tracing the continuity from Old Testament origins to

118

New Testament specifications, I begin with a famous text from the Book of Micah:

> What is good has been explained to you, man;
>
> This is what Yahweh asks of you:
>
> only this, to act justly,
>
> to love tenderly
>
> and to walk humbly with your God. (Mi. 6:8)

Justice, as Jesus taught it, involved a conscious and explicit integration of those two ideas, "to act justly," and "to love tenderly." Cold, impartial "treating-equals-equally" or "every-man-his-due" understandings of justice fall short of the mark set by Jesus for the Christian. From either a personal or social perspective, the root problems he set out to correct, it seems to me, are all reducible to powerlessness, poverty, and indignity. The means he chose to employ in correcting them were educational. He taught by word and example the unity of justice and love. "To act justly," according to the example and teaching of Jesus, meant also "to love tenderly." Love without justice is not Christian love. Justice without love is not Christian justice.

Where do I find this New Testament specification? The Fordham theologian Charles H. Giblin, S.J., suggested in a lecture some years ago that Luke 15 presents justice in a new way, in the context of mercy and love. That particular chapter in Luke contains three parables on God's mercy. They were addressed to the Pharisees and the scribes who "complained," says Luke, because "the tax collectors and the sinners...were all seeking his company to hear what he had to say" (Lk. 15:1). The most famous of those three parables, directed in Luke's grouping toward the scribes and the Pharisees, is the story of the Prodigal Son. But as Father Giblin observed, it is the dialogue with the elder son that reveals an underdeveloped notion of justice, an unawareness of the necessary integration of justice with love. The dutiful ("every man his due") elder son will have to change his notion of justice in order to enter into the celebration. If he chooses not to change, he may not go into the house. He must "repent," undergo a *metanoia*, if he is to accept the new understanding which is there "at hand."

In the tenth chapter of St. Luke another duty-obligation story makes the same point, but much more dramatically. It is the parable of the Good Samaritan. First there is the question, "What must I do to inherit eternal life?" In reply, Jesus repeats the Old Testament instruction to love your neighbor "as yourself." Then the lawyer who had posed the prior question asks, "And who is my neighbor?" The reply this time is a parable about an abandoned victim of a roadside beating and robbery. Along in close succession come a dutiful priest and a dutiful Levite who see the victim but pass him by. Their sense of duty did not move them to assist the man. According to their assessment, apparently, duty required no action of them in that particular situation. "But a Samaritan traveler who came upon him was moved with compassion when he saw him." Compassion enters the instruction, and through the instruction compassion, mercy, and love enter the structure of a Christian response to powerlessness, poverty, and indignity. The rest of the parable further elaborates the notion of justice as Jesus taught it.

This, it seems to me, is a specifically Christian development. It is a development of, not discontinuous with, the Old Testament teaching. Consider Hosea:

> And I will betroth you to myself forever;
>
> I will betroth you to myself in righteousness and justice,
>
> And in kindness and mercy. (Hos.2:21)

All the elements are there in Hosea. They are specifically integrated in the person and teaching of Jesus.

Consider Amos proclaiming the Lord's preference for right over rite:

> I reject your oblations,
>
> and refuse to look at your sacrifices of fattened cattle.

Let me have no more of the din of your chanting,

no more of your strumming on harps.

But let justice flow like water,

and integrity like an unfailing stream.(Amos 5:22-24)

As Shalom Spiegel points out, the very word that Amos used, *sedaqah*, came to mean in later times "justice made clairvoyant by love, i.e., charity."

The "startling and distinctive note in the Christian message," according to Johannes Metz, is the idea that the love of neighbor is not something different from the love of God; "it is merely the earthly side of the same coin." Similarly, the startling and distinctive note in the Christian view of justice is the conscious and explicit integration of justice with love. The beaten and robbed traveler, the oppressed, deprived, and subjugated human person is also, as a result of the Incarnation of Jesus, the image of God himself. In our encounters with such persons, we encounter God. When we pass such a person by, we pass by our God. "Our human brother now becomes a 'sacrament' of God's hidden presence among us, a mediator between God and man." Such is Metz's expression of the Christian view.

So much for my first point concerning the new reality involved in a Christian approach to justice. It remains now to explore the differences between social and interpersonal or individual justice, and to examine the implications of those differences for those who would educate for social justice.

"As He died to make men holy let us die to make men free," is a solemn and familiar line from the "Battle Hymn of the Republic." Many prefer to substitute "live" for "die" as they sing those words. This is one way of stating the dramatic challenge confronting the Christian in quest of social justice. Let Christians, in their various social groupings, live in a way that promotes freedom for those in other social groupings. Such living will reflect the values of Him who died to make us holy. One such value is justice integrated with love.

In considering social justice, I have in mind group-to-group relationships. Hence, relatedness between the groups must be presupposed before one group may be said to have a justice relationship to another group. I find it helpful to use the framework of the traditional symbolism of the scales of justice to look for relatedness in situations of social injustice. Social injustice affects a group, a disadvantaged group occupying the up tray on the imbalanced scale. What group occupies the down tray? In matters of social injustice, the occupants of the counterpart down tray will normally have to "let go," give something up before the trays can be brought into balance. And balance, of course, symbolizes a condition of justice between the groups.

Social justice includes both legal justice (which intends the common good) and distributive justice (which intends the good of each individual as a member of the group), but social justice focuses not on legal rights and obligations but rather on the natural rights and obligations *of the group* in relationship to other groups.

It is a mistake, in my view, to label certain one-to-one relationships as relationships of social justice simply because the disadvantaged beneficiary of that particular exchange is black, or poor, or identified with an oppressed minority group. A helping or saving initiative from the advantaged individual to the disadvantaged individual may, indeed, be not only an act of charity but an instance of justice as Jesus taught it. Recall the Good Samaritan. But it is not necessarily helpful to the group — either group, the helping or the helped. Hence, it is not really an instance of social justice. If the repentance, the change of heart, the *metanoia* does not touch the group which takes its advantage at the expense of the other group (that is precisely what relatedness may imply), then the structural support for the imbalance will be neither weakened nor changed.

Similarly, if a person-to-group initiative (say, an individual landlord to an entire neighborhood) benefits the disadvantaged group without moving others in the advantaged group toward structural change, this falls short, in my view, of a social justice relationship because there is no social group (in this case, say, a board of realtors) on one side of the initiative although there is

122

such a group on that side. It is difficult these days to get people to do things together! All the more difficult is it to get groups to take justice initiatives toward other groups.

Social justice looks to all members of the group. In a context of obligation, social justice looks for a group initiative, a group response to a need. Typically, such a need will be rooted in powerlessness, poverty, or human indignity, three signs of the absence of the Kingdom of God. Each member of the group (however defined, by whatever affiliation) has a personal obligation to be just. Not only is it a personal obligation to be just in individual-to-individual and individual-to-group relationships, it is also a personal obligation to promote one's proper group response to social injustice.

So although I take the position that the just act of one person toward a disadvantaged person or group is not, strictly speaking, an act of social justice, I do not at all deny that an individual can place an act of social justice. Such actions would be taken within and toward one's own group in an effort to activate a justice response from that group toward another. Perhaps I am being too restrictive. If so, it is only to make an important point about where education for social justice might best begin.

If education for social justice might be characterized as educating "persons for others," it is important that attention be given to appropriate strategies and stages of the outward thrust. It will avail little if it is an isolated, individual initiative. This is not to say that isolated, individual initiatives are of no avail. Evidence to the contrary includes a glorious Christian tradition of heroic individual and even small-group initiatives. But despite these, the Kingdom remains "at hand" as we approach the year 2000 — still out of reach for the millions who experience powerlessness, poverty, and human indignity.

Education for social justice must begin with the group that impedes the flow of justice, that fends off a reign of justice and peace that has been "at hand" for nearly 2000 years. Such education must begin inside the Christian community, within its various groups and affiliations. Such education will have to be specialized as well as general. It will have to touch both young and old. It will have to be especially effective with those who have access to power. Education for social justice must be based on good theology and good social science. Social justice deserves a high place on the agenda of the intellectuals of the Church.

That which is to be understood and taught at all levels is a sense of solidarity with all of humankind, an awareness that solidarity means power, and an understanding of the techniques of organization needed to activate power. Whether power is directed toward just or unjust ends, as the Christian gospel defines them, depends in no small measure on whether or not the Christian conscience sets the direction of human activity. The challenge of all of this to Christian education is awesome, so too is the importance of the Christian educator. Let me conclude with a special word about the teacher in the task of social justice.

Sigmund Freud saw that a great person's influence on others would happen in two ways:

> ...through his personality and through the idea for which he stands. This idea may lay stress on an old group of wishes in the masses, or point to a new aim for their wishes, or, again, lure the masses by other means.

Perhaps there is no older "group of wishes" in the people than the wish for justice, particularly that justice which the Christian tradition views as inextricably bound up with love. The Christian teacher who would educate for social justice must embody both love and justice at the level of personality and must internalize the justice-love integration as an "idea for which he stands." More is called for here than Greek impartiality or the "blind" justice of American jurisprudence. A bias toward the poor is called for. A continuing sensitivity to powerlessness and indignity is essential for anyone hopeful of educating for social justice.

A sober self-assessment and practical humility should also accompany the teacher's approach to groups or individuals within groups. Such an assessment can be taken by reflecting on Henri DeLubac's words:

124

If you are not yourself in a position to profit from injustice and if you do not have to make any effort to overcome this temptation, you must show complete moderation in your manner of fighting injustice in others. It is important not to forget, too, that many who protest in the name of justice would only like — in good faith perhaps — to be the strongest and most favored themselves.

It is DeLubac who also offers the caution that "teachers of religion are always liable to transform Christianity into a religion of teachers." The Church is not a school; it is a community of believers, an incredible assembly of loved sinners. Such awareness is an indispensable part of the Christian perspective on education for social justice.

A teacher should be courageously prophetic. The truths about justice are not likely to comfort those who face a reduction in property, prestige, or power as the principles of justice gain wider acceptance. The prophetic teacher can expect resistance, rejection, and even unjust retaliation. But the quality of the great teacher which is not always part of the prophetic charism is the gift of patience. Some mistake this as timidity or unenlightened conservatism. But this need never be the case. What the teacher lacks in prophetic courage may be offset by a reserve of patience sufficient to retain serenity and peace of soul in an imperfect world where diverse peoples and nations are, by God's grace, becoming less and less unequal. The process is underway. The power to bring about a rule of justice resides in the Lord. The patient and persistent educator can help to lower the resistance and thus bring that hoped-for reign of justice that much closer in his or her own time. As more teaching hands turn to the task of education for social justice, the rule of justice will remain less elusively "at hand" and become more fully grasped and comprehended.

12 Bread and Blackboards

Education for social justice would be inexcusably incomplete without some systematic attention to the problem of hunger in the world. Americans like to think of themselves as a problem-solving people. Perhaps no greater problem than that of eliminating world hunger will challenge both the competence and the conscience of those American citizens who now populate the nation's colleges and universities. Their working lives will coincide with the span of time that remains for a growing world population to find a permanent solution to the problem of feeding itself.

To say that this is not an American problem exclusively is correct but dangerous. It tends to ignore the appalling extent of domestic hunger and malnutrition. It tends as well to ignore the range of possible causal links between American power and affluence over against foreign poverty, hunger, and even starvation. It tends, moreover, to ignore America's opportunity and responsibility to exercise true world leadership in a campaign to end hunger everywhere. To ignore these considerations is — there is no other word for it — to remain ignorant. And ignorance of such vital issues presents both an opportunity and a major challenge to education.

"The profound promise of our era," said U.S. Secretary of State Henry Kissinger to the World Food Conference in Rome in 1974, "is that for the first time we may have the technical capacity to free mankind from the scourge of hunger. Therefore, today we must proclaim a bold objective — that within a decade no child will go to bed hungry, that no family will fear for its next day's bread, and that no human being's future and capacities will be stunted by malnutrition." The American Secretary of State pledged his nation's willingness to "work cooperatively" with other nations toward achievement of the "bold objective." He added that the nations gathered there in Rome should "resolve to confront the challenge, not each other." "And let us make global cooperation in food a model for our response to other challenges of an interdependent world — energy, inflation, population, protection of the environment." In bearing down together on the hunger issue, we may indeed find a way to work together to remedy some of society's other pressing problems.

In 1975, the Bread for the World Educational Fund instituted a Decade of Commitment on World Hunger (DCWH) by convening at St. Louis University more than 80 representatives of the church-related higher education community across the country. The purpose was to organize a response from faith-committed educators to the Kissinger challenge. It was evident that the Secretary of State and other top officials of the Federal government would be moving on to other pursuits. It was equally obvious that the hunger problem would remain. Through DCWH, a small but significant group of Americans could find ways and means of moving toward the "bold objective." The purpose of a DCWH workshop is to bring together for information exchange persons who can influence the direction of college and university research, curriculum planning, campus ministry, and career placement.

Corresponding to each of the four DCWH categories is a set of educational issues to which higher education must address itself if it can claim to be preparing people at all adequately for the decades ahead. Before listing the research agenda, curriculum possibilities, campus ministry contributions, and the issue of career choice, I want to borrow from a chapter in a book I highly

127

recommend and list ten causes of the world hunger problem.

It is always a mistake to substitute blame for analysis. Pinning blame is much simpler than analyzing the relatedness of factors that impinge on the hunger problem. This list of causes is not exhaustive, but it is useful in suggesting steps that might be taken by an educational institution desiring to remain appropriately academic but also engaged with the hunger issue. I shall list the causes as C. Dean Freudenberger and Paul M. Minus, Jr., present them in *Christian Responsibility in a Hungry World* (Abingdon, 1976) and then add several more.

1. The colonial legacy.
2. Resource abuse.
3. Complexity of agricultural development.
4. False assumptions on the part of Americans.
5. Low status for agricultural (as compared with industrial) development.
6. Recent business expansion.
7. The dearth of agricultural and rural community leadership.
8. The arms race.
9. Disenchantment with international assistance programs.
10. Population growth.

In addition to these, there are the problems of weather, consumption patterns, and trade practices including the tendency for poor nations like Mexico to "cash crop" for export to wealthy nations, leaving insufficient produce for the domestic market. These and other factors are discussed in a book I edited, *The Causes of World Hunger* (Paulist, 1982).

By the "colonial legacy," Freudenberger and Minus are referring not only to the present gap between landed and serf classes in nations formerly under colonial rule, but also to those colonial systems which fostered the production of rubber, coffee, timber, spices, and other crops which were useful to the colonial powers but did not feed the producers. After independence, the formerly colonialized area finds itself with an economy based on non-food crops and a population without enough to eat.

"Resource abuse" is easy to understand. Grassland, cropland, and forest resources around the world are being ruthlessly exploited. Arable land is shrinking at an alarming rate. Deforestation and desertification are widespread. There is a serious question whether the world has sense enough to preserve the four biological systems needed to sustain the world's population — grasslands, forests, oceanic fisheries, and croplands.

Agricultural development is indeed complex. Weather is one factor in the complexity. Another is relative fertility or infertility of different soils and the virtual impossibility of restoring most impoverished soil to productive status.

The "false assumptions" that Freudenberger and Minus identify as impeding America's response to the hunger problem are: (1) the assumption that we can transfer temperate zone agricultural technology to the tropical and monsoon areas of the globe, and (2) that the solution to world hunger lies in our ability to produce more in order to feed the hungry. Temperate zone technology simply will not work in parts of the world where the need for food is greatest. And the ultimate solution is greater production not here but in the food-deficit countries with the obvious exception of those relatively small areas of desert or polar extremes.

Decision makers around the world tend to be urban minded. Agricultural development enjoys low priority and lower prestige compared to industrial development. This is a result of the so-called "demonstration effect" of western economic development on the aspirations of poor nations.

When Freudenberger and Minus list "recent business expansions" as a cause of hunger, they are referring to economic growth in the developed nations since 1950. Life in the Affluent Society has put unprecedented demands on natural resources and food supplies. Grain reserves have hit alarming lows in the United States as fuel and fertilizer prices hit new highs. In either case, the poor nations are, as a result, less agriculturally secure.

Agricultural and community leaders are in short supply in Third World countries. Their absence is due in part to colonial failures and to the low priority enjoyed by agriculture in poor countries. Training of agricultural leadership, and research leading to the development of techniques and technology those leaders might employ, have been largely restricted to temperate-zone situations.

The arithmetic of expenditures for armaments in the United States and virtually every other nation is so staggering that it eludes practical comprehension. The common-sense conclusion that footnotes the bottom line of any consolidated international defense-expenditure statement is simply this: if less were spent to purchase or produce arms, more would be available to purchase or produce bread for the world.

No less a patriot and military expert that Dwight D. Eisenhower said less than two months after he became President, "Every gun that is made, every warship launched, every rocket fired signifies, in the final sense, a theft from those who hunger and are not fed, those who are cold and are not clothed."

Additional arithmetic that is easily forgotten and awkward to interpret is bound up with the statistic concerning the share of America's annual Gross National Product that goes to foreign assistance. U.S. foreign economic assistance has been dropping since the 1960s. In 1974, the year of the World Food Conference, only one-fifth of one percent of our GNP went to foreign economic aid. Without past assistance, the problem would be far worse today in the food-deficit nations. Without future aid from the United States and other prosperous nations, the food-deficit nations will be denied the means to the ultimate solution, namely, the means to produce more food for themselves.

In countries where social security systems and pension plans are non-existent, a large number of offspring provides the hope of security in a parent's declining years. In such countries, moreover, infant mortality rates are high (a condition not unrelated to the hunger issue) and consequently more children are brought into the world in the hope that a sufficient number will survive to work the tired soil. So goes the cycle of poverty, and so grows the population dilemma.

Other causal considerations include weather which can both create emergency shortages in poor countries and prevent the build-up of emergency reserves in grain-exporting countries. Consumption patterns in wealthy populous nations can have causal links to hunger abroad, hence the growing concern over the need to simplify lifestyles in the affluent nations. Finally, "trade not aid" is more than a slogan. It makes the analytical point that barriers erected in wealthy nations against the exports of less developed nations will deny those less developed nations access to foreign exchange needed to purchase agricultural equipment and other capital needs to produce more food. If hungry nations are exporting food — e.g., Mexican vegetables to nations which could produce their own — then those particular trade patterns are keeping poor people hungry. Moreover, cash crops for export, like coffee or sugar, enrich the exporters, not the plantation workers. And such crops pre-empt acreage which could be used for basic food production for the domestic population.

Related to the trade issue is, of course, the way prices are determined in international transactions. Another complicating factor is the role of international financial intermediaries in setting interest rates and conditions of loans to food-deficit nations interested in increasing food production. At times, conditions associated with loans or grants to developing nations reflect inappropriate and unjust political demands, not to mention military considerations. As I indicated earlier, this list of causal considerations is not exhaustive. Land reform, multinational agribusiness, the politics of food and fertilizer — these and many other considerations should be researched and discussed on campuses which claim to be educating for social justice.

It is my intention now to take the four DCWH categories — curriculum, research, campus ministry, career choice — and suggest ways in which the higher education community might address itself to some of the elements of the very complex world hunger issue.

Professor C. Lee Miller, of the State University of New York at Stony Brook, provided insightful commentary to a speech I gave about hunger and higher education at Villanova University in October, 1978. An ethician, Lee Miller was then working with another philosopher, Patrick Hill, in the World Hunger Unit of Stony Brook's innovative "Federated Learning Communities," an interdisciplinary approach to undergraduate education.

Food, Miller points out, is handled within the same structure of power and profit that have been keeping people poor for centuries. Hunger is a symptom of poverty and underdevelopment.

The problem of world hunger has to be seen as part of the pattern of domination and dependency that is found wherever justice issues like poverty, powerlessness, and violation of basic human rights exist.

Creatively, and to the delight of the students in the audience, Miller suggested a parallel between the way professors relate to students and the way world powers relate to less developed countries. In either case, the relationship follows a pattern of domination and dependency. "We have colonized our students and their independence is a threat to us," claims Professor Miller. He makes a point of no small significance for the classroom teacher. Most students have, in fact, experienced elements of domination and dependency in structured academic settings. Out of that experience, they can begin to "see" for the first time some of the root causes of persistent social problems. Following upon this insight, further analysis may generate creative alternatives to the ways we now have of understanding and responding to the hunger issue. Courses have to be developed to make such growth in understanding possible.

The Bread for the World Educational Fund keeps an inventory of syllabi and course designs that deal with hunger and have met with success in college classrooms. Here are some examples of what has or might be done.

"Perspectives on Food and Hunger" at Duke University applies perspectives from the natural sciences, social sciences (particularly political science), and the humanities to the hunger issue. "The Politics of World Hunger" has been a successful interdisciplinary course at St. Joseph's University. The College of Steubenville offers "The Challenge of Hunger" in an effort to develop "principles" that are independent of a religious tradition but consistent with a coherent set of ethical values.

During my presidency at the University of Scranton, an Indian physicist and an Indian economist, each interested in their native country's hunger problem, joined with colleagues from chemistry and theology to present a team-taught course on the "Dynamics of World Hunger."

Short, intensive workshops are fitted into the academic calendar by some colleges in the hope of reaching students who are unable to take a full semester-length course. Out of such experiences, James B. McGinnis, of the Institute for Education in Peace and Justice at St. Louis University, has produced a book, *Bread and Justice* (Paulist, 1979), for the non-expert. It offers analysis of the economic causes of world hunger and organizes large amounts of economic data. McGinnis also provides a Christian justice perspective in evaluating the so-called New International Economic Order and the food policies of developed nations. He includes an action guide for structural change.

The World Hunger Education Service in Washington, D.C., offers "seminar/praxis" sessions in Washington. They are designed for adult learners and last two weeks. The two-week sessions promote understanding of the problem of hunger and poverty at home and abroad, while fostering more effective response activity at the policy level.

No more need be said here about curriculum. New courses emerge each year. Much more remains to be done, however, by academic administrators and faculty with respect to the many books, articles, films, course models, and training institutes on hunger which are now at hand but not yet grasped by most of those who inhabit the higher education learning community.

Research is important both to the life of a university and to the solution of the hunger problem. The search for knowledge about all aspects of reality is endless. When a college student consults a dictionary, or even an encyclopedia, that can hardly be called research. What does deserve the name research? And what might be said concerning research directed to the problem of world hunger?

As I indicated earlier in a chapter on research and teaching, I like to think of research as the discovery of new understandings. If the discovery is absolutely new, in the sense that no one has grasped that understanding before, I would call it *original* research. If the discovery is new for me and nuanced by me to broaden or update an older understanding, I would call it *derivative* research. Finally, if a discovery in one sphere of knowing, say, biology, can be joined to a discovery in another sphere, say, engineering, and then in combination the two understandings generate a new understanding of an old problem, I would call that *conjunctive* research.

The traditional categories of "basic" and "applied" research are, of course, both valid and useful in the context of the hunger issue. The problem that I have with them, however, is that "basic research" tends to be associated with high-powered, generously funded centers in government, isolated institutes, or research-oriented universities. And "applied research" relative to hunger is easily presumed to belong in experimental stations overseas. Opportunities as well as responsibilities for hunger research in mainstream and mainstreet American colleges, in faculties of arts and sciences, in ordinary libraries and laboratories, will be largely ignored if the academic imagination is locked into basic research centers at home and application stations overseas.

Daydreaming, "what if?" and "why not?" questions turned over quietly in the mind and later shared with colleagues, provide agenda for research. The academic imagination is stretched by interdisciplinary stimulation whenever more than one mode of discovery promises to enlarge our understanding of a problem or issue.

It is not my intention to outline an organized research agenda here. There are simply too many disciplines that are capable of focusing the academic imagination on the hunger issue. There are, moreover, too many interactive issues relative to hunger that invite interdisciplinary research but defy orderly cataloguing. Politics, economics, ethics, biochemistry, history, biological science — the list of disciplines could run on and on. Energy, land, trade, weather, fertilizer, capital, culture — the list of relevant issues is endless. Case studies, all too readily dismissed by sophisticates, are necessary to advance our understanding of what helps or hinders human efforts to eliminate hunger. Who really knows which projects in our much maligned U.S. foreign aid program have helped the poor and which have not? More important, who can tell us why? The data are there at the World Bank and at the Agency for International Development. In some cases, supplementary and evaluative data will be available from other sources. Senior theses, master's theses, and other student and faculty research papers could be produced from these data. This is derivative research, of course, but not the least of the benefits to be derived is a better understanding of one element of an extraordinarily complicated problem. Not to be able to deal directly with the central element (which I would identify as the problem of activating agricultural development along a self-propelling path in the food-deficit nations themselves) is no excuse for not dealing at all with any related element.

Both conjunctive and derivative research could involve the historian who wonders these days, more often than in the recent past, about relevance and survival in the face of declining enrollments, rising career concerns on the part of collegians, and mounting evidence of a weakening commitment to the humanities on the part of liberal arts colleges themselves. An imaginative historian might organize a survey course or even a textbook around incidents of famine, drought, malnutrition, and hunger-related events. Most adult Americans have pegged their historical memory to dates of wars and the development of weaponry. The possibility of pegging the story to developments in food and famine is worthy of a place on the historian's research agenda.

Similarly, American and world literature, either in survey form or in microscopic examination of metaphor, might be organized in terms of food and hunger. It is worth a try, in any case, unless humanistic researchers are prepared to concede that the hunger issue belongs exclusively within the domain of scientific and technological research.

Poets, philosophers, artists, theologians, historians, and litterateurs must be sensitive to the hunger issue and communicate that sensitivity if a foundation is to be laid for the political will to act on the hunger issue. Action — world-wide action — must be taken on five fronts over the next quarter century. As Henry Kissinger told the World Food Conference, these action-imperatives are:

1. Increasing the production of food exporters;
2. Accelerating the production in developing countries;
3. Improving means of food distribution and financing;
4. Enhancing food quality;
5. Ensuring security against food emergencies.

The original, derivative, and conjunctive research activities in America's colleges and universities over the next few decades could facilitate or impede the realization of these goals.

In discussing Campus Ministry earlier in this book, I omitted an in-house Jesuit joke of the 1950s which suggested the desirability of establishing a Newman Club at places like Fordham and Georgetown. Today, "campus ministers," working almost always in teams that include male and female, ordained and lay, Catholic, Protestant, and Jew, are an appreciated and budgeted presence at the Fordhams and Georgetowns as well as on secular campuses. Campus Ministry is expected to raise the value issues, to challenge the meaninglessness of so much that is so prominent in contemporay culture. Campus Ministry confronts the student with the question, "What are you going to do with your life?" Education of the will is often neglected in the classroom; that neglect generates an agenda for the campus minister who also serves the pastoral-counseling and workshop needs of the campus community. It is to Campus Ministry that I look for both witness and guidance on the issue of lifestyle.

The campus community's eyes and ears may be opened sufficiently in the library and lecture hall to personal lifestyle implications of the hunger issue, but our hearts must be readied by Campus Ministry. We need help in choosing to stop our sinful waste of food, energy, and natural resources. We need encouragement in containing our greeds and scaling down our material aspirations.

I admire the competence and conscience of the British economist Barbara Ward who gave a speech in 1977 that might be excerpted and repeated in worship services on college campuses:

> We need a voice in North America, we need a voice in Europe, crying out that these overwhelming needs of the poor people of the world can only be met by some degree of unselfishness — by some "moral development" among the rich. And if Christians cannot say it or feel it, who in heaven's name will do instead? It is as though the good Lord were presenting us with a direct challenge to our affluence and saying: "Look, for 25 years you have had the prosperous years. Now come the lean years. What are you going to do to make sure that they do not become years of deepening malnutrition, famine, and despair? The trends are for the poor to get poorer. They continue thus because you, the rich, have not the courage and the negotiating readiness to make these capital transfers, to secure a better trade balance, to make available the right kinds of technology and to give food production, clean water, education, and employment your top priority. For although these things sound technical, I tell you, as your Lord and Master, that in the end of the 20th century, all these things are the concrete meaning of loving your neighbor as yourself."

Lifestyle links between overweight Americans and malnourished Asians and Africans can and should be examined in the classroom. The moral implications of those links must not go unnoticed. Campus Ministry can provide the forum for examination and fuller discussion of those moral implications. This is happening in U.S. colleges and universities in a variety of ways under Campus Ministry sponsorship: retreat weekends; days of fast and prayer for the hungry of the world; cafeteria campaigns to "stop waste"; film forums and liturgies on hunger and justice themes; collections of money and food for the hungry; overseas service opportunities; near-campus volunteer assistance to the hungry; and organizing citizen support for legislation designed to help the hungry. Campus Ministry leadership has an advocacy role to play for the poor and hungry by keeping the collegiate community honest enough to recognize its position as a privileged little province capable of eventually aggravating or easing the global problems of hunger and poverty. From the classroom comes word that something can be done. From the chapel a stronger voice is starting to say that something must be done. If the starting point is personal lifestyle, the end point may well be the kingdom of justice and peace.

When students graduate, they move on into careers. In the middle 1970s it occurred to me that U.S. college students were becoming caught in a cultural contradiction. As a generation, they were the best educated their nation had ever produced. Yet, for many, their diplomas were passports to nowhere. The new scarcity of meaningful job opportunities for graduating seniors said in effect to the young, "Your nation doesn't need you." Simultaneously, starving African children, pictured on the covers of news magazines, were crying out for help. Basic human needs for food, shelter, education, employment, and health care were evident and real in distant nations. One would expect the ability to meet some of these needs, or at least the ability to assist the needy in organizing their own resources to help themselves, to be present in the well-educated North American who was experiencing frustration in finding a job in his or her own country. Real needs should be convertible into employment opportunities for those with the commitment, compassion, and skills required to meet those needs. Yet real needs overseas coexisted with an unemployed but educated elite in the United States. In a "global village" this is a cultural contradiction.

The disappointed pre-medical student is a prominent part of this puzzle. In this same time period, many liberal arts colleges noticed that the pre-medical program had suddenly become the most popular undergraduate major. It was also the most pressure-producing and competitive. It is still a popular major, but less so at the end of the '80s than it was in the decade of the '70s.

At the end of freshman year, many pre-meds transfer to other majors. More follow at the end of sophomore year. As everyone knows, not all of those who complete the pre-med program gain admission into medical school. Feelings of personal failure are distressingly deep; frustration runs high. In virtually every case, the disappointed pre-med is an intellectually gifted person with a truly impressive record of academic achievement. Unknown to most of these trained, talented, and terribly disappointed young Americans is the fact that some readjustment of their career goals and refinement of their training could put them to work on some part of the complex problem of world hunger.

Academic advisers and career counselors are failing the young if they cannot or do not point the way to meaningful career alternatives for the frustrated pre-med and other collegians who are suffering real anxiety about future employment.

In earlier generations, the young spoke about "landing a job." Members of this generation find themselves "stacked up" over the places where they would like to land. Some have a nervous eye on the fuel gauge. Others are "crashing" psychologically. A few are deciding to land in other places.

I suspect that the decade ahead will witness small but significant numbers of United States college graduates working their way out of a recognizable cultural contradiction but not without personal sacrifice. Their grandparents or great-grandparents came away from poverty to this land of opportunity, and this nation eventually became a land of affluence for the children and grandchildren of immigrants. Now there is evidence, slight but real, of a reverse migration. It is a movememt away from a land of affluence and inadequate opportunity, out to parts of the world characterized by poverty and pressing human needs which are convertible into employment opportunities for those willing to work without the material rewards promised by the

American economic system. This does not mean working for nothing. It does mean working for a lot less than the American dream has conditioned our young to expect.

I look for no stampede away from affluence toward poverty. But I see the beginning of a movement in that direction. The jean generation is confused and caught between an egalitarian impulse and the seductions of an overprivileged materialism. Some few will find (and perhaps fight) their way out by applying their talents to the service of the poor. Curiously, such a choice may prove to be the way out of the ambiguity that has moved in on our young like a closing circle since 1960. As Henri DeLubac observed, "When we choose the poor, we can always be sure of not going wrong. When we choose an ideology, we can never be sure of not being at least partly wrong."

Typically, career choices on the part of young collegians have been permeated with unexamined ideology. Unreflective advisers and counselors are for the most part unaware that no real choices are being made. Instead, a dominant materialistic ideology is pushing the young into career corners from which there is no easy escape. The colleges will have to do better.

Just as there is a cultural contradiction in the global village, there is a curious cross-purpose at work in the campus community. An appropriate meeting ground for clearer identification of this crucial problem would be a campus forum designed to foster interaction among and between reflective persons responsible for curriculum, research, Campus Ministry, and career choice. Of course, responsibility for what you decide to do with your life is ultimately your own. But educators, including advisers and counselors, have an obligation to identify needs and clarify options.

Those whose careers keep them on college and university campuses are not thereby removed or absolved from involvement with the hunger issue. If they do their jobs well, the hungry will be helped. There is a connection between bread and blackboards.

13 Teaching Economics, Learning Justice

As a student at St. Louis University in the early 1950s, I learned from Richard L. Porter, S.J., that "economics is the study of man in relation to his external material environment in so far as that environment is the material basis for the whole of his existence." I recall that St. Louis University had a motto in those days — "Forward in a Great Tradition." And I assume that the University had a more detailed mission statement which informed the work that Richard Porter did in the classroom.

The "great tradition" at St. Louis was Catholic and humanistic. In the days to which I refer, that tradition was usually further specified as scholastic and Thomistic. Moving "forward in a great tradition" was, to my mind then and now, the best possible phrase and face that one could put on conservativism; for *conservare*, after all, had to mean something more than embalming the tradition.

There in the Commerce and Finance Building on Lindell Boulevard, I was protected, by the tradition, from a mechanistic view of economics because I was encouraged to think of economics as a study of man — not markets, merchandise, and machines — but man. Today, of course, "man" would translate to "person" or "humankind," and this reflects forward movement on another front. But the basic point is clear and constant: The University's Christian humanism provided reference points as well as starting points for the work of academic specialization in the University's several schools and separate disciplines.

Other courses and other professors at St. Louis (notably an offering by Philip S. Land, S.J., on "Theory of Social Economy") convinced me that economics was by no means "value free." I also learned that ethics and economics were intended to be partners in human progress, not strangers and certainly not enemies. But the closing lines of a textbook written and taught by another professor of economics at St. Louis, Joseph P. McKenna, persuaded me of the need to remember that although economic theory is a guide to policy, economists, as such, are not policymakers. "Economists can only delineate the alternatives, while others make the choice. One need not conclude, as did the classical economists, that society should never try to help those in need. It is clear, however, that a kind heart without a clear head may do more harm than good." (*Intermediate Economic Theory*, Dryden Press, 1958.)

My own teaching of economics, both with and without the assistance of a published statement of institutional purpose, has tended to focus on human persons and human values. A clear goals statement does, however, facilitate the humanistic approach.

Just as Christian humanism outdistances secular humanism in attempting to respond to the boundary questions of life (the meaning of suffering, failure, death; the understanding of the incompleteness and imperfection of the most nearly complete and nearly perfect human experience), so an economics that adds Christian humanism ("kind heart") to the best of secular science ("clear head") can come to a better understanding of that part of the human condition which is the proper study of the economist.

This is the appropriate point to acknowledge with regret that no Catholic college or university in the United States has yet succeeded in blending the best of scientific economic analysis with the best of the Catholic humanistic tradition. At neither the graduate nor undergraduate level is there a Catholic-sponsored departmentof economics regarded as excellent by the profession at large. Some are quite good, but none is first rate. Since challenge is not unfamiliar to the Catholic intellectual tradition, it should be neither disheartening nor surprising to acknowledge this present challenge to Catholic higher education.

The task of this chapter is to share a few experiences and suggest a few directions that might be taken by those who are scientifically equipped as well as faith-committed, and who are also content to labor in the classroom for the eventual betterment of humankind.

To say it all begins with theory could be misleading. As I indicated in chapter 10, one of the ongoing debates in the academy touches the twin question of whether it is preferable to *act* your way into new ways of *thinking* or to *think* your way into new ways of *acting*. The educational establishment tends to favor the second alternative. There is nothing so practical as a good theory, it is said. Learn the theory first and then put it into practice. A solid pedagogical argument can be made, however, that runs in exactly the opposite direction. Experience first, reflection later. Just as students may have been unaware that they were speaking prose long before they "saw" prose for the first time in a classroom, so all of them were economic decision-makers long before they ever heard of Adam Smith. The pedagogical task is to help them see, to understand. Experience and reflection upon experience prepare the way for understanding.

During a graduate course in microeconomics at the University of Maryland, I recognized for the first time (thanks to an essay by Milton Friedman) that the words *theory* and *theater* are related etymologically. Each is constructed to focus the attention of the viewer. It is important, therefore, to make the point early with students that theory is a way of looking at reality, and without a theory they will simply miss seeing important parts of reality.

I was teaching at Loyola of Baltimore when the riots following the assassination of Martin Luther King put parts of nearby Washington in flames. Within a day, the burning and looting came to Baltimore. The city was stunned. For Baltimore, in those anxious days, nothing was more real than the so-called "civil disorders." I invited my students to examine this reality from several perspectives — sociological, historical, psychological, ethical, political, and economic. Each angle revealed more of the reality. The economic perspective gave us the opportunity to turn the telescope around and examine various economic theories in themselves. To the extent that the troubled reality had economic causes, the uses of economics might contribute toward a solution. Meanwhile, people were hurting, and the city was burning. We put faces on the unemployment statistics and noticed how labor markets can malfunction. We also looked with great interest at the distribution of wealth and income in Baltimore and noted that those maldistributions were not unrelated to the complicated phenomenon we were trying to understand. And we did all this because our college understood itself as part of the city; its problems belonged in our classrooms.

In my labor economics course in Baltimore, each student had to do a term paper derived from non-library sources. They went to the Bureau of Employment Security, to the Chamber of Commerce, private employment agencies, skill training centers, and similar private and public organizations. As part of the term project, experience in the local labor market counted a lot, as, for example, the experience of presenting oneself for a day's employment at one of those "rent-a man" offices which broker the services of unskilled, marginal people to match the temporary heavy duty needs of port city businesses. To insure, however, that the library did not recede to a position of irrelevance in the minds of those same students, all were expected to follow a reading list and each was called upon in the classroom for an oral presentation of a preassigned journal article. The Jesuit system encourages *eloquentia perfecta* as well as reflection based on experience.

Similarly, we examined the dynamics (or inertia) of the labor market for ex-offenders in Baltimore. In this connection, we brought to campus both job-seeking released prisoners and a good cross-section of personnel administrators, the gatekeepers to jobs in Baltimore.

144

I taught a course in managerial economics to Loyola's MBA students, most of whom were middle-level executives going to school in the evening. At the bottom of managerial economics is price theory. The term paper required in this course was an "archaeology" of a given price, preferably the price charged for the good or service produced in the place of daytime employment. This exercise taught the students a lot more than the application of price theory. The impact of market structure on decision making and economic efficiency became clear. The difficulty of gaining access to information in some firms raised questions about the freedom of the free enterprise system. Market imperfections were more noticeable than before. Students raised questions about the fairness of the returns to the factors of production, particularly the human factor. As costs were stratified, profits were revealed. Debates began (during oral presentations of the projects) over the reasonableness of rates of return on investment. In many cases, students "saw" for the first time what they had been looking at every day of their working lives.

Another course taught by me at both the graduate and undergraduate levels in Baltimore dealt with "The Legal Environment of Business." It was easy in that setting to take cases and probe their ethical as well as their legal and economic implications. It was also easy to travel with student groups over to Washington and visit with the regulators at the Interstate Commerce Commission, the Federal Trade Commission, and the Antitrust Division of the Justice Department, and also talk to spokespersons for the regulated in the offices of Washington-based trade associations.

Some students, particularly at the undergraduate level, made better career decisions as a result of this exposure. And many students appeared to become, as a result of all this, just a bit more sensitive to justice issues and a bit more aware of the human and personal side of economic activity.

My teaching took an interdisciplinary direction when I left Loyola in 1969 to join the Woodstock College faculty for work in social ethics. All my students there were graduate students, but very few had any prior exposure to economics. They were train-

145

ing for priestly ministry, most of them, and they were interested in a better understanding of the society in which they would be working. Woodstock's mission statement encouraged efforts to understand the dominant social institutions that affected the lives of human beings.

"Justice in a Business Society" was one of my Woodstock offerings. "Ethics, Economics and the Development of Peoples" was another. Probably the most popular and useful course I offered there was called "The Economic Dimension of Society." This was half macroeconomic theory and half highlights of the Federal Budget. We used the annual Brookings Institution report, *Setting National Priorities*, to examine, as the title suggests, the national priorities reflected in the way the federal government budgets its income and expenditures. I considered the course to be good training for informed citizenship and often thought that students in other professional schools, especially medicine, dentistry and law, could benefit from a similar classroom opportunity. A minor amendment of the mission statements of these professional schools would facilitate a movement in that direction.

In 1973, as a new interest in institutional mission statements began to emerge around the country, I left Woodstock to become Dean of Arts and Sciences at Loyola University in New Orleans. Two major developments immediately prior to my arrival at Loyola of the South set the agenda for my work there. The first was the publication of an institutional goals statement; the second was the conversion into new course formats of the new and reduced general education requirements.

Here are excerpts from the published "goals of Loyola University":

> "Loyola is committed to the ideal that the Christian gospel presents a world view which can be integrated into the thought of any age."

> "The Catholic institution must foster among its students, its faculty, and the larger community a critical sense. To think critically, one must have a place to stand. Loyola stands on its Catholic commitment."

146

> "They (Loyola's graduates) should be capable of principled judgment in the face of complexity and ambiguity...."

> "In sum, Loyola wishes to provide those services which will help the developing human person become more aware of the problems of the society in which he lives and of his ability to correct these problems — a person who has firm moral convictions regarding his obligations to himself, to his fellow men, and to God, and who has the moral self-reliance to live up to his obligations."

The other noteworthy development immediately prior to my arrival at Loyola in 1973 was the establishment of the "Common Curriculum," that portion of every undergraduate's program which was there to guarantee a liberalizing dimension to his or her education. This was chiefly the work of Joseph A. Tetlow, S.J., my predecessor as Dean of Arts and Sciences.

Common Curriculum was Loyola's term for the general education area; it comprised blocks three and four of a five-block curriculum. Block One was the major; Block Two consisted of cognate courses viewed by the department as necessary adjuncts to the major. Block Five included electives. The two-block Common Curriculum was made up of Dialogue Courses (DC) and Mode-of-Thought courses (MT).

Each DC was designed to foster a discussion of values in the context of the great ideas. Typically, a DC was scheduled to meet three times weekly. Enrollments ran between 20 and 25. All enrolled in the course met together once a week to hear a 50-minute "master lecture" and to receive an assignment for a short "position paper" to be brought to a scheduled "dialogue session." If the course were scheduled on a Monday-Wednesday-Friday 50-minute timetable, half the class (10-12 students) would meet with the professor for dialogue on the value question on Wednesday; the rest of the students would gather for dialogue on Friday. A given student met with the professor and other students only twice a week; the third period was free time for private reading or writing.

The whole purpose of the position paper and the dialogue session was to encourage students to locate the presence or absence in themselves of the value under discussion.

What were some of the values studied in the context of great ideas (as recorded in literature, films, drama, poetry, and in the writings of the theologians, philosophers, historians, scientists, and others)? Justice, love, courage, faith, hope, and many more. Students were encouraged to approach their readings, their personal essays and discussion itself with the "critical sense" called for in the Goals Statement.

I encouraged faculty members to view the "master lecture" presentations in the DC format as potential chapters for a book; research the lectures, listen to student reaction and discussion in the dialogue sessions, learn from the student essays, and polish up the lectures for another semester and another class. A publishable manuscript could emerge from a goodDC offering the second time around, and this in fact did happen in several cases.

Block Four, or the other half of the Common Curriculum, contained course material presented in the Mode-of-Thought (MT) format. The MT design was deliberately interdisciplinary. Normally, MT courses were given only in twice-weekly, 75-minute sessions. (At Loyola, all Tuesday and Thursday class periods were 75 minutes long.) No small-group discussion was part of the MT design. The focus was on the front of the classroom. Each participating professor represented a different discipline. Each professor was committed to attendance at all class sections. MT courses were not team-taught in the sense that professors came and went in sequential fashion; interaction between professors (and hence the disciplines) was expected at every class session. If three professors taught an MT course, each was credited with three hours on a normal teaching load. We planned enrollments for MT on a ratio of 25 students to each participating faculty member. Frequently, three disciplines were represented in an MT; fortunately, we had a sufficient number of large classrooms to accommodate the large enrollments.

In designing a mode-of-thought course, faculty members had first to select a truly significant problem area on, in, and around which the disciplines could interact. Next came the division of labor — assigning segments of the course to the appropriate discipline. Perhaps an example will be helpful.

I invited an historian and a professor of American literature to join me (an economist) for a course on The Great Depression. We opened the course with a newsreel, a "March of Time" film-documentary on the Depression. Students began working on a reading list which included novels, historical accounts, journalistic essays, records of oral history, and a simplified textbook on macroeconomic theory.

The first third of the course was turned over to the historian who would lecture for the first 50 of each 75-minute period. Comments on his lecture (somewhat in the fashion of reactors at a professional meeting) came from both the economist and the litterateur. American literature (Steinbeck's *In Dubious Battle*, Agee's *Let Us Now Praise Famous Men*, Wright's *Native Son*, and several other selections) occupied the middle third of the course. Economic theory and policy filled the third segment. Macroeconomic theory, as we now know it, was in fact a response to the problem of widespread unemployment and economic depression. An interest in the problem, prompted by the experience of the first two-thirds of the course, prepared the students for a better understanding of the theory. It also prepared them for a better understanding of the public policy debates over the relative merits of tax cuts and public spending as economic-stimulus mechanisms.

We attracted 158 students to this course. We succeeded in holding their interest and most of them evaluated the experience quite positively. I enjoyed it and learned a lot. Colleague ties were strengthened. All three of us who shared the teaching responsibility for that course agreed that the MT format is an effective device for on-the-job faculty development.

If I were working at Loyola today, I would certainly try to bring several disciplines together for an MT on "The American Family." World hunger is clearly a significant problem area that invites interdisciplinary reflection. The list of possibilities is endless.

149

In 1975, I became president of the University of Scranton and helped to fashion that institution's excellent Goals Statement.

Scranton is Catholic. "This means, first of all, that the University is committed to the person and gospel of Jesus Christ as the source of values and attitudes which should characterize the campus culture."

Scranton is Jesuit. "This means that the life of the University is inspirited with the vision contained in the Book of the Spiritual Exercises of St. Ignatius of Loyola." And the mission statement specifies that the contemporary Jesuit accent on "the service of faith and the promotion of justice" must characterize what the University does.

Scranton is committed to liberal arts education. "Career-oriented course concentrations will, at the University, always be accompanied over the full course of undergraduate study by a general education curriculum which, in the judgment of the faculty, gives every student, regardless of major, an adequate exposure to the disciplines of the liberal arts."

The mission statement says much more — about personalized education, about innovation, about community service, and about academic excellence. The University translates much of what it says from goal-statement rhetoric into classroom reality. The departments of religious studies and political science have gotten together for an interdisciplinary offering that relates faith to justice. Similar cooperation has produced a good course on world hunger. When I left Scranton in 1982, conversations with several of the theologians were preparing the way for new courses on Christology and on prayer, simply because without them the mission statement will not ring true.

Then-recent publications like Joseph Gremillion's *The Gospel of Peace and Justice* (Orbis, 1976) and *Renewing the Earth: Catholic Documents on Peace, Justice and Liberation,* edited by David O'Brien and Thomas Shannon (Doubleday, 1977), were bringing the latest Catholic social teaching to the attention of our students. But we acknowledged that we still had a long way to go. Assistance along the way will come from the 10th and final section of the

Statement of Goals: "This Statement of Goals is intended to give direction to all that the University does. Progress toward these goals will be measured first by the ability of each academic department and administrative unit to choose, and announce the choice of, specific objectives pertaining to each division of this Goals Statement. Second, progress toward our goals will be measured by the actual achievement of the stated objectives. The objectives, clearly stated, quantified, and specified within a time frame, will be means to the ends spelled out in this Statement."

That paragraph is the "engine room" of the Goals Statement. So long as it remains in place, it will protect the institution's value orientation. It will touch classroom life, however, only by first touching the teachers who lecture there.

Part III
Curriculum

14 Preparing for the Conversation

Colleges and universities are falling down on the job. They are failing at least on their portion of the large, long, and complicated job of preparing the young for the responsibilities of marriage and the family. Other parties to the preparation process may be failing to a greater degree, but the process is in trouble and the colleges and universities have reason for concern.

Through the marriage contract, better described as a covenant, a commitment is made. The strength of that commitment, of the love relationship that establishes a marriage, provides the structural foundation for family life. Where family life is unstable, the fault line is almost always reducible to a weak commitment on the part of those who established a family through their marriage covenant.

Colleges and universities educate the young for careers. Learning centers that stand in the liberal arts tradition speak of education for life as well as work. Few schools have much to say formally and explicitly about educating their students for married life, although the vast majority of those students are headed directly for marriage. The schools that do recognize their awesome responsibility in this regard would be slow to claim full success in meeting it.

The schools, of course, cannot do it all. But more can be done in the classroom, in research, and in extracurricular campus life to assist the young prepare for marriage.

155

Here, as I see them, are several of the major problems of the young on the way to marriage in the U.S. today. First, there are the false expectations entertained by the young with regard to marriage. Second, there is the evident inability of contemporary young adults (and their parents as well) to communicate effectively and in depth in any of the languages of interpersonal relationships. Third, there is the question of the possibility and desirability of a permanent commitment in a world of rapid change. A fourth consideration, deserving of separate notice although tightly linked to the problem of false expectations, is the issue of money management.

Additional problems could be listed. These four will be sufficient to promote the kind of reflection which could lead to subsequent action on the campuses.

1. False expectations. Reinforced by materialistic, even hedonistic advertising, fiction, films, and popular music, the young groom fully expects to have a 22-year-old mate for his entire married life. His bride, subject to the same cultural influences, is encouraged to expect a wedded life marked by adulation beyond any spouse's power to sustain, and a secure living standard higher than the income potential of all but the most affluent newlyweds. "Love in action is a harsh and dreadful thing compared to love in dreams," says Father Zossima in *The Brothers Karamazov*. Dreams are not the stuff of solid marriages. The humorist James Thurber, writing in *Life* magazine in 1960, put it this way:

> My pet antipathy is the bright detergent voice of the average American singer, male or female, yelling or crooning in cheap yammer songs of the day about "love." Americans are brought up without being able to tell love from sex, lust, Snow White, or Ever After. We think of it as a push-button solution, or instant cure, for discontent and a sure road to happiness, whatever it is. By our sentimental ignorance we encourage marriage as a kind of tranquilizing drug. A lady of 47 who has been married 27 years and has six children knows what love really is and once described it for me like this: "Love is what you've been through with somebody."

The antidote of realistic expectations, coupled with simple protections against the seductions of materialism, can be encouraged through good education. Moreover, true education will favor the immaterial and spiritual dimensions of the human person. Attention to these in the classroom will serve to deepen personal formation as well as lay a permanent foundation for the communication needed to keep a marriage alive. The colleges can help.

2. Inability to communicate. The problem of poor communication in marriage has reached epidemic proportions in the United States. Any generalization is hazardous, but I would hazard the guess that poor communication in marriage is both a symptom and a cause of a significant amount of family instability. Parents tend to permit their own communications with one another to travel an indirect course through and about their children. Alternate routes scan the headlines or run through and about activities and personalities encountered in otherwise mute televiewing. Direct interpersonal communication, to and about themselves as persons, is less frequently, in some cases never, realized.

An elderly widow, looking back over a long and happy married life, once recalled for me the words her husband used to propose marriage when she was only sixteen: "Will you have a conversation with me for the rest of your life?" Without good communication, there will be no lasting conversation, no lasting marriage. The colleges have a responsibility to help prepare their young for that conversation.

Intergenerational communication is also a problem in families today. Few parents claim to be skilled in talking to their growing children through all the stages of development. Children all too rarely learn interpersonal communication skills. Moreover, they tend to welcome the encircling protection of withdrawal from their native openness and trust that are prerequisite to good communication. As these "crippled" children arrive on college campuses, we find them fumbling with intimacy in their search for meaningful communication. That ever-elusive "meaningful relationship" is really a quite obtainable ground of communication. The colleges should be doing a better job of helping the young to find that ground. On such ground, better marriages can be built. From better marriages, greater family stability will result.

3. Permanent commitment. It is evident that growing numbers of the young in the United States have been shying away from permanent commitments over the past three decades. They acknowledge their unease with the word "forever," but they cannot explain, even to themselves, why. Understanding — its discovery and communication — is the business of a college or university. Analysis, clarification, and discussion leading to a deeper understanding of the commitment problem are needed today on the campuses.

Observers note that children do not develop well in an unstable, emotionally insecure environment. Passing through unstable family environments into marriages of their own, the young adults of the present decade, like the young adults of the two decades immediately past, are sure to contribute, without willing it, to the continuing decline of family stability in the United States. If only our young could bring themselves to "make the promise" and regard it seriously, even reverently, as Thornton Wilder has Mrs. Antrobus regard it in Act II of *The Skin of Our Teeth:*

> Mrs. Antrobus (calmly, almost dreamily): "I didn't marry you because you were perfect. I didn't even marry you because I loved you. I married you because you gave me a promise." (She takes off her ring and looks at it.) "That promise made up for your faults. And the promise I gave you made up for mine. Two imperfect people got married and it was the promise that made the marriage."

Writing about marriage in the December, 1979, issue of *Notre Dame Magazine*, James T. Burtchaell, C.S.C., calls it "The Implausible Promise." He outlines the "growing work" of marriage. "Always more. Never enough. Always to stretch, to accommodate, to put away preference." But putting away preference is becoming harder by the day. One of the developing preferences is the pursuit of challenging career opportunities for married women outside the home. "I expect that much good will come of the enormous renegotiation now under way between men and women, their worth and work," writes Father Burtchaell. "It will bring new freedom and honesty and rid many homes of exploitation." A guided pre-negotiation is needed now on the campuses. How will parenting responsibilities be shared? Whose career will determine geographic location? Is all income shared income? Whose responsibility is it to be with whom, where and when? Who owns what? Child care, house care, home-making, spouse-care — all belong on the pre-negotiation agenda. I will not follow that agenda now except to offer one suggestion related to the fourth problem identified earlier, the question of the management of money.

4. Money management. A young working couple approaching marriage would be well advised to gear its standard of living, after marriage, to one salary only, a veteran marriage counselor has remarked. Income from the other salary should be set aside for major, non-recurring expenditures. It should not be used to support a level of entertainment, travel, wardrobe acquisition, or other lifestyle expenditures higher than the one full salary can support. Why? With the arrival of the first child, the mother sometimes withdraws from the job market and family income drops. Even if she soon returns to work, the family is faced with new and significant child-care expenses. If the couple has grown accustomed to a double-salary lifestyle, the sharp drop in income opens the door to discontent and resentment. This is not uncommon. Criticism of the one provider's earning power surfaces. Resentment turns in some cases toward the child. Discontent, invited by an already present but unrecognized materialism, moves in with the family to stay. That problem only grows worse with time.

Realism requires the observation that many mothers have to work if basic family needs are to be met. Labor market participation rates of married women will continue to rise. But the one-salary-support suggestion, allowing for coverage of job-related expenses by the paycheck related to that job, still holds for the first few years of marriage where two, like it or not, should do their level best to live as cheaply as one. The resultant self-imposed simplicity will prove to be the least costly and most profitable investment any couple can make in laying the foundation for their own family stability.

A couple smart enough to work out successfully the earliest problems of money management in marriage will grow strong in the process and also wise. Since wisdom is a hoped-for outcome of the college and university experience, perhaps higher education should require of itself a better effort to address these problems before they arise. How might the schools meet this challenge through the curriculum, research, and by management of the extracurricular campus environment? At stake is the level of stress and strain in many marriages not yet established.

If the schools do well what they are intended to do, they will find themselves addressing the cultural illness identified by Robert Bolt as too many persons whose "center is empty when the hours of business are over." This is a major portion of our problem — the empty center, the lack of substance and integrity, in a word, the hollow person.

Colleges and universities are surely busy centers in the United States. In virtually every case, the hours of business are long and regular. Those in the liberal arts tradition claim quite properly to provide avenues toward wisdom, a wisdom that forecloses on flights to the periphery.

It is certainly not an unreasonable expectation to look to the colleges to begin filling what might otherwise remain an empty center in the developing human person. Nor is it unreasonable to expect such a developing person to want to share the task of human development with another in the project of marriage. If filling up the center, which is the task of human development, is not seen by both partners in marriage as a lifetime process, their education has been neither liberal nor humanistic (it has not been education at all), and their marriage will, before long, feel the predictable stress and strain present wherever restless and unrelating persons are caught in close confinement. Then the house becomes a cage.

What might a liberal arts college do in the face of present threats to family stability? Only a given college can answer that question for itself. And the answer will not be found in any formula wrapped in the rhetoric of a president or a dean. The answer will be written in department meetings, academic councils, campus senates, student and dormitory councils, student activity planning centers.

What follows is nothing more than an outline sketch of some possibilities. I begin the outline at the beginning of the liberal arts tradition.

There were seven liberal arts when the liberal education tradition began back in the early Middle Ages. Lowrie Daly's *The Medieval University* (Sheed and Ward) cites a description of the seven arts provided by Gregory of Tours (538-593) in his *History of the Franks*:

> ...Our Martianus has taught you the seven arts, that is...by means of grammar he has taught you how to read, through dialectic to discuss statements for debate, through rhetoric to know the kinds of verse, through geometry to figure the measurements for planes and lines, by astronomy to study the course of the stars, through arithmetic to determine the characteristics of numbers, and through music to harmonize different tones in songs of pleasing accent....

Grammar, dialectic, and rhetoric formed the *trivium*. Arithmetic, geometry, astronomy, and music comprised the *quadrivium*. Philosophy and theology would enjoy a higher, later place.

Grammar, of course, meant Latin grammar. By extension, it came to include the development of reading habits as well as facility in writing and speaking.

Dialectic dealt with reasoning skills, rules of argument and logic, elements of what we might call communications skills.

Rhetoric, not surprisingly, referred to speaking well and in public. Arithmetic, as might be expected, focused on numerical calculations. Geometry originally included geography and surveying.

Astronomy was then, as now, a study of the stars and even then astronomy was confused with astrology.

Music, although more theoretical and mathematical then, was essentially what we delight in recognizing as music today.

To the intellectually curious, the seven liberal arts still hold great attraction today. My purpose here is not to urge the launching of a revival. I would, however, like to propose a contemporary trivium and quadrivium for a curriculum sensitive to the challenge of preparing the young for marriage. On the contemporary U.S. campus what I have in mind might be better imaged as a three-pack and a four-pack. The inserted containers may share a common brand name but the content of each would differ.

My *trivium* would include the language-based arts, psychology, and communications skills.

Music, economics, theology, and the visual arts would form my *quadrivium*.

Around that outline I would organize a curriculum, or at least a portion of a curriculum intended to address the issue of preparation for married life. Somewhere in that curriculum I would find a place for a general course called "The Project of Marriage," and I would simply trust the competent and interested professor to develop the content along any one of an infinite variety of creative lines. Marriage is a project. Students should have the opportunity to regard it as such in the delightful detachment of the classroom experience.

Learning, like love, is immaterial. It is not necessary for one person to have less of either so that another can have more, as would usually be the case in the sharing of material things. If both learning and love are recognized as mutually reinforcing as well as growth-producing, the importance of shared learning for the development of the marriage project will also be recognized. There are so many great books waiting to be read, shared and talked about! What types of collegiate learning can start this process along? I turn first to my *trivium*.

For me, the language-based arts include not only poetry, drama, and all great literature, but history and biography as well. The meaning of psychology is familiar to all; no less evident is the importance of psychology to marriage. Under the heading of communications, I would include philosophy, not to stand reality on its head and attempt to argue that the search for ultimate meaning is a subordinate category to communications on the ladder of the disciplines, but only to make the point that interpersonal communication about ultimate reality can strengthen the connectedness which defines married and family life.

Within this *trivium*, separate or interdisciplinary courses can be designed with an eye toward the marriage project. Students can be enlightened, inspired, instructed, entertained, and motivated to explore further for themselves. There are family histories to unfold, love themes to be compared, psychological relationships — both interpersonal and intergenerational — to be understood. The damage that can be done by unloving or incompetent parents to developing children, as well as the delights that only the experience of marriage and the family can provide, can be dealt with in the curriculum without any threat to academic integrity.

My *quadrivium* of music, economics, theology, and the visual arts offers great potential for preparing the young for the marriage project. Their values, so often unexamined, are sung in their songs. And the opportunity to gain an appreciation not only for music in itself, but for good music as a bonding mechanism in marriage, is all too often lost in the collegiate years.

Economics, like ethics, is a science of choice. It deals with the measurable, edible, vendible, practical world of scarcity. Knowledge of that world, its procedures and practices, its potential for argument and envy, is essential to anyone moving toward the responsibilities of married life.

Theology, on its own terms and in its ongoing quest for a better understanding of divine revelation, looks at God's design for marriage. It is also beginning to listen to what believers have to say of their experience, as believers, in the married state. Theology, of course, examines the sacramentality of marriage and stands open for interdisciplinary exploration of marriage rituals, the history of the family, and the moral responsibilities incumbent upon persons called to the service of life within the vocation of marriage.

In selecting the visual arts for inclusion in my *quadrivium*, I am acknowledging the impact of the image on our contemporary young, as well as our general failure to appreciate how much we learn and communicate through signs, symbols, and all forms of visual art. I am aware, moreover, of the immeasurable impact of the film on the education (usually informal education) of the young, of the film's potential for the translation of great literature, and the film's value as a stimulus for discussion. Just as the colleges cannot do it all in the overwhelming task of preparing the young for married life, so the film cannot do it all for the colleges. But the medium is there awaiting creative application to the problem.

The success of any pedagogical approach to the problem depends on whether or not the potential spouse and parent participates actively in discussion opportunities generated by this *trivium* and *quadrivium*. One must talk about the multiple challenges of marriage and locate within himself or herself the presence or absence of the information, values, wisdom qualities, personal depth, moral, cultural, and historical perspective necessary to make the marriage project work. Good liberal education will facilitate this process. It is all a question of filling up the empty center.

It may strike the reader as strange that a discussion of this length on this topic would make no specific mention of sex education, family planning, the "how-to" techniques of parenting, communicating, and budgeting in marriage. There have been no suggested course investigations of domestic violence, child abuse, family health, nutrition, divorce, or countless other issues that arise in discussions about marriage and the family. My concern is with the preparation of persons, as persons, for the marriage commitment. My concern, moreover, is with what colleges in the liberal arts tradition have to contribute to the preparation process. And my assumption is that family stability rests on the strength of the marriage commitment. I also assume that the colleges can develop in their young the potential they already possess for a commitment that is both deep and permanent.

In his June 22, 1979, *Commonweal* review of Jane Howard's *Families*, Thomas V. McGovern mentioned that half of the students in his Virginia Commonwealth University course on mental health and personal adjustment had divorced or separated parents. Almost all of these students, he commented, "yearn for the stability, the certainty, and the emotional support and intimacy which a traditional family is supposed to provide." They were aware of and took seriously, he said, "the finding reported in Vaillant's recent research, *Adaptation to Life*, that mid-life mental health was most highly correlated with the presence of stable, intimate marital relationships."

The probability of achieving mid-life mental health will be raised for the present collegiate generation to the extent that the colleges link up liberal learning and preparation for marriage. If it is true, as William Bennett has remarked, that "the most important contribution the study of the humanities makes to public policy is the sound education of the young men and women who will make public policy in the future," why should it not be equally true that the greatest contribution liberal learning can make to the stability of family life in the United States is the sound general education of the young men and women whose love will create the nation's future families? The least the educators can do is start talking about it now. The "it" to be discussed touches upon the quality of those conversations not yet begun but expected to last a lifetime.

15 Coherence in the Curriculum

Dreams and debates about "what every college student should know," or "what anyone graduating from this place should have read," tend to focus on sequenced content. Content because the dreamers and debaters are typically those who "profess" content — organized subject matter presented in the classroom. Sequence is always part of the discussion because of frustrations faced by those same professors who cannot count on finding students on the first day of class adequately equipped with knowledge considered to be prerequisite for the course.

I recognize the problem and like to think about it in terms of coherence in the curriculum. It helps, I find, to begin consideration of this issue by looking to the day after commencement, to the first day of the rest of the intellectual lives of those whose diploma bears my signature. If I expect them to have read all the "great books," met all the great minds, explored all the great questions during their four-year undergraduate experience, I am entertaining an illusion and inviting disappointment. Graduation Day should, in my view, be Registration Day for self-propelled lifelong learning. I do not worry if a period of history has not been studied or a whole body of literature — not to mention a branch of science or a school of philosophy — has been missed along the way to a baccalaureate degree. I worry only if the intellect has not been given a full-enough stretch and the appetite for learning has not developed sufficiently to guarantee uninterrupted nourishment for the life of the mind for decades to come.

A college curriculum should deliver competence in a foreign language and in a significant segment of one's national literature. It should produce people capable of reasoned argument in philosophy and science, sensitive to the movements of history, and intellectually aware of the tenets and development of doctrine in a theological tradition. Mathematical reasoning must be practiced as part of the undergraduate experience, so must oral and written expression of English. I see all of this as so many layers or foundational slabs upon which more narrow specializations of knowledge, imparted on the way to a degree, can be placed.

For me, coherence in the curriculum means literacy, numeracy, and linear reasoning. These should be surrounded by a circular ring of the creative and imaginative, but never suppressed by the non-cognitive. As I make this point, I also want to cite, with admiration, Georgia O'Keeffe's explanation of her self-expression in art, "I found that I could say things with color and shapes that I couldn't say in any other way — things that I had no words for." And I find not at all uncongenial Robert Bridges' remark about music "being the universal expression of the mysterious and supernatural, the best that man has ever attained to, it is capable of uniting in common devotion our hopes with a brighter promise of unity than any logic offers." As I mentioned in the last chapter, there is a place for music in a modern "quadrivium."

My bias toward the linear and literate is no judgment against the circular and emotional in human expression. It does not preclude curvilinear reasoning and creative thinking. Even in politics, where solid policy analysis and clear, crisp decision-making are necessary for good government, experience shows that reason has anything but an uninterrupted reign. It must be acknowledged that Washington lobbyist Fred Dutton's comment makes a point to be considered seriously by those involved in the education of future policy-makers: "Washington isn't all that thought out. So much of it is improvisation."

My bias is rather a principle of selection for what we do in our collegiate classrooms and laboratories as part, the central part but part nonetheless, of the undergraduate experience. No undergraduate experience should be confined to classrooms and laboratories, nor should it be assumed that what is not central has no place in the formal curriculum. It is my fear that we are losing our powers of reasoned argument in American literature, law, politics, and life itself. Just listen, if you will, to our private conversations, public debates, and mass communications. Not only are our young not writing well; they are not thinking clearly. Our nation is by no means illiterate, but we see mounting evidence of a-literacy. We negate reading of any consequence in our lives; we choose not to read.

When I note the absence of serious reading among college graduates, I wonder why they have no appetite for reading. And then I wonder about preventative measures to be taken now so that the next generation of college graduates might be more inclined to value their library cards on some level of equivalency to their credit cards. Those thoughts carry me back to considerations about what should be done in the limited confines of a core, or general, curriculum which would touch all students on their way to variously specialized degrees.

It would be absurd to provide all incoming freshmen with an academic shopping cart and invite them to roll it through the aisles of a collegiate supermarket eight times, once at the beginning of each semester, during their undergraduate experience. Well-stocked shelves of quality products will not an education make. We who stock the shelves should provide a consumer's guide and a whole lot more. We should provide personal advising. And the advice should reflect a community consensus, set by the faculty, on the question of sequencing the course selections.

I began my teaching career at the college level in the days when few if any high school students had any classroom exposure to economics. It was a pleasure to open up for college freshmen the "principles" course in economics. True, some did not have a sufficiently strong mathematical background to grasp with ease the functional relationships or the expression, in equations or graphs, of theoretical principles. They found the "institutional" side of political economy interesting and found the policy debates enlightening. They selected upper-division courses accordingly, but rarely chose to major in economics unless the quantitative skills were part of their academic tool-kits. Virtually everyone who took the principles course and an appropriately sequenced upper-division course in, say, development, labor, or public finance, found the exposure to this discipline intellectually broadening and useful by way of education for citizenship. The majors, of course, took much more and followed a well-defined course sequence. Professors of physics might recount something of the same experience. It is not so simple in most other disciplines.

"Foundations of..." and "Introduction to..." are familiar expressions in course catalogues. "Elementary," "Intermediate" and "Advanced" are labels generously distributed throughout course listings. They give the illusion of careful sequencing, but that proves often not to be the case.

Coherence in a course of study is one thing; the "arithmetic" of coherence, or the number of courses available to construct an undergraduate program, is quite another. Typically, a complete baccalaureate program of study will consist of 40 courses or 120 academic credits. How might they best be spent (remembering, of course, that Graduation Day is Registration Day for independent, life-long study)? Institutional purpose and identity — expressed in a mission statement — will influence the answer to that question on any given campus. If that influence is not felt, the campus should acknowledge that it has a serious problem. Attempts to answer the question provide a point of entry for frustration on the part of academic administrators caught in the crossfire of competing claims from various disciplines.

I would assign three of those forty courses to philosophy, two to mathematics (permitting one of those two to go to computer science). I would give two to a foreign language (allowing one or both to the exploration of literature in a language where grammar is already in hand). I would also assign two courses each to science, history, English, and social science. My list would reserve space for three courses in theology. And I would want to see one course of interdisciplinary design with a conscious intent to begin the integration not only of previously departmentalized (or compartmentalized) knowledge, but also a conscious interaction of different disciplinary approaches to the study of reality. Finally, I would add a single course in the much-neglected field of geography and hope that this would whet the appetite for travel and provide a partial foundation for appreciation of different cultures.

When arrayed in a column, these "core" or "general" courses total 20 and can be listed, by area of study, as follows:

3 Theology
3 Philosophy
2 Foreign Language
2 Mathematics
2 History
2 Science
2 Social Science
2 English
1 Geography
1 Interdisciplinary
20 Total

The arithmetic of this distribution leaves 20 courses for a "major" and its "cognates," or for a "concentration" and "subconcentration." The remaining 20 courses are there to be consumed by the "specialization" and those courses (other than the core) considered to be prerequisite to the major, or concentration, or specialization.

Not everyone will agree with my choices — the 20-20 split and the spread of two- or three-course expenditures on areas of general learning not directly related to the major. I make no curricular provision for music or visual art, not because I regard them as unimportant (recall my inclusion of both in the *quad-*

rivium I sketched out in chapter 14), I simply used up my 20 before I could include them. I'd gladly lengthen my list to 22! And my assignment of three courses to theological investigation will be unintelligible to some educators and simply unworkable in many higher educational settings. Substitutes for the entries on my list are possible; but only by consent (consensus) of the faculty. That is where the responsibility for core selection lies.

Some will view these general requirements as wasteful. Pressures from narrowly-focused certifying bodies, if not from regional accrediting associations, will mount to reduce the number of courses in the core and enlarge the number available for specialization. But even if there were agreement on the arithmetic, the problems of appropriate sequencing and content remain.

In the spring of 1988, Stanford University's faculty voted to change a required course in Western culture for first-year undergraduates. The content would be enlarged to provide a foundation in "global" culture. The new course bears the title, "Culture, Ideas, and Values." It will include the study of non-European cultures. The works of blacks, women, Hispanics, Asians, and American Indians will have a place on the reading list for this freshman course, along with selections from Plato, the Bible, Augustine, Machiavelli, Rousseau, and Marx. Whether outsiders agree with the Stanford faculty's decision on content areas and required reading for this core course, all should admire the seriousness with which the faculty took its responsibility to make decisions in an area that contributes significantly to the definition of the Stanford experience.

It is no exaggeration to say the faculty "owns" the curriculum. It is clearly, therefore, a faculty responsibility to provide coherence in the curriculum and to guarantee that the curriculum is a faithful expression of the mission of the college or university. No need, therefore, to defend theology in the core of a church-related college or university curriculum; just explain it. I will attempt to do that now from a Catholic perspective.

I view theology as an exercise of human understanding. It is subject to a discipline, as is any formal exercise of human understanding. Theology employs methodology. It respects rigor in reflection on its data, the data of revelation. It requires skill in the use of tools, particularly as one approaches the sources of theological data.

Most of those who undertake this exercise of human understanding called theology possess a distinctive datum called faith. Not all, by any means, but most. Presumably, theological effort on the part of both apprentice and journeyman in a Catholic college will reflect respect for and, in most cases, possession of the Catholic faith. It is precisely the desirability of reflecting systematically and academically on the data of faith, in tandem with systematic reflection of the data dealt with by other academic disciplines, that wins for theology as a discipline a place in the college curriculum. Those who see this as undesirable or of little value choose, presumably, to teach or learn in other settings. The Catholic college would abandon not only its commitment to the compatibility of faith and reason, but its sense of purpose as well, if it were to lose interest in the discipline of theology.

Care for the discipline of theology on a Catholic campus is the task of the theologians on the faculty. Care for the faith-needs of a campus community is primarily the responsibility of the Campus Ministry team which offers a sacramental ministry, spiritual direction, religious counseling, and retreats. For insight related to psychological problems, Campus Ministry will ordinarily refer people to the Counseling Center. For systematic understanding of the data of revelation, Campus Ministry will look to the theology classroom. For celebration of the gift of faith, and for a faith-deepening ministry of the word, the Catholic college community looks to the services regularly rendered by Campus Ministry.

It seems to me that the centerpiece of the undergraduate Catholic college theology curriculum should be Christology. The central truth in Christianity is Christ. This is a truth to be explored academically and systematically in a Christian collegiate setting. If Christology is the best organized and best taught course in the undergraduate curriculum, it will attract students and establish itself as the centerpiece. Best taught means best teachers. The Catholic college should address its resources, its recruiting efforts and its rank-and-tenure decisions toward the realization of this goal.

Assuming the Christology course designed, the centerpiece will have been put in place. What should come next in a three-course requirement in theology? I like to think of a three-course centerline in undergraduate theology; what comes next as the centerline is traced out? I would opt for a course on "The Church." I am thinking here of a community of believers, a community with societal dimensions. It would be a course, therefore, with an opening into social as well as sacramental theology. It would equip the student with tools to be used their whole lives long in dealing with papal encyclicals, bishops' pastorals, and other documents of a teaching Church.

Christology first, Church next. What third course belongs on the centerline? Here we confront what some in other contexts have referred to as the "tragedy of the excluded alternative." Examine the typical catalogue listings for undergraduate theology in a Catholic college: Introduction to Theology, Old Testament, New Testament, Biblical Exegesis, Pauline Letters, Prayer, Spirituality, Marriage, Christian Ethics, Peace Theology, Political Theology, Protestant Thought, Jewish Studies, Eastern Religions, etc. Which one belongs as the third link in my centerline?

In third place, I would put a course "On Prayer." If we are educating students for life, we ought not fail to invite them to theological reflection on prayer. Here especially the faith question can be dealt with directly, for prayer provides a window on one's faith. Various spiritualities, differing traditions of prayer in the East and West, great biographies of men and women whose prayer enriched their lives, all these threads could be woven into the course. And specific attention could be given here to a theology of the Holy Spirit who, as the Catholic theological tradition attests, prays within us.

If these three courses (Christology, Church, and Prayer) were taught well and with enthusiasm, they would generate their own student demand. Quite probably, students who traveled the centerline would want to find time for other courses in theology and religious studies. I would hope so.

As a one-time professor of social ethics, I would hope that a well-traveled centerline would lead into special theological considerations of injustice and other concerns related to a Theology of Kingdom.

If I were asked to fill the philosophy bracket of the course list I identified earlier with three course titles, I would choose: (1) "The Nature of Argument," (2) "The Idea of Justice," and (3) "Meaning." I would leave it to faculty to select the authors and the sequence of topics. These three course "containers" could accommodate logic, ethics, philosophical questions about science, art, human destiny, and all the boundary questions of life; the third course could open up inquiry into the "meanings of things." These topics would open naturally toward great literature; they would lend themselves easily to interdisciplinary reflection. They could equip the student to notice the absence of coherence in matters personal as well as educational. They could have an extraordinary impact for good on the young developing person.

Academicians should be engaging one another in honest argument about what they regard as important in the common educational experience all students should have on the particular campus, with its declared mission, where they are. From that argument, they should produce a consensus that can be expressed in 20, more or less, course "containers." It will be one task, not necessarily easy, to label those containers. It will be much more difficult to sequence them and map that sequence for the guidance of students. Most difficult to achieve will be consensus on what those containers should hold. But that is not so large a problem as it may seem. Knowledge is a changing, developing, dynamic reality. It will always be a mixture of the old and new. Nor should it ever be assumed that learning is confined to courses and classrooms. They help to organize learning. They target some specific things and, more importantly, methods to be learned. The coherent curriculum will provide the learner with the right targets and the most appropriate methods of inquiry needed to reach them.

Faculty consensus on the core or general areas of inquiry to be covered by any student member of their academic community will, when translated to a course map, leave another 20 or so courses to be "spent" in an area of specialization and other areas related to that specialty. This next round of argument should first be conducted within the confines of the department of specialization but later opened to the full faculty body. It will be instructive for all to see what colleagues in a given specialty regard as a coherent course path within that specialty. Familiarity with the broad core and the narrow concentrations will enable faculty members to meet their advising responsibilities much more effectively. It will also invite them to more care in meeting their "ownership" responsibilities with respect to the curriculum they are expected to provide as a coherent expression of the mission of their college or university.

If the arithmetic of all this could be reduced to blocks — forty of them — arranged in eight sets of five, on a single piece of paper, some interesting questions would surface. Are there too few or too many courses in the curriculum? Are course offerings rotated in a way that enables most students to follow a predictable sequence? Is normal academic progress characterized by a balance between general and special courses in each semester? These are the questions faculty members must ask among themselves, discuss with their students, and follow through to conclusions that are consistent with the declared purpose and stated mission of the college or university.

One indication that these questions (and their implications for registration and scheduling of courses) have been adequately addressed will be the absence of student complaints about the deficiencies of the academic advising available to them. Such complaints are widespread in higher education today. They point to the absence of coherence in the curriculum. They also outline an important challenge that faculty and administrators simply must not ignore.

16 The Impact of Metaphor on Education for Business

This is a special, even narrow case of curricular concern. "Business" is an extremely popular undergraduate major. The world of business is the vocational destination for most college graduates. Yet education for business is often separated in practice from the "nobler" and more lofty goals of higher education. Catholic higher education can make a special contribution toward meeting the contemporary challenge of humanizing the business curriculum.

The text I want to employ to launch a reflection on the relationship of Christian humanism and the world of business is drawn not from the *Summa* of St. Thomas, nor the *Spiritual Exercises* of St. Ignatius, nor from Lonergan's *Insight*, nor even from the *Wall Street Journal*. And yet I want to consider, now, education for business in a university setting that is Catholic and rooted in the best humanistic tradition. Let me begin instead with a paragraph from Thomas Wolfe, the great novelist from North Carolina who died in 1938. Wolfe observed the United States business system in the 1920s and '30s and saw with his novelist's eye the impact of the Great Depression on some of the persons who populated, even dominated, our business establishment in those days. In *You Can't Go Home Again* he wrote:

> What happened in Libya Hill and elsewhere has been described in the learned tomes of the overnight economists as a

breakdown of "the system, the capitalist system." Yes, it was that. But it was also much more than that. In Libya Hill it was the total disintegration of what, in so many different ways, the lives of all these people had come to be. It went much deeper than the mere obliteration of bank accounts, the extinction of paper profits, and the loss of property. It was the ruin of men who found out, as soon as these symbols of their outward success had been destroyed, that they had nothing left — no inner equivalent from which they might draw new strength. It was the ruin of men who, discovering not only that their values were false but that they had never had any substance whatsoever, now saw at last the emptiness and hollowness of their lives. Therefore they killed themselves; and those who did not die by their own hands died by the knowledge that they were already dead.

But the learned economists of "the system" do not bother about this. For them, it belongs to the realm of the metaphysical — they are impatient of it, they will not trouble with it, they want to confine the truth within their little picket fence of facts. But they cannot. It is not enough to talk about the subtle complications of the credit structure, the intrigues of politics and business, the floating of bond issues, the dangers of inflation, speculation, and unsound prices, or the rise and decline of banks. When all these facts are added up, they still don't give the answer. For there is something more to say.

A good portion of that "something more to say" is available in Catholic higher education, especially education for business which, in the Catholic view, is not confined within a "little picket fence of facts."

Catholic educators have long been aware of the potential for reciprocal influence of persons on systems and systems on persons. Catholic educators, no one of whom is completely free of a missionary impulse, have not, however, always noticed the significant impact for good or ill of business institutions on persons at all levels of our society; nor have they recognized sufficiently the potential for good to be exercised within the business system by persons imbued with values, equipped with technical and scientific competence, managerial skills, human compassion, and a desire to serve.

Education for business, although widespread in Catholic higher education, still remains an opportunity to be seen and seized by perceptive educators concerned about faith, justice, and the building of a better world. Those concerns characterize Catholic higher education.

The opportunity can be framed within a choice of metaphors, a choice between The Machine and The Workbench as capturing the meaning of the American business system. The impact of metaphor is strong in shaping our often unexamined assumptions and preconceptions about what we do. If we think of the economy as a machine, we all too easily adjust to assumptions that place property over people. We view people as factors of production, interchangeable, even disposable parts. Our measurement of value is mechanistic.

If we apply an alternate metaphor, The Workbench, to the economy, our assumptions will be shaped by an alternate logic. The bench is there for the person, not the other way around. The bench is of a piece with the table where other persons gather for shared activity. They are viewed no longer as factors of production. They are participants in a process leading, of course, to a product but not diminishing the person along the way. In the light of this metaphor, the measurement of value is humanistic.

We are comfortable in thinking of bench and table as the locus for the breaking of bread, the place where individuals become com-*pan*-ions. Prescinding altogether from the eucharistic implidations of the bench-and-table metaphor, let me simply say it is regrettable to find no suggestion of bread-breaking, of fellowship, of companionship in our economic vocabulary when we use the word "company." Lost is the notion of *cum-pane*.

Well, as we all know, machines — sturdy, metallic, enduring — are more efficient than workbenches — wooden, warped, and anything but automatic. Play with metaphor as you will; when your whimsical and wordy reflection arrives at the bottom line you have no choice but to choose The Machine — no matter how noisy, gritty, and uncongenial that mechanistic embrace may be. Let's take another look at that.

Writing in *The Philadelphia Inquirer* on April 3, 1983, Peter Binzen noted:

> When the Great American Economic Machine began to sputter and stall a decade ago, analysts differed on the causes. Some blamed the Arab oil embargo, which ended the cheap-energy era. Some cited government regulation of industry that, they said, stifled free enterprise. Others pointed accusing fingers at labor unions for allegedly exorbitant wage demands. Still others attributed the decline to a general breakdown in American society and virtual abandonment of its vaunted work ethic.

> For a long time, corporate management escaped the salvos. In fact, it was the top executives of major companies who had been credited with masterminding an economic miracle after World War II. But starting about 1980, all of that changed. The analysts finally began training their guns on the managers. And they have been firing away with deadly aim ever since.

> Now the best and the brightest in American business are widely viewed as being part of the problem, not part of the solution. A *New York Times* analyst finds the nation "strewn with evidence of managerial failure." David Ogilvy, the advertising man, says flatly that "the majority of businessmen are incapable of an original thought." At the Harvard Business School, professors Robert Hayes and William Abernathy say that we may be "managing our way to economic decline."

Leaders in business and government are concerned about this problem. Their first impulse is to say, "Let's sit down and talk about this." Wherever they sit — in board room, cabinet room, conference room, or dining room — they are not likely to notice the metaphorical link between the business roundtable and the workbench.

Perceptive educators are alert to the same problem. They reflect on their schools of business, of administration, of management, and they wonder about the potential of these schools to meet this problem. They, too, gather around the conference table to search for a solution. Most will assign the problem to a machine — the computer — and await the solution on a print-out.

In my biased opinion, no group of educators anywhere in the world today is in a better position than the Jesuits to examine this problem through the lens of companionship, to appreciate the fullest meaning of the expression "The Company," and to provide for the young an education for business that rests on correct assumptions about the nature and unique value of the human person. Jesuits, whose personal spiritual formation, community governance, and apostolic outreach are all characterized by a 450-year tradition of *cura personalis*, have something special to bring to the education of men and women for business in a highly technological society.

Advertisements emerging from the heart of that society invite us all to "reach out, reach out and touch someone" without leaving our isolated living quarters and without touching anything warmer than a telephone. Similarly, managers of the highly technological U.S. business system are "interfacing" without seeing each other and "communicating" without any meaningful participation in community.

Jesuit Father John Staudenmaier of the University of Detroit, a visiting professor not long ago at MIT's Center for Science, Technology, and Society, sees the birth of the telephone in 1876 as "the first time in human history that we could split voice from sight, touch, smell and taste." He also remarks that spatially closed relationships (hometown, street, neighborhood) "have been eroded" by the telephone "because the real relationships in my life are not the people on my street and not the people in my apartment building. They can be strangers because I have 'real' friends connected by electronic rather than physical, bodily connections."

Neither he nor I would argue for disconnection from the electronic ties that bind us together in our spatial apartness. My point, for the moment at least, is that Jesuits and their lay colleagues can meet a need today in the education of innovators and managers for American business. Those Jesuit "products" (notice the depersonalized, mechanistic appelation still in use from the days of its first application to graduates of the Jesuit classical system!) can indeed help to shape the American enterprise system in a humanistic direction, or be shaped by it in a way more mechanistic and less respectful of human values. Much will depend on the selection of the guiding metaphor. And this, in turn, depends on the metaphor at work within the educational system itself.

The Jesuits, of course, have no corner on this educational market, no monopoly position. They do, however, have something of a comparative advantage stemming from their humanistic tradition. All of Catholic higher education has something of deep and lasting value to bring to the preparation of men and women for life in the world of business.

There is no stopping technology. That is not the question. Nor is there any question, at least in my mind, that machines will continue to displace people in the U.S. business system. The question, as well as the challenge, is how can humane business managers be best educated for service in the enterprise system, as well as for citizenship in the larger society. Within the enterprise system, goods and services will inevitably be produced, but their suitability for the good life as well as the quality of work life for the producer will depend on the humanity as well as the competence of the manager of the enterprise. Outside the enterprise system — in government, the schools, the arts, the volunteer and not-for-profit sectors — the quality of life for those excluded from the production side of the enterprise sector will, to a large extent, depend on the humanity and social conscience of those citizens who serve as managers in the enterprise system. They will always have power and influence. The related question is: will they always have social responsibility?

Catholic higher education has something meaningful to say to these important questions. Much of what it has to say will be said in its departments and schools of business. Perhaps students and faculty who will meet over the years in the teaching-learning transaction within a Catholic business school will come to view that setting as their common workbench. If they do, they may more easily come to see all the means of production in our nation and our world as Pope John Paul II sees them in his encyclical *Laborem Exercens*, as the "great workbench" of human society. And when graduates of Catholic business schools take their places in managerial positions at their assigned section of the great workbench, they will apply all they learned in college in a way that can make our economy not only more productive but also more human. They will do so in a manner that opens the way for a fuller realization of human potential than will ever be available to those who think of themselves as a spare part in the Great American Economic Machine.

A distinct but not unrelated opportunity awaits Catholic colleges and universities to prepare persons for management positions in the not-for-profit fields of diocesan management, emergency management, refugee management, management of the arts, management of local, regional, and national Church organizations. There are high levels of idealism and commitment among young and second-career Catholic laypersons now looking for non-ordained service opportunities in Church-related enterprises. Catholic higher education can surely attract them to an academic workbench where the needed competencies can be acquired along with a systematic understanding of the body of Catholic social thought. This is a distinctively Catholic contribution that cannot be anything but good for that off-campus collection of machines and workbenches that help to shape the American economy.

17 Books as Bridges Between Students and Parents

If the student is at the center of everything we do in Catholic higher education, and I certainly believe that to be the case, it will surely be helpful to consider for awhile not only the development path the student has traversed on the way to our campuses, but the key role the high school plays in that development. Specifically, I want to dwell in this chapter on the opportunity high schools have to "reconnect" teenagers with their parents. There is some institutional or occupational self-interest at work here; reconnected teenagers perform better in college than do their peers who continue to wage psychological war with parents.

Books can help bridge the gaps between teenagers and their parents, between pairs of related people who happen not to be relating very well. Not books about parenting or adolescent psychology, but books that deserve a place on those lists of works that any educated person should read. Again, self interest; it is nice to welcome freshmen who have already read a long list of such books, and nice to know their parents have somehow shared in that exercise. But this is getting ahead of the story. Let's begin at the beginning.

The newborn child constitutes the center of significance in his or her unfolding life. All experiences, all surrounding influences — pleasure or pain, heat or cold, hunger or satisfaction — all are measured in reference to self. Self constitutes the center of significance in the infant's life. The self-centered reference remains fixed through many months of being held, fed, changed, and bathed; it is reinforced by tactile and vocal attention provided by significant others. All the while the center of significance remains the self.

As both the presence and awareness of siblings and peers enter the world of the developing child, parents move into the center of significance in that child's life. Parents become a point of reference for what the child begins to value, how the child attempts to walk and talk, where the child goes, and who the child knows. Parents can expect to hold this spotlight position in the center of significance for about a decade. At some point in the pre- or early-adolescent years of the developing youngster, it is clear that the parents no longer hold the central reference position. They no longer constitute the center of significance for the child. The center, however, is never vacant for long. It can be filled with a "hero" from the world of sports or entertainment. It can be filled by an older brother or sister, a friend, an uncle or aunt, a neighbor. It can be filled by the child himself or herself, thus signaling reversion to infantile self-centeredness. Or it can be filled by a significant adult in the school setting — a teacher, coach, or counselor.

In the process of development, there is a natural and inevitable separation from parents. At some point in the early teen years, there should be a natural but by no means inevitable reconnection with parents. The reconnection must not be forged in terms of parental domination and infantile dependency. Ideally, it should be mediated by a subsequent occupant of the privileged position I have defined as the "center of significance." The reconnection should, moreover, be based on revised relationships and new choices involving parents and children.

Parents may and do choose to have children. They do not, however, choose the unique child-person and personality who is related to them as daughter or son. Children, of course, don't choose their parents. But young adults do — or at least they can. And so can parents choose their teenage children. That's the

184

meaning of reconnection. Teenagers and parents should choose one another, should choose to relate to one another in new and perfectly appropriate ways for persons of separate identity, unique personality, and relative independence. They should relate on new ground, beginning with the shifting ground of adolescence.

In my view, the high school (by that I mean the significant teacher, coach, or counselor who occupies the center of significance for a high-school student) should mediate the process of reconnection. If incapable or uncaring others occupy that center, the reconnection will be made badly, if at all. Most entertainers and sports figures are unlikely to be mediators of reconnection. But it is a natural role for the high-school professional. It is not, however, a natural for the high-school peer group. There can be good or bad peer pressure. The "right" high school for a youngster will be "right" to the extent that it fosters contact with positive and productive peer relationships. Hence the importance of a choice of high school — one whose teachers and coaches are desirable candidates for filling up that vacant center of significance, and one where peers are likely to provide pressure that moves in the right direction.

Not all parents will be willing to make their own the attention-getting opening words from an American Heart Association newspaper advertisement which pictures a punk-rock teenager and directs to him the following message: "We don't care if you paint your hair blue, rip the sleeves off your shirt, or pierce your ear. But don't smoke just to be like your friends. Or to be different from your friends. Or to be nothing at all. Because with everything we know about cigarettes today, there is only one thing you'll be if you start smoking now. And that is sorry."

Parents will echo the conclusion more readily than the opening assertion. They should note, however, that blue hair, pierced ears, and smoking are just symbols of some pressures that come from peers. Good schools will encourage positive pressures. Smart parents will use the schools as helps in getting reconnected with their youngsters. They will not use the schools as surrogates for themselves as parents. Nor will they point to the schools as reasons to believe reconnection is unnecessary or even unachievable.

One reason parents do not reconnect with children in the early teen years is that parents appear to be too busy. Fathers in particular seem to be too busy. Or at least fathers seem to be less interested and less capable of conversing with their teenage children. Researchers James Youniss and Jacqueline Smollar at The Catholic University of America's Center for the Study of Youth Development find that teenagers have a different relationship with their mothers than they have with their fathers. Mothers fare better than fathers with both male and female teenagers, and girls especially seem to have strained relationships with their fathers. This is not to say that the adolescent-parent relationship is characterized by hostility; but there are strains. And to the extent that youngsters are talking to their parents, both boys and girls are talking much more and about every conceivable topic to mothers, not to their fathers.

Both mothers and fathers, as equal partners, should be conversing with their children. It is interesting to speculate whether the conversation is a cause or effect of parent-child reconnection. But it is important for many reasons that the conversation take place and be ongoing. One of these reasons relates to positive influences on moral behavior. The National Center for Family Studies at CUA analyzed data on more than 200,000 graduates of Catholic grade and high schools and found that the most important factor influencing student moral behavior was whether parents and their children discussed moral situations.

Discussion, in the reconnected years, is not the instruction of the early developmental years. Some parents will find themselves incapable of this. It involves respect for the other's opinion, listening to the other; it requires reasoned argument and consistency of principle. Parents denounce smoking by their youngsters, but continue to smoke themselves. Youngsters say parents "never listen" as they themselves repeatedly "forget" the plainest and simplest communications. And when either side starts

186

shouting, both sides know that reasoned argument has come to an end.

How can the good high school help? The good high school, once it seriously takes the question into consideration, will come up with answers of its own. It will be able to test and revise its answers if it maintains interest in the question over time. The suggestions I offer here are intended simply to get the experiment going.

If parents and teenagers are to reconnect, they will need things to talk about and projects to share. The school, by definition, should be providing students with things to talk about. But what can the school do to encourage conversation about such things with parents? One device is the joint book report. The book, assigned by the teacher, is read by both student and parent. The report would have each summarize the thesis or theme, and disclose one's personal judgment of its value and relevance. The parent's work would not be graded, just noted.

Written composition (the good school should insist on frequent written homework) offers many opportunities for shared assignments. Film, play, or television program reviews are possibilities. In order to write joint reviews, the production will have to be viewed by both parent and student, and discussed together. Assigned interviews are additional possibilities. Specific assignments on interesting aspects of American life before the youngster was born can bring a student with a prepared set of questions to a parent for structured interviews about an endless range of topics, each capable of stimulating intergenerational conversation.

What about students without parents, or worse, students with parents who are unwilling to cooperate? The good high school will find ways of adjusting; it will also have in this an early warning system to detect the presence of problems at home.

Oral histories are good conversation stimulators; so are efforts to trace the family tree. A guideline in all of this which the school can easily invoke, and which will preclude the wrong kind of competition between families on projects of this type, is to insist that the shared experiences be home- or community-based and the cost of doing them be reasonably close to zero. Aside from protecting economically disadvantaged students, this norm will encourage families to discover that "doing things together" does not imply large outlays of money for travel or expensive tickets of admission.

The good school should expect its teachers to publish and distribute something resembling a course syllabus. It should also provide a set of such syllabi to the parent.

It would be easy enough for a school to require every student to keep a standard, pocket-size notebook for recording homework assignments on a daily basis. Parents should be expected to display an interest in the contents of that notebook. Indeed, parents can keep notebooks of their own — logs of homework assigned to and completed by their youngsters at home. Parental logs can stimulate student productivity.

Scheduled opportunities for parents (particularly fathers) to meet with teachers should be frequent and regular. Such meetings are quite helpful to the school in its role as a facilitator of the reconnection process. They also provide the school with an opportunity to assess parental involvement at home with the learning process. Light involvement can be expected to correlate with low achievement.

I mentioned earlier the finding of the CUA Family Center that the most important factor influencing students' moral behavior was whether parents (not teachers, but parents!) and their children discussed moral situations. How can the school help to structure these discussions? The "roundtable" is a device that can be employed in school or at home. It is much more likely to be tried at home if both parents and children have had the opportunity to share a roundtable experience together in school. Success of a roundtable discussion is virtually guaranteed if the topic question is a good one, and if a preassigned reading can open that question up sufficiently for the discussants.

The resourcefulness of both school and family can be depended upon to produce the questions and the useful preparatory material. Often the only thing required for a good roundtable is a stimulating newspaper or magazine article. Much more difficult, it seems, is the problem of finding an occasional hour in a hectic household routine for gathering around the table. One thinks, of course, of conversations at the dinner table. Theoretically, there is probably no more stable impulse in America than the gentle force that draws chair to table as the American family sits down to dinner. Practically, however, the theory isn't working very well. Families are sitting down to fewer meals together; table talk is on the wane.

Schools have a scheduling advantage over families and are thus able to make time for shared conversation on moral or other topics. They will do it if they are convinced that discussion with parents shapes moral convictions in the young. Interested parents will find themselves turning to the schools for help in getting those conversations going.

Reconnection is the objective here. There is the inevitable separation of child from parent and the uncertain reconnection through the mediation of the school. Much depends on the success of the school, or significant adults within the school, in holding for a while the center of significance in the student's life. Many good schools miss the opportunity.

Several years ago, *The Washington Post* reported a disturbing story. "Some of them seemed to have everything: private schooling, cars for cruising their suburban neighborhoods, silver spoons tucked away since birth.

"But America's middle- and upper-class youths are showing signs of startling unhappiness. They are fleeing their homes by the tens of thousands."

According to the *Post*, an estimated 1,500 suburban Washington area teenagers would spend at least one night in a local home for runaways that year. A social worker employed at the home is quoted as saying, "The runaways we are seeing today have far more complex problems and more of them. One of the reasons is that the parents of the '60s never learned how to parent. They wanted to be kids' pals and thought the enlightened way was to let the kids do what they wanted." A survey of 210 shelters which cared for 50,354 youths that year revealed that fewer than half, 19,411, left home voluntarily. The others left with the consent of their parents, or were "throwaways" forced to leave home.

Joint book reports are not going to eliminate that problem. But the problem itself is certainly not going to run away, and America's high schools should be innovative negotiators of a reconnection process that will depend for its success on the ability of both teenagers and their parents to carry on conversations in a new key and under new terms of trade.

I would hope the conversations will continue on through college. It is widely acknowledged that parental participation in the schooling process is essential for success in elementary and secondary education. I hear little about efforts to encourage parental participation in the higher education process, and I have to wonder why. The most convenient campground for this kind of shared adventure is the humanities. Colleges are under some legal restraints about sharing some of the contents of student records with parents without student consent. But there is no reason not to share reading lists with parents. Few parents would be unable to read along at a comfortable pace in the humanities. Many, however, will simply be unwilling. And, here again, one has to wonder why.

Part IV
Management

18 Fund Accounting

When independent college presidents look to the future, they do not reach for binoculars; they size things up with the help of four buckets. Not real buckets, of course, but accounting buckets — the four funds devised by accountants to track financial activity on a given campus in any given year. When college presidents and their financial officers map out their capital strategies, these four funds, bins, or buckets provide the analytical framework for their strategic planning.

The first bucket — the Current Fund — might be thought of in terms of the old-fashioned watering-can — one, however, of grand proportions. The watering-can is filled from an outside faucet, and its contents are poured out over a thirsty flowerbed. In the case of a college's current fund, annual operating revenues flow into the bucket from tuition, fees, gifts, grants, and other sources; these revenues are then poured out as expenditures that pay for instruction, research, and the support necessary to keep the operation running for an entire fiscal year.

The second bucket is the Loan Fund. This is a revolving fund — something like a closed, circular-flow system which lends out and takes in dollars that can serve no other purpose but that of financial aid to qualified borrowers.

The third bucket, much like an underground tank, holds the institution's endowment. The yield on endowment can, if restric-

193

tions permit, be used for current or capital expenditures, but the tank itself (assuming strict endowment) cannot be tapped to meet current or capital needs.

The fourth bucket is the Plant Fund. A useful image might be the large, round, and relatively squat refinery tank used by petroleum companies in their distribution systems for automotive fuel. The Plant Fund "contains" dollars for repair, replacement, and additions to the institution's physical plant, but it also "contains" the dollar value, at cost, of the entire campus plant. Hence, the above-ground visibility of this fourth bucket.

All four buckets have compartments or subdivisions which I have chosen to ignore, except for one. The so-called "Unexpended Plant Funds" are dollars not yet embodied in brick and mortar and thus distinguished from "Funds Invested in Plant." (A useful exercise for trustees and others responsible for, but relatively unfamiliar with, the financial realities portrayed by the four funds, is to take the columns of data on the audit sheet listed as the "Statement of Changes in Fund Balances" and simply draw an outline of a bucket over each of the four activity areas: Current, Loan, Endowment and Plant. Within the bucket will appear the columns representing the sub-categories I have chosen to ignore in this broad-stroke description.)

The Unexpended Plant Fund category is an important bucket-within-a-bucket. It is a "bank" where a college can "save up" enough dollars to prepare for some capital (as opposed to current or operating) expenditures. The strategic question, of course, relates to how a college or university can put money into Unexpended Plant in order to be able later to make capital expenditures that will add to the value of "Funds Invested in Plant," not simply for the sake of adding value, but for the crucially important purpose of providing a suitable physical plant for the institution's academic, extracurricular, and resident life activities.

An institution can build up its pool of unexpended plant funds by:

1) Borrowing from itself (e.g., from endowment);

2) Borrowing from outside lenders (tax-exempt debt financing,

194

taxable, variable-rate commercial paper, lines or letters of credit, etc.);

3) Receiving gifts from outside sources;

4) "Selling" its depreciation (and other benefits related to its tax-exempt status) to outside investors;

5) Searching out various "joint venture" opportunities with partners from the for-profit sector; and by

6) Transferring dollars from a current fund surplus—i.e., from bucket No. 1 to bucket No. 4 — whenever the current fund reaches the end of the fiscal year in sufficiently robust condition to permit such a "non-mandatory" transfer.

The non-mandatory transfer mechanism is worth examining. Accounting conventions have, in the past, not provided for depreciation of a university's physical plant. Presumably this is because it is assumed that the benefactor whose largesse built, say, the university's library, will be succeeded a couple of generations later by another benefactor who would be willing to replace that library. We all know it does not work out that way. We also know that there are tax considerations in the for-profit sector which make depreciation accounting attractive; these would not apply to non-tax-paying colleges and universities. But this is now changing. Depreciation may soon have to be shown in order to obtain an "unqualified opinion" from the outside auditor. This will cause unwelcome and, in my view, unwarranted deficits to be shown in the Current Fund.

Colleges and universities have always been free, of course, to impose upon themselves a quasi-depreciation expense. Many simply charged against current income an allowance, in addition to mandatory debt-retirement allowances, which would follow the non-mandatory transfer route over into the Unexpended Plant Fund. This is easier said than done. If such a self-imposed levy were charged at a fixed rate, it could easily throw the Current fund into a deficit position. If it were a planned, fixed-sum transfer, say, $1 million on a $50 million current fund, it would, in effect, be a budgeted expenditure competing with other budgetary needs, notably needs for higher faculty compensation, more generous applications of institutional dollars to unfunded student aid, and more dollars applied to the library acquisitions budget. The list of competing claims could easily be lengthened. The auditors, or better, the professional accounting standards, are now reducing the choices for colleges in this regard.

I think colleges and universities should always plan to transfer a small but fixed percentage of their operating income to the Unexpended Plant Fund at year's end. Those transferred funds, together with other dollars that find their way into unexpended plant, should then be expended for capital purposes. Thus, a capital budget clearly distinct from an operating budget, and lagging that operating budget for one year, would become part of a university's way of conducting its business. This procedure would reduce, if not eliminate, the problem of deferred maintenance. So much to the good. But predictable opposition to this way of doing business will arise from those campus constituencies which have good reason to want to stake a claim on the surplus.

A Current Fund surplus (i.e., a positive fund balance) should, in my view, be the result of planning, not a matter of luck. Not to plan to be able to make non-mandatory transfers to the Plant Fund is to admit defeat in the annual battle against deferred maintenance, even with depreciation accounting. To lose this battle with annual regularity puts the institution on a crumbling foundation of a decaying physical plant. Morale drops as do applications for admission. The correlation, although clear, is usually noticed much too late.

There are short-term reasons for wanting to have a year-end surplus in the Current Fund. There are obvious needs for cash on the first day of the new fiscal year, a day on which revenues do not necessarily flow in. A year-end positive fund balance enables institutions to avoid short-term borrowing to support current operations. Another reason is the desirability of having a "hedge" against those accounts-receivable which are carried as assets on the year-end balance sheet. Not all of those receivables are going to be received!

Competing claims over a Current Fund surplus most commonly pit an inflation-wounded faculty against a sympathetic but maintenance-conscious administration. Cooperation between administration and faculty in budgeting for a Current Fund surplus is essential, not just for systematic capital budgeting, but for the long-term well-being of the institution.

It is to that long-term future that independent college and university presidents are looking with the four-fund rangefinder that is part of their managerial toolkit. They need help from their auditors. Although outside auditors are often regarded in academic circles as the people who arrive after the battle to spear the wounded, presidents and trustees appreciate their expertise and the importance of the role they play. What the auditors themselves may not recognize, however, is how helpful they can be as consultants to academic managers by providing them with guidelines within which capital decisions can be made with greater confidence.

What, for example, would be a "normal range" for a given institution regarding the percentage of current revenue applied to debt service? Auditors, who look at many comparable academic operations every year, are in a position to say. How high should an institution permit its unfunded student aid to rise measured as a percentage of total tuition income? The measurement is a simple matter; the establishment of a norm cannot be done without the experience of many institutions that auditors alone possess.

How might a university's asset-liability ratio be compared to the same ratio in the for-profit sector as an indication of credit worthiness? What advice might the auditors have with respect to the president's problem of accumulating capital in that Unexpended Plant Fund? Auditors, of course, are not bond counsel, or bankers, or venture capitalists. But just as physicians who are neither nutritionists nor trainers dispense good advice about diet and exercise, so the auditors might be expected to tell presidents and trustees something of the ways in which institutional financial health might be improved, and something of the

197

means to measure the institution's capacity for improvement.

No one need worry about "malpractice" risks in this regard. What I have in mind would be an opinion communicated apart from the certified statement and also apart from the management letter. Perhaps it would be opinion for a fee. But I would hope that the general guidelines and norms for financial health could become as easily quantified and popularized as the information on diet and exercise that all presidents, trustees, and their financial managers receive from their physicians. This medical information, incidentally, helps them remain physically fit to do battle with their financial problems, particularly the problem of mapping their capital strategies!

It has been remarked that a college budget is a theological document — long on mystery and short on revelation. The annual audit, with its four-fund focus, can be laid out at year's end beside the budget to lift a bit of the mystery. Performance ratios, fashioned and explained by the auditors, would be a welcome revelation to those on campus who "sit in darkness" whenever the institution's fiscal condition is not clearly understood.

19 Entrepeneurial Management

The notion of entrepreneurship is rarely associated with the groves of academe, and the responsibility of managing the higher education enterprise is usually regarded as an executive, not faculty, function. But faculty members manage much of the enterprise, even before they become deans or higher administrators. Faculty members should grow comfortable in thinking of themselves as entrepreneurs at all stages of their academic careers. The faculty member who manages a department or division in an institution of higher education has a manifold role to play. Such a person is not only a manager, but also a planner, evaluator, recruiter, innovator, motivator, and entrepreneur. All of these elements are, moreover, "add-ons" to this special person's professional responsibilities as teacher and scholar.

Before examining the functional role and what I would regard as desirable personal characteristics in this key academic manager, the department or division head, I want to post a few comments about the industry in which this person works — its students, faculty, and institutions. Indeed, higher education is an industry. Some would say a "regulated" industry; others, who keep an eye on demographic decline, are afraid it might become a "depressed" industry. There are arguments pro and con over whether or not it is a "competitive" industry. But in any case, it is an industry — an important industry — and those who work there can gain a helpful perspective on themselves and their future by regarding it as an industry. Some comments then about the students, faculty, and institutions within the higher education industry:

1. Students. Our students are coming to us out of a culture that is materialistic, violent and aliterate. It is not a question of not being able to read; it is a question of a-literacy — choosing not to read. The violence of speed, noise, destruction of property, and assault on persons is the environment that dulls our students' sensibilities and tightens the grip of stress on their lives. The seductions of materialism place formidable challenges in the path of the educator who really believes there is a priority of mind over matter. Our students are getting a different message from the world around them.

Family reinforcement for the cultivation of the life of the mind, once presumed to be present in achievement-oriented ethnic groups, is diminishing. Escape, fantasy, and "can't cope" are on the rise. "Insist on the cultivation of the real in your midst," urged John Tracy Ellis, The Catholic University of America historian, in a 1984 speech to college presidents. "The present disarray in society has driven many to an unhealthy indulgence in fantasy and to the world of make-believe that so frequently ends in disillusionment, cynicism, and ultimate despair. A sense of the real, the ability to face the inevitable occurrence of the unpleasant in life, must be recaptured if the young are to find a durable peace of mind."

Their elders in the academy find peace of mind eluding them as they stare at demographic data which show shrinking cohorts in the 18-22 age range. These elders are, for the most part, faculty members, the group from which managers of departments and divisions are drawn. What might be said about the condition of faculty in the industry of higher education?

2. Faculty. The faculty function (as distinguished from the faculty person among other persons in academe) is central and of greatest importance in the higher educational enterprise. Yet faculty morale is not high. Neither are faculty salaries. Nor is faculty status or prestige as the nation compares this profession with others. Faculty members are certainly not a-literate (just the opposite!); but the print-oriented professors are, by and large, uncomfortable with the new educational technologies. Some are not yet comfortable with typewriter and telephone. This technological backwardness impedes faculty productivity and thus aggravates the economic problem each faculty member faces. More on the productivity issue below.

On most campuses, institutional researchers track median-age trend lines that show an aging, tenured faculty with a tendency toward occupational stability and geographic immobility. Some will tell you the faculty is simply "stuck" — psychologically and economically, as well as occupationally and geographically. Some who teach undergraduates regret not having chosen the legal profession for themselves instead of a life of preparing others for law school. Some faculty wish they had become physicians rather than choosing an unappreciated and undercompensated career in classroom and laboratory with the young who are on their way to "success" in medical and other health-service professions. Some indeed never really made a choice and are now "stuck" with a career that somehow happened to them and from which they seem unable to escape. Not all, by any means, but some. There is no precise measure of the personal and professional discontent, but there is no denying its presence in our industry.

President Richard Cyert, of Carnegie-Mellon University, holds an interesting thesis concerning the implications of all this for the management of higher education in the decades ahead. Our problems, he suggests, will be similar to those we have witnessed in the railroad companies over the last few decades. According to Cyert, the bright young business and engineering graduates of the 1950s took a look at the railroads and noticed they were "tenured up," so to speak. So the bright young graduates entered other industries. Twenty years later that talent was simply not around to help the railroads solve their management problems. The point, of course, is that this is happening today in the education industry. Bright young men and women hear our complaints, notice our discontent, recognize the tenure problem and conclude that our industry is not for them. Not only is the higher education industry losing potential scholars, as talented youngsters opt for the M.D., J.D., or M.B.A. instead of the Ph.D.; our industry is also losing its potential managers. They simply won't be there, the best and brightest of today, to fill those vacant deanships and presidencies twenty years from now.

Perhaps the railroads did not fully realize that they were in the transportation business. Their narrow perspective was locked between the rails, as the planes literally took off and the trucks ran circles around the rail component of a much broader transportation industry. If the education industry confines its vision to three-credit courses in four-walled classrooms over semester-long segments of study, it will surely suffer the fate of the railroads. This unhappy outcome is by no means inevitable.

Alongside the Cyert thesis I would want to post what I call the "September thesis." There is no better place in the world of work than the American college campus in September of any year. The weather is great. Everyone is fresh and rested. New faces reflect optimistic expectancy. Older, more familiar faces offer reminders and reassurance of the value of colleagueship. No football team has yet had a losing season. No student has yet failed an exam. It is not yet time to argue over salary increments, promotions, terminations, or vacancies for faculty for next year. The campus is just a great place to be. If only the spirit of September could be extended, month by month, through May, our industry would have no difficulty in attracting and holding top talent. The central elements of September-on-the-campus are there all year: young human potential waiting to be developed, mature colleague ties waiting to be enriched. We just have to try our best to protect the special environment within which we relate to one another in the cultivation of the life of the mind — our own and those of others in the campus community. No other industry defines itself in terms of that enobling dimension of human life.

202

3. Institution. The third area within our industry that requires comment before examining the role of academic manager is the institution — the campus, as we tend to call it. Institutions in our industry are characterized by an aging physical plant. "Deferred maintenance" is not an unfamiliar phrase in academic board rooms.

Our institutions, with very few exceptions, have insufficient depth of endowment. Public sector institutions face fiscal constraints from state legislators who are unable or unwilling to raise taxes in order to provide the institution with more operating revenue. Authorities are often unwilling to permit managers of state-supported campuses to raise their low prices, their tuition and fee charges. This defines, for public sector educational managers, an "economic bind." Some turn to external fund raising: pursuit of the philanthropic dollar, thus raising howls from the independent sector about the inappropriateness of tax deductibility of gifts to government (i.e., to government-run campuses).

The independents define their "bind" most often in terms of rising pressures on compensation levels and downward pressures on tuition levels. Some see evidence of what the economists call "price-elasticity of demand." Rising prices (tuition) depress the quantity of private higher education demanded and thus drive students to lower-priced (due to public subsidies) educational alternatives. Some of the private managers cry foul: "predatory pricing" in the public sector. But no one is planning an antitrust action. All look to various forms of fund raising to replace facilities and build endowment for scholarships and faculty salaries, while working hard to maintain federal- and state-government financial aid to students.

Every institution is caught in the access-excellence crossfire. Most are uneasy with the word "elite." All, however, want to enjoy prestige and pursue excellence.

Most institutions are not doing strategic planning. Some do not know how. Others do not see its value. But most fail to plan because they don't have the data base that can support a good management information system. I think of a data base in terms of bins or buckets. Someone should be responsible for dropping data every day into five large bins (we typically think of them as large; the computer has a way of reducing them to size): (1) students, (2) curriculum/programs, (3) facilities, (4) finances, (5) personnel. Subdivisions within the bins can be multiplied, and should be, to match the manager's purpose.

Most institutions are simply not well managed. Managers, who should indeed delegate and hope for results through the efforts of others, have to ask themselves on occasion, "where does trust end and neglect begin?" If they happen also to be parents of teenagers, they will recognize the importance of the question. Managers should inquire, inspect, and encourage, without undue intrusion or interference. No small order.

Most higher education managers are ignorant of ratio analysis which, when known, is often regarded as inappropriate for the academy and proper only to business. Without ratio analysis, however, academic managers are simply "flying blind." Financial ratios and efficiency ratios belong on the academic manager's instrument panel.

A lawyer friend of mine refers to himself as a "manual laborer" and illustrates his point by putting a pen in one hand and a long, yellow legal pad in the other. If he does not put pad and pen together, the job doesn't get done and payment is not received. Faculty members should not take offense at the suggestion that their hard work is indeed labor not easily delegated to subordinates. If faculty members can increase their productivity, their institutions will be in a much better position to increase their compensation.

This is not a depersonalized, mechanistic consignment of faculty members to a "factor of production" category. Nor is it a refusal to recognize the differences between plumbers and philosophers. But the point must be made that increased faculty productivity would make increased compensation more readily attainable in tuition-dependent institutions. And without some measures of productivity more sophisticated than the student-faculty ratio, academic managers are not going to get a handle on the problem. The wage-price guidelines fashioned by the Council of Economic Advisers in the Kennedy Administration embodied a simple principle: to avoid inflation, average increases in compensation in the economy must not be permitted to exceed average increases in productivity. In the higher education industry, of course, the question is how to measure productivity. A related question is how to measure the institution's rate of inflation. The well-informed manager will know.

The productivity issue will not go away. Some higher education institutions will not be able to bear the weight of declining productivity ratios. Kempis said of one definitional problem in the late Middle Ages, "It is better to feel compunction than to know how to define it." Academics today would agree that it would be a lot better to enjoy productivity in higher education than worry about defining and measuring it. But if productivity is on the decline in a college or university, the institution must do one of three things: (1) freeze salaries and prepare the life boats, (2) find revenue other than tuition to pay for the decline, or (3) use work-measurement devices as handles for the application of productivity controls.

One such control touches upon the sequencing of courses, the cycling of a given course by semester, year, or longer intervals, and the elimination of courses that carry insufficient enrollment. Duplicated course offerings often signal the presence of a productivity problem. Since the elimination of courses leads to the elimination of majors and perhaps departments, the devices used to measure the problem of declining productivity must be well-designed and carefully applied. In addition, the institution's position on what is essential to its mission and what program areas simply must be subsidized (and to what extent), must be clear to all concerned. All of this is part of the management responsibility in higher education today.

It should be noted that unattended productivity problems abound in the non-faculty, non-instructional areas of campus life. Coopers & Lybrand noted some of these in its March, 1984,

Higher Education Management Newsletter: underutilization of athletic facilities, administrative space, and data processing equipment; excessive insurance costs; improper investment of available cash; failure to attract the paying public to campus events; inefficient custodial operations; inadequate attention to admissions. The list could be lengthened. It points to potential mismanagement, or at least poor performance by the academy's full-time managers. But even where the central administration is performing exceptionally well, there will be management challenges waiting to be met in the departments, divisions, and schools which provide the academic programs.

The Manifold Role. Of all the elements in the manifold role that describe the management function in divisions and departments, the one that comes across to academics like a fingernail on a blackboard is that of entrepreneur.

Not all persons who choose the academic life have passive-dependent personalities. But the teaching profession may well attract a disproportionate number of persons who tend to be more passive than active when it comes to risk-taking, venturing into unexplored "business opportunities," not to mention "chasing the buck." Teachers are used to finding students in place on the first day of instruction, the class schedule and academic calendar set by others, and the institutional support systems like library, audio-visual, and computing services ready to go. The teacher's responsibility centers on the preparation of self to perform the teaching function for students recruited by others, in a setting arranged by others, and, not always but often, with support services provided by others. Even the most successful classroom "performer" must, when invited to add a management responsibility to teaching duties, check to see if his or her teaching *persona* is sufficiently "outward bound" to provide the necessary managerial momentum.

The entrepreneurial academic manager should be willing to go into the market — for students, for faculty, and for ideas. This attitude will lead naturally to collaboration with development officers in approaching foundations. Collaboration with other department or division managers in developing joint majors, interdisciplinary programs, and special events is also natural to the entrepreneurial manager. So is competition with other academic units for fellowships, awards, and other symbols of superior student achievement. One's department or division thus becomes "well known," is seen as "standing apart," begins to win for itself the precious prize of prestige.

The entrepreneurial academic manager normally finds librarians more than willing to respond to requests for special services. All one needs to do is ask! Similarly, off-campus entities, such as museums, government agencies, social services, businesses, and research centers, respond well to proposals from resourceful academic managers. But the proposals must first be thought of inside the academy; more precisely, they have to originate between the ears of the entrepreneurial manager.

Here are a few possibilities:

> Faculty members in four-year colleges need renewal opportunities and more money. The manager of a particular academic unit can negotiate short-term (summer, January, spring break) paid-employment opportunities for his or her faculty in business. New surroundings, new problems to be solved, extra compensation to be pocketed, and, quite probably, a more content and productive professor upon return to the classroom.

> When the entrepreneurial eye notices press reports that Congress is likely to respond to, say, the "math-science crisis" by providing summer workshop funds to colleges willing to assist in the updating of elementary and secondary school teachers, the alert manager's immediate response is one of planning to convert this development into an opportunity for one's own faculty. Joint ventures between and among faculties of education, mathematics, science, and computer science come to mind. As does the suspicion that the entrepreneurial manager will probably find in all of this an opportunity to pick up a few personal computers along the way without, of course, using institutional funds or unbalancing the departmental or divisional budget.

> Budget officers would surely be intrigued and possibly persuaded by a special request for a "loan" rather than a "grant" to

cover a specific project in the next budget year. Academics tend to think of expenditure budgets as being made possible only through grants of institutional funds to the academic unit. Institutional budget officers might be willing to try a small loan program to cover some of those projects that have income-generating potential but are not essential to the unit's mission and thus not first in line for a commitment of institutional funds. But if the project (e.g., a recognition dinner, a festschrift, an artistic performance, a weekend workshop, a special lecture) succeeded, it would presumably enhance the work of the department or division and the success would, by design of the manager, also produce revenue sufficient to offset the expense. The extent of the risk is a measure of the resourcefulness of the manager.

> In more routine matters like new course development, the entrepreneurial manager can offer "challenge grants" to faculty in terms of released time for course preparation and paid advertising (flyers, box ads in the student press) for new courses. The released time can often be created out of the thin air of more efficient class scheduling and enrollment planning; the funds needed to provide special advertising for new courses are so small that it is not difficult to think of ways of coming up with the dollars or the barter arrangements.

> There are adult learners waiting to be attracted to campus. There are younger students who want to do degree work part-time. There are enrolled students who want to cover the course work in three years. The entrepreneurial academic manager will respond with creative and persuasiveplanning as well as imaginative rescheduling of teaching loads.

> The teaching load can, through the wonder of telecommunications, be simultaneously increased and lightened. This speaks directly to the problem of productivity. The availability of interactive telecommunications systems and the exploding market for video cassette recorders invite the academic manager to address the quantity side of the productivity challenge with quality academic programming. The market for educational software created by the home computer represents potential revenues and enrollments for well-managed academic units.

I have stressed the entrepreneurial role because the maintenance of both quality and quantity in the higher education enterprise (particularly its private sector) depends on it. But something should be said of the manager simply as manager.

This person must be an enabler, a facilitator of both faculty and student energy. The manager is, of course, one who trusts, who delegates, who achieves results through the efforts of others. The academic manager should set performance standards. These should somehow be embodied in syllabi, bibliographies, and outlines which are required of all professors for all courses and retained on file in the manager's office. Moreover, the performance standards are tested in a variety of ways each year. One of those tests is the examination sheet prepared by the professor and presented to the student at the conclusion of the course. This test, new and updated each year, should also be on file in the manager's office.

The manager is a supervisor of both instruction and advising in the academy. This supervisory function is carried out, of course, in a fashion consistent with professional protocols, academic freedom, and respect for the rights of faculty and students. But it must be carried out. This is the place to make the point that the manager is also an encourager — an affirmative person who affirms others. As I mentioned earlier, one veteran and wide observer of life in the academy thought it should be standard procedure "to spray the place with praise." Expressions of appreciation do not ordinarily top the list of managerial excesses in the academy. Even when the flow of recognition is regular and generous from the manager out, it rarely attracts a reciprocal response of gratitude flowing in. Such is the world in which we live and work; such is the environment that impedes the spread of the spirit of September, month by month, throughout the academic year.

The good manager is also a planner. He or she will want to have institutional goals clearly articulated, and departmental or divisional objectives clearly defined in function of those goals. Objectives are shorter steps toward longer and larger goals. The planning function requires the development of action strategies to be pursued over time. The planner must therefore have a useful data base, workable measures of progress, and knowledge of the efficiency ratios. Again, the question of which gauges are necessary and useful on the instrument panel.

The academic manager is also a "hiring boss." Responsibility for searching out and signing up new faculty resides with the manager of the unit. In these days of steady state, if not decline' in the industry, the hiring decision must be taken with care. Here the good manager will not simply refer to the institution's mission statement, but use it to ferret out the right person. It is not enough to inquire whether the central theme of the mission statement (e.g., emphasis on the liberal arts, or a religious tradition, or community service, or the higher education of women) is agreeable to the applicant. The candidate must be asked, "Will you commit yourself to helping us advance this mission, achieve this purpose?" And the manager must be shrewd enough to evaluate the response correctly in today's depressing and depressed academic job market, where some candidates would be willing to agree to just about any mission statement in order to get the job.

Another desirable quality in the unit manager is innovation. Although John Tracy Ellis warned leaders of higher education, in the speech referred to earlier, to "avoid the national craze for innovation," he acknowledged that Newman said "to live is to change and to be perfect is to have changed often." Change for the sake of change is undesirable. But genuine innovation is energizing. It awakens the tradition and conserves it by moving it forward. The good academic manager will have a fertile imagination and serve the institution well by injecting new ideas into his or her academic unit.

All of the foregoing presupposes that the person who chairs a division or department is a teacher-scholar. Hence the faculty member who holds this manifold managerial role is presumed to be one who believes in quality and insists on quality when dealing not only with those whose efforts he or she facilitates, but with the central administration as well. Indeed the teacher-scholar with managerial responsibilities can be expected to do everything in his or her power to shame the administration into pro-quality decisions!

The managerial task will be all the more effective to the extent that the manager writes well, does team-teaching on occasion, and feels a personal responsibility to be a working member of the profession. The academic manager may not be able to stay on top of his or her discipline, but should never lose touch with the discipline either. Familiarity with, and contributions to, the higher-education management literature also serve to enhance managerial effectiveness.

Not only should this special person be able to represent colleagues and students well to the central administration, he or she, functioning as an enabler, will never lose an opportunity to open up avenues of development for the persons he or she is privileged to serve.

Service somehow says it all. Neither our industry nor our larger society is comfortable yet with the notion of "servant leadership," but that may well be the best possible way of reducing to two words what the academy needs today in its divisions and departments. (Additional words on leadership are the content of chapter 22.) The spirit of service which, by the way, is not at all unrelated to entrepreneurship, productivity, planning, innovating, evaluating, and motivating, is quite capable of pushing the spirit of September on into the colder and darker months of the academic year.

One last word from John Tracy Ellis, a true elder statesman in my own academic community and the dean of American Catholic church historians. In his January, 1984, speech, given when he received the Association of Catholic Colleges and Universities' Hesburgh Award for his "significant contribution to the advancement of Catholic higher education," Monsignor Ellis left the assembled college and university presidents with this bit of advice: "Place a supremely high premium on the value of work, and hard work, for every member of your academic community. In the pursuit of what so many today designate as fun, the imperative of strenuous work that helped to make this nation great has become enfeebled." Presidents, and all other participants in the academic enterprise, can unfeeble their troubled industry by heeding his advice. In the process, they will have discovered to their own deep delight the meaning of productivity. Good management, particularly in the departments and divisions, can make it happen.

20 Generating Options for Improved Compensation

Catholic colleges have distinctive characteristics that set them apart from their secular counterparts. It is not my intention here to explore the differences or probe again the identity issue. What makes the schools "characteristically Catholic" is of less concern to me now than the question of what the Catholic character of an institution has to say, first about collective bargaining in that institution, and then about the compensation question in general.

Collective bargaining deals with job security, wages, and working conditions. I would assume that a Catholic institution would be careful to provide working conditions consistent with the dignity of the human persons employed there. If not, the institution is not "characteristically Catholic." I would also assume that Catholic institutions would not take lightly the concern for job security on the part of the worker. That issue rises in importance as job opportunities elsewhere decline. But even if an institution does respect the job-security concerns of employees, does provide them with both voice and choice in matters affecting their work environment, there will always be the distribution issue, the complicated question of remuneration. Wages are part of a larger picture. They relate, in the private sector at least, to price, to the charges borne by the recipient of the institution's services. In hospitals and schools ("non-profit" institutions), wages do not compete with profits. They do, however, represent a competing claim — on the expenditure side of the budget — with management salaries, necessary operating-fund surpluses, plant fund needs, overhead costs, reserves for contingencies, "venture funds" for the development of new services, discounts or waivers of fees for the poor and others unable to pay for services the institution provides. The list of competing claims could be easily extended. Judgments about their relative importance will understandably differ. These differences set the stage for a collective bargain, a resolution of the competing claims.

Paternalism, not unknown in the history of the very best Catholic institutions, resents and rejects intrusions in the process of deciding what is "best for all concerned." Collective bargaining, backed by law, forces such intrusion. It takes a while for paternalistic (or maternalistic) managements to get comfortable with the presence of others in the decision-making process. Opening up the process voluntarily is an obvious way of avoiding the imposition of collective bargaining.

Whatever the forum for discussion, the focus of decision-making will center on remuneration. The issue will naturally enlarge itself to include the "fringes," benefit considerations that move beyond mere *vivere* to *bene vivere*. But, in my view, the heart of the remuneration issue, and thus the core of the bargaining debate, relates to gain sharing. If the debate is to be honest and productive, the gain must be clearly defined. For the gain to be defined, management must have measures that are agreeable to, and can be audited by, the other party to the decision.

Despite their sometimes bombastic language, frail people sit on both sides of any bargaining table. The process would work beautifully if only the participants would not posture and pretend. All too often what Kermit Gordon once called "forthright evasion" lines up against bellicose bluffing. The words least likely to be believed are, "this is our top offer" and "this is our rock bottom demand." Thus, a cloud of distrust and ambiguity descends. Out of the confusion rise honest management fears about ability to pay while holding charges to a reasonable level, and honest labor concerns about keeping up with rising prices and making enough to get ahead. Encircling these concerns are honest fears about the interruption of necessary, even vital, services in the event of a strike. Such fears, in a Catholic institution, are, it must be presumed, prompted by professional integrity on both sides of the argument.

Survival of the institution is another deep-down concern. The presumption, often unfair, is that management takes a longer view than the more immediate paycheck perspective of the workers. The judgment made by one side against the other in this regard is usually faulty; the perspective on neither side is as long and altruistic as the proponents pretend. Moreover, there is nothing in Catholic doctrine that grants any Catholic school existence until the end of time. There is, though, a time-honored Catholic social principle that attaches a simple conclusion to the argument of inability to pay a living wage: Dissolve the enterprise.

Catholicity clearly requires of its adherents in the world of work an openness to collective bargaining. Creativity, enlarged by supernatural grace, can make the Catholic enterprise function in a way that collective bargaining (with its added financial costs, litigiousness, potential for distrust, and penchant for acrimony) can be rendered unnecessary. Or, if needed to bridge communication gaps and meet unattended problems, collective bargaining in a Catholic context can itself exhibit Catholic characteristics. Aside from charity, patience, justice, honesty, courage, and compassion on both sides, collective bargaining in a Catholic context should be characterized by creativity.

There is no such thing as Catholic collective bargaining. The process is a human construct, a social institution. When Catholics engage in the process, their Catholic principles and character can make the process work in new ways. Only creativity can make this happen. In the context of collective bargaining, creativity means generating new options all the time.

It must be said that not every good, service, or way of doing things in the world of work is always good for the use of everyone. To put it another way and simply, collective bargaining can be abused. It can provoke participants (all of them, as noted earlier, "frail" and in need of healing grace) to behavior less than virtuous. Not all negotiators are selected on the strength of their moral character or the depth of their faith. Nor is intelligence always a prime criterion. Sadly, force is a sometimes acceptable substitute for thought in the collective bargaining process. Collective bargaining is a device of human construction. It is open to abuse on either side.

It must be acknowledged, however, that collective bargaining is a useful structure for communication. In the process, things get talked about. Sometimes endlessly! I was impressed by the remark of novelist C. P. Snow's wife who explained that "something to talk about" can help a lot in keeping a marriage together, as was the case in her marriage of many decades. Honest talk in a bargaining context can keep an institution together. But honest talk and fair dealing are possibilities, of course, in many workplace arrangements other than collective bargaining.

It is often remarked that the most effective union organizer is an unresponsive, heedless, doctrinaire manager. Case histories of unionization in Catholic institutions will not infrequently substantiate that assertion. If the "Son of Man came not to be served but to serve, and to give his life as a ransom for many" (Mt. 20-28), one might expect institutions that embody Christian principles to be sufficiently sensitive to employees to listen to them. The employees, in turn, should be sufficiently responsible to communicate in unexaggerated and unprovoking terms. But frail, fallible, and limited people line up on both sides of the communication gap. Often before they know it, they are saved from their own excesses by the mechanism of collective bargaining.

Once the mechanism is in place, parties to a potential bargain relate to one another differently. This is not necessarily bad. What previously may have been random, even arbitrary, decision-making on remuneration issues is now formalized. Procedures are rationalized. Accountability is focused.

As employee security increases, management freedom decreases. The relationship is not necessarily causal. A fully free and fully responsible (there's the rub!) management can use spontaneity, generosity, and surprise to advance the enterprise and benefit the employees. But a free and irresponsible, or at least insensitive, management can fail its employees and leave them with little choice but to organize. In the wake of the Yeshiva decision, this option is no longer open to faculty members in independent colleges and universities. It is, however, a path still open to many other employees on independent campuses.

Once organized, workers can choose some of their own to represent them or opt for outside negotiators. From management's viewpoint, there are advantages and disadvantages either way. If the union negotiators are insiders, full-time employees, one might presume easier communication, greater familiarity with the enterprise (particularly with students or other "clients" the institution serves), and deeper loyalty to the institution. Catholic management would consider all this important. It would hope for a commitment on the part of the negotiators to the institution's religious mission, an understanding of its purpose, a disinterested desire for its survival. But inside negotiators are, at least in the early years of unionization, inexperienced negotiators. They sometimes misapply the "big industrial union" model to themselves. They begin clumsily and end excessively dependent on outside legal counsel. Parallel problems appear on the side of management.

When an outside (national or international) union represents employees of a Catholic institution, administrators in that enterprise have, in addition to their discomfort over the "intrusion," the genuine fear that the institution's Catholic purposes will be misunderstood or ignored. There are further fears that the institution's "clients" will be at best unknown and at worst disregarded, and the institution's survival will not count for much on a long list of outside negotiators' concerns. All of these fears represent possibilities that need not be realized. Each one of these fears, moreover, is a measure of the responsibility management has to attend to the problems that prompt workers to organize in the first place. In no case, however, can an institution call itself

Catholic and attempt to suppress its employees' right to organize.

I have mentioned creativity more than once in this chapter. In those pursuits most obviously creative — acting, writing, composing, painting, sculpting — the format provides an opportunity to start all over again. A new play, poem, or performance is a new creation.

Contracts expire and the opportunity is there to start all over again. Collective bargaining represents a new beginning (so does a fresh budget for the next fiscal year). The material to be shaped into a creative agreement is limited in that one important respect — it is material. It is subject to constraints. There is just so much to go around. The question is how much, and this brings the discussion back to the notion of gain sharing.

As men and women work for pay in a shared enterprise, they derive satisfaction from the achievement of measurable results. They also receive pay for their labor, for the time and skill they devote to the enterprise. If they work well together, they can realize economies; they can produce more for less. Gains of measurable dollar value, thus produced, should be shared. In a market economy, the expectation of sharing in the gain keeps all participants in the enterprise going.

Because the gain is by no means assured before the fact, management is unwilling to commit itself antecedently to wage payments that would presume the gain.

Labor, for its part, is unwilling to concede, long before the fact, that no gain will be there to be shared. Labor is thus reluctant to settle for a wage which, over the life of the contract, may prove to be significantly less than the wage an as-yet-unrealized gain will enable the enterprise to pay. So before the fact, labor holds out for more and management holds back.

If a non-profit institution has a good management information system grounded on a reliable data base, a form of gain sharing can be worked out which will ease anxieties on both sides of the bargaining table, hasten arrival at agreement, and provide a guarantee of increased remuneration if the year ahead proves to

218

be a good one. How is all of this to be achieved before the fact?

Budgets, which are planning documents prepared before the fact, embody assumptions. In a college, budgeted revenues will assume a certain number of "paid credits" or a "full-time equivalent" student count for the period in question, multiplied by a set price (tuition) which is pre-announced and will not change over that same period.

College faculty may argue that enrollment projections are too conservative and that the revenue picture will be brighter than the budgeted number of paid credits would indicate. Rather than arguing over the estimates and pushing the institution into a high risk position of antecedent commitment to a compensation bill it may not be able to meet (not to mention pushing the price to a level beyond the reach of its clients), why not agree that if paid credits (or whatever previously agreed-upon, measurable, suitable number has been used in the revenue assumption) exceeds the estimated level, the consequent revenue gain will be shared with the workers on the basis of a formula that reflects labor costs as a percentage of costs incurred in providing the service?

Would the gain be shared as a bonus or fitted somehow retroactively into the wage structure? Let the bargainers decide. What if there is no gain? Then the revenue assumptions will have proved to be correct and fiscal damage will have been avoided. What if there is not only no gain but a loss, a revenue shortfall? The remuneration agreed upon in the contract will not change; management assumes full responsibility. What is proposed here is gain-sharing with employees, not risk-sharing. The workers will not pay for management's estimating errors. Worker willingness to accept a gain-sharing arrangement would, one might hope, contribute to a better revenue-estimating environment by properly pressuring managerial competence.

Management's rights are not infringed by an audit of the appropriate records which reveal quite precisely the number of paid credits. The complete financial audit of the most recent fiscal year need not be disclosed. The point of an audit associated with gain sharing is to enable adjustments in pay to be made at the end of a fiscal year but before the "books close" on that year.

Although it would be most unwise to pit student vs. faculty or other staff in the revenue and remuneration context of a non-profit enterprise, it cannot be denied that compensation is related to client payments. Improved compensation normally means higher prices. Rarely is there sufficient room on the expenditure side of the budget to provide higher wages in the absence of a price increase without deferring maintenance, incurring debt, or depriving the enterprise of necessary plant and equipment.

Careful management will calculate on an annual basis and communicate to all concerned the ratio of compensation to a given employee group (faculty, for example) as a percentage of total fees paid by users of the service the institution provides. The calculation involves a simple fraction. In the college example, tuition and fees would be in the denominator, faculty compensation would be in the numerator. If a reasonably fair arrangement is already in place — i.e., the price is fair, the compensation is reasonable although subject to improvement — then management will want to hold that ratio as constant as possible to safeguard the financial security of the entire enterprise. Hence, adjustments leading to improved compensation (the numerator) must be made with an eye to offsetting adjustments in price (increasing the value of the denominator). If the numerator grows and the denominator stays the same (no price increase) and if there is insufficient growth in other revenue sources like endowment income or external fund-raising for current operations, then serious problems will develop elsewhere in the enterprise. The gain-sharing idea is one way of preventing irreversible problems from developing. Gain-sharing can enable the institution to stay on the safe side of financial exigency.

Management will understandably resent, but must come to expect as normal, employee pressure. A certain pressure, from management to labor, to produce is not unusual. Pressure for pay and for a voice in production decisions is not unexpected from labor to management. When those pressures bear on concealed deficiencies, understandable resentment turns into self-justifying defensiveness that is unworthy of those who are there "to serve and not to be served."

If reciprocal pressures in the workplace are held to normal levels, communication can be constructive and differences will not become entrenched. This can be the case in or out of a collective bargaining context. With or without collective bargaining, labor and management can, in John Gardner's words, "tolerate extraordinary hardship if they think it is an unalterable part of life's travail. But an administered frustration — unsanctioned by religion or custom or deeply rooted values — is more than the spirit can bear." (John W. Gardner, former Secretary of Health, Education, and Welfare, in a commencement address at Cornell University; quoted in *The Wall Street Journal*, November 26, 1968.)

Administered frustration can force workers to organize. But the collective bargaining process itself can produce administered frustration. Pressure management remains a challenge with or without collective bargaining. Creativity is the best control. And the best application of creativity in this regard is the identification of potential gains and the design of an agreement to share those gains in a way that serves the balanced interests of all parties to the enterprise. If there is no unexpected gain to be shared, the shared commitment of workers and management to the purposes of the service-rendering enterprise will keep the organization together. And the Catholic view would see the organization remaining together as long as the Lord wills it to be so.

21 Academic Antitrust

The system of U.S. higher education really depends on student choice, on each student having the capacity to choose and the freedom to exercise it. This fact should please every educator because the educator, more than most others in society, will acknowledge that a person is, after all, the sum of his or her choices.

But what is the contemporary student's *capacity* for choice? This, of course, is a question about student maturity. What is the *freedom* of the student to choose? This is a question about faculty trust. No simple answer is available to either of these questions. But they stake out an area for constructive discussion as educational managers consider their future options in strengthening and advancing the educational enterprise.

Many students are not mature enough to choose wisely when they arrive on college campuses. This, of course, is not to say they should have no choices. Faculties, for their part, often display a trust of students that is less than total; they are reluctant to grant freedom of choice. This is not to suggest that the faculty should have no voice and no control concerning the choices made by students in their collegiate experience.

Beneath these questions is a tension between respect and control. It is not unlike the dilemma seen by the radical psychiatrist Thomas Szasz, writing in *Harpers* in March, 1973:

> To the child, control means care and love; to the adult, disdain and repression. Herein lies the fundamental dilemma and task for society: to encourage parents to love and control their children; and politicians to respect their fellow citizens and leave them alone (except when the latter deprive others of life, liberty, and property).
>
> Modern societies are well on their way to inverting this arrangement: They encourage parents to fake respect for their children and thus justify their failure to control them; and politicians to fake love for their fellow citizens and thus justify their efforts to exercise unlimited control over them.

A faculty, as such, is neither politician nor parent. Yet there are faculties that fake a respect for their students to justify the abdication of all responsibility to control the educational process. There are also faculties that are overzealous in regard to their control responsibility and fake a love for their students in order to justify treating them like children and repressing all freedom of curricular choice, sometimes for job-security motives on the part of faculty.

There is a tension, therefore, between respect or love, and control on the side of the faculty, and a corresponding tension between freedom and the need for direction on the part of the student. Believing, as I do, that a person may be defined as the sum of his or her choices, I would look for something constructive to emerge from these tensions. This positive result would, it might be hoped, emerge in the form of student choices based on principle (not on whim or simple desire), supported by personal guidance (not repressive dictation). In choosing and in committing himself or herself to those choices, the student will progress in the practice of life. But for this to occur, there must be options; and where, it might be asked, have all the options gone?

Many of the options in higher education have gone the way of vocationalism, of specialization. The basic option is toward a specific career, leaving relatively few curricular options after the career commitment has been made. This is a current trend that constitutes both a threat and a challenge to the quality of the collegiate experience.

Approaching the question from another direction, one might comment that many options in higher education have receded behind a cloud of ambiguity. Many young people have no clear vocational orientation, but neither are they comfortable with the prospect of selecting leisurely from a four-year menu of higher studies. They don't know what they want. Often, this is symptomatic of another problem — they don't know who they are. Until they acquire a sense of selfhood, they will have no self to commit. The options are deferred until a self is located. Here there is less threat and possibly greater challenge to the quality of the collegiate experience. And here the custodians of the curriculum, the faculty, must be particularly wary of a fake respect that might be used to justify their heavy-handed application of pre-packaged solutions to the problem of student choice in an age of ambiguity. Above all, faculty interest in the form of job or department preservation, should never influence student choice.

A third approach to the case of the missing options follows a middle path, where most students who have chosen to enroll in college find themselves. They have opted at least for a general direction in their academic program. More often than not, they have a career objective in that same general direction. They are pre-professional or readying themselves for unspecified managerial, political, social-service, or other creative pursuits.

They come to college and select a major field of study. In that field, the student encounters a set of designated courses that must be taken to meet the major requirements. Next, the faculty which offers the major courses normally specifies other courses from other departments as "adjunct" to the major and necessary for the program. As I suggested in chapter 15, the entire faculty, in a genuine collegiate setting, has the responsibility of seeing to it that no one department denies its majors access to liberalizing studies by insisting on an overburden of major and adjunct coursework. If it is to be faithful to the aim of a true college education, the entire faculty must meet a concomitant responsibility of seeing that a core of liberal studies is available to and taken by all students regardless of their major. The discharge of this responsibility differs, quantitatively and qualitatively, from college to college. The difference is easily detected by simply examining the way the so-called General Educational Requirement is handled. Here, the issues of respect, trust, control, and freedom become most visible; for only after the major, adjunct, and general educational requirements are accounted for can a count of electives be made. Electives are free choices, courses taught and taken for no immediate utilitarian purpose, courses taught and taken because of interest and value and connection with the great liberal tradition. Chapter 15 dealt with the question of coherence in the curriculum. The issue now under consideration is the management of choice within a curriculum.

A good college will respect persons, foster values, be open to the transcendent, pursue truth for its own sake, encourage eloquence, and delight in beauty in all its forms. Excessive rationalism and a preference for prescription of curriculum over freedom of student choice can work against these objectives. So can random selection of courses by unguided students, semester after semester, on a path of credit accumulation. Students need guidance, but they also need freedom. When the student feels repressed, unfree to speak out or raise questions, then the last real option is gone and learning is all but impossible. It all comes down to a question of balance.

Students do have freedom of choice; many, however, are looking for firm direction, some would even prefer command. And those students on a comfortable middle path between career orientation and unfocused liberal studies are not in the best of all academic worlds either, because they suffer from the absence of an Academic Antitrust Law. By that I mean that they are consumers in monopolistic markets. In most colleges, every department is a monopoly, hence every department is capable of monopolistic behavior — restricted output, inefficient and outmoded methods of production, resistance to change, disregard of consumer demands, even excessive pricing, although this

225

might be measured in units of frustration and loss of intellectual enthusiasm rather than in units of dollars and cents.

Where one department "services" another with adjunct courses, various forms of monopolistic or oligopolistic behavior are possible. Collusion is always a possibility in these days of heightened interest in the student-faculty ratio. You send me your students, I'll send you mine! The opposite behavior pattern is also possible: unilateral setting of course content, time schedule, and prerequisites on the part of the offering department without prior consultation and approval of the receiving department. In either case, the consumer — the student — suffers, as is always the case in an unfree, optionless market.

Where will antitrust activity originate on the campus? With the students, of course. Just as the Federal Trade Commission, an antitrust agency, was intended from its beginning in 1914 by President Woodrow Wilson to "punish with pitiless publicity" unfair trade practices, students are now evaluating and publicizing the results of their evaluation of stagnant courses and ineffective teaching.

As more curricular options come their way and attendance requirements are relaxed, students are voting with their feet and sending market signals to producers of ill-prepared and unpopular courses. But where monopoly control remains tight, as is often the case in major and adjunct offerings, students have no recourse but to stop or drop out, or to grit their teeth and go for the grade while battling the boredom.

Antitrust activity will never be effective unless it becomes a faculty- rather than a student-cause. Professional pride as well as professional ethics should drive any professor toward constant personal renewal and curricular improvement. For the fact is that some degree of monopoly must always exist in academe, and the professorial product in very many cases will never improve except by personal professorial decision. The matter is complicated by the fact that the very product is really a process — a motivational process aimed more at the will of the student than the intellect. The student has to want to learn. Learning is a

self-propelled activity. If all options disappear, the self-propul-
sion stops and the student becomes a passive receptacle rather
than an active learner. This is of capital importance to professors
of the liberal arts who deal with the communication of imagination, of unrealized possibilities, from human mind to human
mind. "A mind is a terrible thing to waste," say the advertisements for the United Negro College Fund. The statement should
give all educators pause.

I think of professor and student as fitting the ironic imagination of Thomas Hardy, whose poem "The Man He Killed" tells a
sad story of two men who happened to meet on a battlefield
rather than at an inn.

> Had he and I but met
>> By some old ancient inn,
> We should have sat us down to wet
>> Right many a nipperkin!
> But ranged as infantry,
>> And staring face to face,
> I shot him as he shot at me,
>> And killed him in his place.
>
> Yes; quaint and curious war is!
>> You shoot a fellow down
> You'd treat if met where any bar is,
>> Or help to half-a-crown.

Yes, "quaint and curious" college classes can be, as professors
and students sometimes realize. "Had he and I but met" elsewhere, or if our classroom had been more like an inn than a
battleground, a communication of imagination might have occurred. Minds don't die easily, but even so, a mind is a terrible
thing to bore, or ignore, or leave unchallenged and unstimulated
in a joyless, lifeless learning environment. And how often is the
remark, "He shot him down!" heard in collegiate corridors as the
classrooms empty out?

I have not alluded at all to the radical critique of what is perceived to be the alienated learning environment in America's schools. Such a critique views the school as servant to the capitalist system, mechanistically preparing students to fit subsequently into an alienated work environment. I do not at all subscribe to that. But I do think it is instructive to note how faculty and administration tend to keep talking to students about a better future while ignoring opportunities for present improvements. Thus the academic establishment opens itself to Camus' charge that "Progress, paradoxically, can be used to justify conservatism. A draft drawn on confidence in the future, it allows the master to have a clear conscience. The slave, and those whose present life is miserable and who can find no consolation in the heavens, are assured that at least the future belongs to them. The future is the only kind of property that the masters willingly concede to the slaves."

Knowing, as they do, that knowledge should liberate and not enslave, educators can quite rightly reject the master-slave categorization. However, they should note carefully the possibility that the promise of a better future can be a phantom substitute for needed present improvements. Monopolistic behavior within the academy can prevent those improvements from happening.

What De Tocqueville noted nearly 160 years ago as a defect in the American character has produced the "vocationalism" we have noticed in our students. He saw a streak of narrow pragmatism in us. "Their life," he observed, "is so practical, so confused, so excited, so active, that but little time remains to them for thought." The narrowness of our pragmatism prompted James F. Fixx, in commenting on De Tocqueville, to remark that "many Americans would rather have no ideas at all than have ideas lacking an immediate and obvious value." Many of these same Americans are sitting today in college classrooms. They are riding the wave of the new vocationalism. They really need what liberal education can give. Maybe they even *want* it, but think it is unavailable, or financially unattainable, or altogether unrelated to real jobs in a real world. If the humanists on our faculties are themselves convinced of the value of what they have to offer, they should mount a tireless campaign to explain their educational vision to potential students, and point out that four years of disciplined work in the liberal arts is itself solid preparation for many careers. They should also persuade those who hold public and private pursestrings that this kind of education deserves financial support. And they should use their collective influence on campus to break departmental monopolies while retaining coherence in the curriculum. But even more important is the need for faculty in all departments to trust the students they attract, to give them options, and to encourage them to choose for themselves from a rich array of well-taught courses in a balanced curriculum.

All educators recognize that some students have insufficient maturity to choose wisely and thus need (even want) some measure of direction and control. As the level of trust between professor and student rises, the quality of love will also rise, and the present fears about jobs — preserving them for faculty, getting them for students — will diminish. Students will thus be free for the assimilation of values, of beauty, and ideas of substance. Faculty will be free to teach and research. Academic antitrust will be a problem no longer in need of a solution.

22 Leadership

In every corner of U.S. higher education, repeated calls are heard for "leadership." Some of the callers are hoping to find magicians or miracle workers. Others are looking for iron-fisted ayatollahs. Still others would be content with an easy-going Pied Piper. Most, of course, are searching for able educators who can inspire a vision, organize a plan, mobilize resources, and encourage forward progress toward a well-defined goal. What is the nature and purpose of good leadership? Before addressing that two-fold question, it should be remarked that no one should assume that the only leadership on campus is the so-called "top leadership." Leadership is needed in every division and unit ofthe enterprise. What, then, might be the nature and purpose of the all-pervasive leadership I have in mind?

Service. There it is, plain and simple. The purpose of leadership is service. This purpose can be achieved in a variety of ways. Whatever the style, level, or motivation of effective leadership, the outcome will be service.

The nature of leadership is more difficult to grasp.

The leader is an enabler. Good leadership empowers and releases a potential in the follower.

"Followership," more easily defined perhaps than leadership, is not so easily identified. Most leaders have many followers, at least they have manifold constituencies. A political leader serves persons who identify themselves in terms of age, race, gender, geography, property, party, creed, a specific public policy issue, or some such compartmentalizing category. University leadership looks to students, faculty, staff, alumni, and an array of interest groups beyond the campus. Within the university, deans, directors, department heads, and all other leaders face diversity within the groups they are there to serve. Church leadership, at all levels, presumes a common ground of creedal commitment but presides over different forms of expression of that common creed. Also different are the levels of commitment, the depths of understanding, and the degrees of participation by the members in church affairs.

In theological terms, the root of Christian leadership runs directly to the one-sentence summary of the mission of Christ found in Matthew 20:28, where the evangelist has Jesus declare that "the Son of Man came not to be served but to serve, and to give his life as a ransom for many." There it is again, service. And ransom, of course, means release. The leader releases the potential in the follower.

A precondition for effective leadership is trust of the follower. Ideally, any organized human activity (the mere presence of a leader-follower relationship is sufficient to identify the activity as organized) should live on the trust of leader for followers and followers for leader. When followership falters, trust in the leader has faltered first. Quite probably both falterings were preceded by an erosion of the leader's trust of the followers. The "uncertain trumpet," famous for its inability to activate the follower, is, in truth, a signal of distrust — self-distrust of one's own ability to lead, or distrust of the follower, a condition which invites the substitution of force for leadership.

It is helpful to look at images of leadership as times and the human condition change and new opportunities for leadership arise. No one model or image is everlasting, although one will be more appropriate than another as human circumstances change. In those situations where goals are necessarily general or even obscure, the vertical, top-of-the-pyramid image of leadership is of little use. Similarly, the DILT-style (Do It Like This) of direction, appropriate in a master's relationship to an apprentice, simply does not work where the pattern is not pre-cut or the terrain is unfamiliar. It produces dependency and impedes integral outcomes.

When the leadership task is to move human activity through a truly complex situation (which is usually the case in large organizations) the horizontal, center-of-the-circle image of leadership is instructive. This model suggests an in-touch relationship between leader and follower. Within the circle, the leader is more likely to ask, "Do they want me here at the center? Is my being here good for the others around me?" Such questions arise less easily in the rarefied atmosphere surrounding the top of the pyramid. Moreover, in order to pass from the center out to the edge — a movement the leader must make with some regularity if the organization is to advance and maintain vital contact with other organized bodies and contemporary movements — the leader must pass through and among the followers. They deserve to be seen and heard. Listening is an important quality of leadership. Whatever one's pedagogical principles might suggest for learning in general, the leader learns best by listening. The listener-learner is off to a good start in the development of leadership skills.

There is a characteristically Christian ring to Denis Goulet's remark that the leader should be "available, accountable, and vulnerable." Availability and accountability are conditions of leadership-service, thus differentiating it from domination and dictatorship. Vulnerability is less a condition than a continuing risk accompanying all human activity in an imperfect world which is open to misunderstanding and flawed by sin. The Christian vision, however, sees redemption in the wound. Hence the Christian leader can accept the wound, knowing that divine power may choose to work through it. The prototype of Christian leadership-service is symbolized by a broken body on a cross. Few leaders will be slain in their efforts to serve, although no one is at a loss to cite tragic instances where this has happened. Most leaders will be treated badly on occasion. All leaders should accept and respect their condition of vulnerability.

> But Jesus called them to him and said, "You know that among the pagans the rulers lord it over them, and their great men make their authority felt. This is not to happen among you. No; anyone who wants to be great among you must be your servant, and anyone who wants to be first among you must be your slave, just as the Son of Man came not to be served but to serve, and to give his life as a ransom for many." (Matthew 20:25-28)

Leadership at all levels requires both vision and values. Values will differ to some extent from leader to leader, from organization to organization. The pagans have their way of approaching the matter, the Christians have theirs. Effective leadership implies a personal embodiment in the leader of the organization's dominant values, coupled with an ability to articulate those values clearly and persuasively. Value conflicts within the group must be resolved before the group can move forward. Resolution of such conflicts is a task for the leader. The effort to reconcile can put the leader on the rack.

Vision, like values, is prerequisite to effective leadership. Curiously, those persons and organizations most intent on supervision are typically deficient in anything resembling a visionary outlook. The vitality of both the leader and the organization is linked to vision. Vision derives from ideas. Ideas depend on creative imagination.

It would be a mistake to look only to the leader for the ideas needed to generate a sustaining vision. This is, of course, an important leadership responsibility, but by no means a leadership monopoly. Nor must all leadership ideas be original. Many great leaders are derivative thinkers. The wise leader will create a suitable climate for the growth of ideas throughout the organization.

The "suggestion box" is hardly an innovation. Nor is it necessarily a sign that leadership is listening to followership. An empty or non-existent suggestion box could be a measure of insensitive and unresponsive leadership. It could also be a sign that more direct avenues of communication are open and in use. A full suggestion box could simply measure the distance between leader and follower. Suggestion boxes, active or idle, are not the issue, of course. The real issue is whether or not new ideas are taken seriously throughout the organization from top to bottom in the vertical model, and at all points on the radius in the horizontal image.

Regardless of the leadership location, idea generation is an unrelenting demand. Leaders have to come up with ideas themselves and draw them out of others. "I get an idea occasionally, too, you know," is a muffled complaint that shuttles through the ranks of most followerships. It is a leadership task to keep those complaints to a minimum by listening, implementing, crediting, and recognizing the ideas of others. Ideas must not only be solicited and cultivated; they must also be communicated.

Popes publish encyclicals. Political leaders draft platforms, make speeches, and issue "messages." Bishops publish pastoral letters and, of course, use the pulpit to reach their people. Leadership in any circumstance faces the twin challenge of articulating ideas and communicating them to the followership. No leader is ever free of a dependence on others for the generation of ideas; all followers look to their leaders for the articulation and communication of ideas.

The most common error in communication is the mistaken assumption that the communication has been achieved. No leader is ever free of this problem. In addressing the problem, person-to-person communication is always best but rarely practicable. Leadership by example has no real substitute, but this form of communication is highly perishable; its only preservative is the repetition of being given and received. For the leader there is no escaping the use of words. They must be "broadcast," "published," "distributed," "circulated" in spoken or written form. The assembled hearers or targeted readers define, in a very real way, the "home country" in which prophets have, over the centuries, experienced difficulty in gaining acceptance. But when the words stop flowing, or worse, become empty of ideas, there

234

is evidence of an abdication of leadership. The followers are no longer being served.

The prophetic voice expects chilly receptions. In its purest form, it denounces injustice and warns of dire consequences if the injustice is left uncorrected. The acoustics are rarely good for prophetic denunciations. The prophetic role is part of the burden of leadership. When compelled to exercise that role, the leader can expect to suffer rejection or worse from those not willing to move. And there lies hidden a problem that touches on the very nature of leadership.

Who can really be sure that genuine leadership is possible in a highly structured organization? Leadership quite obviously implies followership, and followers form part of a movement. Organizations, however, are not commonly regarded as movements. On the contrary, organizations tend to boast of their stability, reliability, dependability. They celebrate adjectives like "solid," "sound" and "permanent." And to guarantee solidity, soundness, and permanence, organizations need managers, not leaders.

Movements, on the other hand, always seem to be underfunded, randomly organized, somewhat unpredictable, and struggling to be understood. They need leaders to articulate the vision and keep it alive, to inspire new followers and protect the veterans from discouragement, to build momentum and foster enthusiasm.

True, an organization "on the move" is not a contradiction in terms. So there must be a form of managerial leadership capable of bringing a balanced stability to an organization while energizing it with forward motion. Like a modern, shoulder-supported movie camera that enables a running camera operator to film a running actor without any choppiness in the finished product, there is a human quality capable of combining in one person the sprightliness of good leadership with the containment of good management. No one holds the patent on it. It does not yet have a name. Call it "balanced creativity" and hope to find it in a person whose potential for leadership is already grounded in trust for the followership, a readiness to listen, a willingness to innovate, and a recognition that availability, accountability and vulnerability are central to the leadership role.

Can organizations, which will always require management, tolerate the best of leadership? Dynamic, creative, innovative leadership may, in fact, be so rare that there is just enough to serve the movements that arise from time to time. Organizations will always have their managers. Some of these may, perhaps, exhibit leadership qualities that are less than best but sufficient to sustain organizational progress. When the leader-manager meets frustration within the confines of the organization, limited and conservative as organizations tend to be, the leadership impulse may have to look to a larger arena beyond the hemmed-in "home country" if it is ever to find full expression.

I suspect that this is often the case in the U.S., where prominent political leaders often enjoy greater influence nationally than they do in their home states or Congressional districts, where bishops can influence Church life beyond their local jurisdictions but cannot resolve certain diocesan difficulties, and where university presidents' ideas can shape national policies but their on-campus pleadings leave curriculum committees unmoved. Indeed there are heads of families (by definition leaders on a small but critically important scale) who are stymied by domestic frustrations as they enjoy effortless and widespread influence outside the home.

Leaders anywhere are expected to unify their followers. The service of unity provides another perspective on the nature of leadership.

A military commander presides over uniformity, controls it, and guides it into a conflicted engagement with an opposing uniformity. The presence of an external enemy is sometimes all it takes to transform uniformity into unity. The troops become "united in battle." But this is a partial unity, not the unity that creates community and thus renders ideological differences anachronistic along with the military arrangements that support them. In deploring our differences we must not lose hope, since it is out of difference that unity is achieved. In moving toward that achievement, however, it will not be useful to rely on the military model of leadership.

Unity invariably suggests simplicity, and simplicity may well be the key to an understanding of the nature of leadership. At the heart of leadership is the human person. That person's leadership service of others will be most effective when those others perceive their leader as an integral person whose central ambition is to be of service, whose authority is an enabling "authorship" of what the followers want to write, and whose perquisites of position amount to nothing more than a necessary "tool-kit" to do the job. When the tool-kit becomes overloaded with the trappings of office, and when the distance separating leader from follower widens beyond the range of meaningful contact, simplicity is lost, trust erodes, and service deteriorates. The need for new leadership now preoccupies the followers who recognize, however vaguely, that the ultimate power is theirs. Power resides with them by law, in those arrangements where governance depends on the consent of the governed, and by virtue of the dignity of the human person in any arrangement where human potential awaits a unified release in response to a leader's enabling service. Since leaders are also human, it should surprise no one to see them come and go, rise and fall, despite the fact that some arrangements permit the leader to remain in place long after the leadership has gone.

What all of this has to say to political entities, to Church bodies, to the universities, and to other movements and organizations which attract the allegiance of people in their transit through life, is a matter to be decided by leaders and followers for themselves. I have not named persons from history or contemporary life whose leadership has been exemplary. Not because there are no exemplary leaders, but only to avoid the risk of obscuring the lines of analysis with swatches of legend, hyperbole, and romanticism that tend to mar the simple stories which seriously attempt but invariably fail to catch the uniqueness of a given leader's life and service.

Let those who would lead in higher education continue to write their own stories in lines of service to their followers. Let those who would search for the nature of leadership look first for evidence of significant service. The more significant the service, the more likely the source will be rooted in simplicity. The simpler the source, the greater the leadership.

Part V
Policy

23 Schooling Can Spell the Difference Between Poverty and Power

John Kenneth Galbraith once noted the possibility of distinguishing two types of poverty. In some societies you will find, he said, a poverty that affects only a minority; in others you will find poverty affecting everyone except a minority. That second type of poverty is obviously more important, in a worldwide perspective, and surely worthy of consideration. I intend, however, to focus primarily on the first. I see between the two a difference in degree, not in kind. And by concentrating here on the poverty that affects a minority — the case as we know it in the United States — I hope to point to solutions that have applicability to those parts of the world where poverty affects all but a minority of the people.

I want to note at the outset that I do not know anyone who is well-educated and also involuntarily poor. That observation suggests to me an important anti-poverty strategy to which I shall return shortly.

Let me first define my understanding of the meaning of poverty. I see it as sustained deprivation. The poor are deprived, in varying combinations and at different stages in life, of income, work, food, shelter, health care, and education. These deprivations are sustained both by systems and circumstances that are open to change but usually beyond the control of the poor themselves. Systems and circumstances—as, for example, public welfare and private charity — are also operative in combating poverty.

Combat metaphors are often used in discussing poverty, but insufficient attention is paid to the obvious question: "Who's on the other side?" Surely, it cannot be a question of fighting the poor; it must be a matter of addressing the causes of their poverty. Why are people without income, work, food, shelter, health care, and education? To ask the question is to suggest the need for a division of the poor population into categories of age, sex, and family status, and further subdivisions into categories that quantify nutritional, educational, and survival (into adulthood) attainments. Further categorization by race and ethnicity is helpful in sorting out the causal influences.

Whether cash income only, or cash plus the value of in-kind benefits, should be considered in setting a defined poverty line is of no concern to me in the present discussion. Nor is the course of my argument going to be altered by a few percentage point changes in the segment of the U.S. population found to be officially poor. It is obvious that too many people are poor in the U.S. today, that blacks suffer poverty that is disproportionate to whites, as do Hispanics. It is becoming more obvious, due to repeated headline reminders, that about one-third of the families headed by women are below the Federal poverty line, which is a dollar-income level adjusted each year to reflect increases in the Consumer Price Index. In 1984, the poverty line (representing money sufficient to meet the basic needs of a family or single person) was $10,609 for a family of four, $5,278 for a single person, $6,762 for a couple, and $8,277 for a three-person family.

What is less obvious, and therefore well worth noting, is the fact that poverty among children in America is increasing, according to Federal government measures. Senator Daniel Patrick Moynihan pointed this out in a Senate speech, on May 22, 1985, introducing the Family Economic Security Act of 1985, legislation designed specifically to relieve poverty among the young.

"In the 1970s, we allowed the benefits for children under the AFDC program to decline by one-third. We cut the children's allowance by one-third while we indexed benefits for everyone else. Only the children got left out. If you are under six years old in the United States, you are six times more likely to be poor than if you are over age 65. We are the first industrial nation in the world in which children are the poorest age group."

How many children are we talking about? Approximately 14 million. Childhood poverty is most prevalent among female-headed households. In 1983, the poverty rate for children living in female-headed households was 55.4 percent—more than four times that for children in male-present households. And, of course, the burden of poverty is disproportionately heavy on the children of minorities. Among minority children, 47 percent of the blacks and 38 percent of the Hispanics were poor in the U.S. in 1983. The figure for non-minority children was 15 percent.

Poverty and family structure are inextricably linked. This means, at the very least, that children's poverty is linked to divorce, to the increasing number of teen-age pregnancies, and to the ease with which a father can leave the home without being held economically responsible for his children. These issues must be addressed simultaneously by opinion makers, moral educators, writers, and advertisers who influence value formation, and by legislators whose responsibility it is to frame public policy. We have no national family policy. Nor do we have effective means of measuring the impact of other policies (tax, employment, and a host of regulatory policies, for example) on the family.

Legislation identical to the Moynihan bill was introduced on the same date in the House of Representatives by Representative Charles B. Rangel, of New York, and Representative Harold Ford, of Tennessee, Chairman of the Subcommittee on Public Assistance and Unemployment Compensation of the House Ways and Means Committee.

The legislation would increase tax exemption for dependents. It would adjust welfare aid for children. All the other Federal entitlement programs (for veterans, retired people, the disabled) have, since 1960, been adjusted for inflation. The sole exception is the entitlement program for children, Aid to Families with Dependent Children (AFDC). The proposed legislation would also establish uniform standards for child welfare aid. As Moynihan sees it, "A child in Mississippi is just as deserving as a child in Vermont."

The Washington Post gave an editorial welcome on May 25, 1985, to a new study by the Congressional Research Service and the Congressional Budget Office entitled "Children of Poverty." The principal message of the study is that

> ...poverty among children has not only increased in recent years but has also become more severe in degree. In 1968 the poorest fifth of families had enough income to meet 90 percent of their most basic needs. In 1983 they could buy only about 60 percent of the same necessities.

> A lot of people take this as evidence that government programs to reduce poverty didn't work. What they conveniently leave out is that some of these programs didn't work because *government spending on poor children declined* over the last decade — and this is true whether or not food, medical, and other non-cash benefits are counted! The big dollar increases you heard about went to offset inflation and to improve benefits for the elderly and disabled.

No one, I suppose, can be said to have an absolute guarantee against poverty. But permit me to repeat a point I made at the beginning, namely, that I do not know anyone who is well educated and also involuntarily poor. Education is an extraordinarily effective anti-poverty device. It does not, however, provide a quick and easy solution. And before education can really take root, the child to be educated must be rooted in a stable family environment.

Senator Moynihan has been calling for a national family policy since the 1960s when he was an Assistant Secretary of Labor in the Kennedy Administration and later a domestic policy adviser in the Nixon White House. He acknowledges today that a bi-partisan consensus on family policy would be difficult to achieve. But he does think there is support for programs that have proved they can work. One example is Head Start, a voluntary education program for pre-school age children. It has worked quite well. Head Start, by definition, helps the child. It also eases the daycare burden on the single parent seeking employment outside the home. The daycare need is more extensive, of course, but Head Start is a help for the mother in need of daycare assistance and a godsend to the child in need of intellectual stimulation.

Mention has been made of the link between children's poverty and family structure. The linkage relates to divorce, teenage pregnancies, and economic irresponsibilty on the part of permanently absent fathers.

The economic effect of divorce on children (of all socioeconomic classes) works this way. According to Stanford University Professor Lenore J. Weitzman, who has concluded a 10-year study on divorce, American women typically experienced a 73 percent decline in their standard of living in the first year after divorce, while their ex-husbands experienced a 42 percent increase. Only 13 percent of mothers with pre-school children were awarded any alimony. Since the divorced woman usually keeps the children, divorce tends to create economic hardship for the child. The children of divorce are more likely to be poor, and poor children tend to be burdened with educational deficits as well, thus making the recovery from poverty that much more difficult.

The teenage-pregnancy dimension of the problem (children having children) raises educational questions on all sides of the issue. Some see sex education as a preventative measure. Too few see the engagement of the young in the life of the mind as a way of breaking away from instant gratification and present orientation, so common among the very poor, and pointing them toward an achievable future that requires disciplined academic work and deferral of childbearing and marital responsibilities. The more sensate we permit our culture to become, the more difficult it will be to foster the life of the mind of the young and the more widespread will become the problem of "premature parents." Study after study demonstrates that teenagers who become

QUADRANGLE CONSIDERATIONS

pregnant know about contraception but choose not to use it. Some are fatalistic. Others want to "show" their parents something. Many low-income teenagers see the "achievement" of having a baby as a way of "becoming someone."

Once an unmarried teenager bears a baby and decides to keep it, there is the dual challenge of educating the child and the mother. The mother typically needs education in child care and in subjects that will enhance employability. In order to be free to get this education, the mother must make care provision for her child. Centers are now springing up in poverty-area high schools that provide, in the same school building, daycare for the child and high-school classroom work for the mother. It is good that this is happening but regrettable that conditions require that it happen.

Conditions are worsening in the United States for the chronically poor underclass — those poor persons who appear to be beyond the reach of social programs. The observance of a national holiday in honor of Martin Luther King in January each year tends to occasion reflection on, and review of, the experience of poverty in the black community in the U.S. over the past 20 or 30 years. It is shocking to note sharp increases in the number of black infants born to unwed mothers. Data show startling comparisons of single parent families headed by women in 1985 — 50 percent of black families fit this description, over against 15 percent for whites. Black unemployment was 14.9 percent in December, 1985, compared to a white unemployment rate of 5.9 percent. Black teenagers had a shocking 41.6 percent unemployment rate over against a white teenager rate of 15.9 percent. Almost 50 percent of the people going to prison these days are black, while blacks constitute only 12 percent of the nation's population.

The headlines and the television documentaries are openly pointing to a "vanishing" black family; insufficient notice is being given, however, to the concomitant erosion of a family base for the necessary education which can prevent destructive poverty.

246

The poverty under discussion is not a black burden exclusively, just disporportionately a black problem in the urban slums of our day. The erosion of family reinforcement for educational development is not a black problem exclusively, nor is welfare dependency and pregnancy among unmarried teenagers. But black children are suffering more than whites from poverty, and black children, more than whites, are in need of immediate educational assistance. Without it, they will never escape poverty. To paraphrase a Polish proverb, a person without education is like a person without legs; he or she crawls but cannot get anywhere.

What can be done to help our black children get somewhere — anywhere out of reach of poverty? Whatever is done must have a high and genuine regard for the value of good schooling. And, as I shall explain more fully in a moment, whatever is done in the schools must include the courage on the part of the community to exclude from the schools those who are unwilling to learn and who make both teaching and learning virtually impossible for others.

We have to begin again to believe that schools can make a difference. This is a principle that needs reaffirmation, particularly in the black community. A 1979 British study called "Fifteen Thousand Hours" (the title refers to the time a child spends in acquiring 12 years of schooling) has had repercussions in America in the form of the following five principles for "effective schools," principles being applied with measurable success in some American cities. Schools should have:

1. A clearly stated mission to raise students' reading and mathematics test scores.
2. Explicit requirements and goals for every class, including rewards for work well done and penalties for poor performance.
3. A uniform basic curriculum.
4. A method of instruction that requires teachers to expect the same high standards from each student. (Teachers are to be evaluated and trained in the

attempt to alter preferential attitudes toward some children).

5. Active parental involvement.

The principles are simple in theory but difficult to implement. Implementation, I would argue, must begin with an affirmation of the principles, especially in the black community. And the basic principle, I believe, is this: schools can make a difference. Involved here is a return to basics, a restoration of strict standards, and, I believe, a grouping of students by ability level. Note that principle #4 would require "teachers to expect the same high standards from each student" and that teachers should be "trained in the attempt to alter preferential attitudes toward some children." Arranging or stratifying students by ability does not violate this principle. Everyone in the group would face the same high standards applicable to others in the group.

What is to be done with the student of ability, but no motivation, whose behavior upsets the order of the class and impedes the teaching-learning process? The teacher should be free to remove such students from the classroom without delay. In the earlier years of schooling, provision should be made for transfer to another classroom within the school; in the adolescent years, the unmotivated student should be removed from the school and placed in an alternate training center (with the option to return whenever the will to learn also returns). The school should be a protected environment for the teaching-learning process. The teacher should be able to turn serious discipline problems over to other professionals, and the students who want to learn should be protected from those who don't. (I am assuming, of course, that the teacher is competent to teach — an assumption that should never go unexamined.)

By giving the teacher power to keep the classroom door open only to those who want to learn, both private and public schools would voluntarily crack the protective professional shell that masks from general public view the impossible working conditions confronting so many urban teachers. Unless teachers have that power, schooling will not realize its potential as an antipoverty strategy. Unless parents agree that teachers should have such power, it is not likely to be given.

If such power were granted to all teachers at all levels all at once, the problem of caring for the non-performing students would be overwhelming. So the place to begin is the first grade, and the pace of change should be gradual—grade by grade over a decade or more.

In both Boston and Baltimore, the business community is beginning to recognize that it has a direct interest in applying remedies to sick schools. The "Boston Compact" began early in the decade of the 1980s with businesses offering to graduates of inner-city public schools a first shot at entry-level jobs. The city school system's half of the agreement is to make sure that the students who apply have met a fairly strict class-attendance requirement. In Baltimore, the business-led Greater Baltimore Committee, in cooperation with a predominantly black, church-oriented, grassroots community organization called BUILD (Baltimoreans United in Leadership Development), has entered into a pact with the city's public high schools to induce more students to raise their grade average to 80 and their attendance to 95 percent so that they'll be able to receive a job "passport" — a certificate which gives those students a hiring preference at over a hundred Baltimore business firms.

I happen to believe that the generals in our domestic war on poverty must be the teachers in our urban schools. I also believe that the persons who have to give these generals their commissions are the parents of the children in poverty. But those parents are, by and large, unwed teenage mothers. They are hardly a powerful force in contemporary American society, yet they represent a social problem of enormous destructive potential for American society. For those who believe in the essential goodness of the human person and the power of maternal love, not to mention the power of divine love, these unwed teenage mothers represent an ironic but no less real possibility for change. For as William F. Lynch, S.J., has put it "...irony deals not with appearances, but with the opposite of appearances...; its main task is to keep opposites together in a single act of the imagination. Thus if we ask the question, what is power? who has the real power? appearance will say the powerful have power, but the beatitudes and the sermon on the mount in the Gospel of St. Matthew say the opposite. Like the imagination itself, faith moves below appearances into existence."

I am taking a Christian faith perspective at the moment but a common-sense perspective as well. Faith tells the Christian that there is a curious coexistence of the low and the high, that lowliness is the basis of power. The Christian expectation is to find through losing, to get by giving, to be exalted by humility — not timidity, but true humility, which is a form of courage. Christian spirituality advises detachment from material possessions in order to gain real power and genuine freedom in this world.

The crisis in today's black family is not just economic and sociological; it is also religious and spiritual. The unwed black teenage mother may be ready for a radically new evangelization that is perfectly consistent with the heritage of black religion in America. The Bill Moyers CBS Television two-hour documentary on "The Vanishing Family: Crisis in Black America" (January 25, 1986) ended with Carolyn Wallace, who with her husband runs a community center in the Newark ghetto that was the location for the documentary, urging Moyers to deliver the moral message of greater personal and social responsibility on the part of young blacks.

"They won't listen to me," said Moyers.

"It doesn't make any difference," she replied. "You've got to say it anyway. They may not listen to me, either. But I'm saying if you say it in your corner, and I say it in my corner, and everybody's saying it, it's going to be like a drumbeat, and sooner or later it will sound. But it's not just for me to talk about, it's for all of us to talk about. And I think it's going to surpass color. And you're not going to be safe, I'm not going to be safe, and nobody's going to be safe, unless we all send out this drumbeat — hey, let's deal with it. Let's deal with the problem."

The part of the problem I have isolated for attention here is the need to bring good schooling to poor children as a means of breaking the cycle of poverty. Dealing with that problem will, from a strategy perspective or community organizer's point of view, be easier if support for teachers and disciplined schooling comes from parents. A related strategy to mobilize the parents should focus on unwed teenage mothers in black urban ghettos. Chief among the influences on their value formation have been television entertainment and recorded music; these media must now become part of the solution. Their role in producing the problem of irresponsible sexuality has gone unchallenged too long. This is all the more worthy of note since the bedrock market for recorded rock-n-roll music is made up of 13-year-old girls.

It is also time to take a new look at religious and moral persuasion as part of the necessary drumbeat. The churches have to start speaking to the young again with new conviction. The churches have to convince the young that the churches believe the young really matter. It is an evangelical moment which the churches cannot afford to miss. For the Catholic Church, Hispanic teenagers have a special need and present a special opportunity in this regard.

The organizers should be encouraged to see the helplessness of unwed teenage mothers as the ground on which a new community organizational effort can be mounted. These young women should be encouraged to see that schooling can make the difference between poverty and economic security for their children, and then organized to demand the necessary changes in the schools. Good schooling can break the cycle of poverty for children now in poverty. For them, knowledge will exercise power over poverty, as the conventional wisdom has always said it would. But this is unlikely to happen unless the teenage mothers in our decaying urban neighborhoods come to recognize the power they do not know they now possess. It is the power the Christian eye is trained to see, by faith, in helplessness and nothingness — the stuff that depressing television documentaries are made of.

If the churches do a better job of explaining this theological reality, and if the community organizers can focus on the schools the force-for-change embodied in a young mother's concern for the progress of her child, education — understood as back-to-basics schooling — might be able to demonstrate once again its very powerful anti-poverty potential.

Family policy may well emerge as the next great national political issue. The erosion of family stability in America should concern us more than most of the issues heralded by the headlines on a typical day. My plea, as family policy emerges for debate, would be to keep it tied to the schooling issue.

Better schooling will not solve all family problems, but stronger families will make better schooling possible. Nor will better schooling heal all the social wounds that are poverty-related. It can, however, break the cycle of poverty for poverty's children who become the beneficiaries of the better schooling.

I am convinced that the world moves on words and numbers, the companion languages of quality and quantity in human affairs. Children now poor have no hope of overcoming poverty unless they gain a mastery of words and numbers, the kind of mastery their schools should give but will not, without parental prodding and community support.

24 National Service

Compulsory national service would mean enforcement by the state of human service in the interest of the state. Just to mention this idea is to heighten tension on the campuses. Compulsion always involves force. The moral implications of compulsory national service touch upon the use of force. At issue would be the right of the state not simply to enforce a law, but to compel human service. Not a very attractive prospect.

If the common good, not just national convenience or comfort, requires it, the state may compel service and do so morally. Few would disagree with that. If a citizen faced with such compulsion to serve refuses, the moral consideration extends to the means the state employs to compel the service of the many by punishing the refusal of the few. Since, however, the use of compulsion is usually a declaration of defeat for the rule of reason, it should be used sparingly; otherwise, more harm than good will ensue as the force of reason gives way to physical force. But that line of reflection is more at home in the philosophy department than the Police Academy.

Typically, the means of enforcement available to the state are the denial of property (fines), the denial of residence (exile), the denial of freedom (arrest), and the denial of life (execution). All would agree that no one of these means is to be employed lightly. Strong arguments can be made against applying the death penalty under any circumstances.

Aside from consideration of the morality of the means the state might choose to employ in compelling service required by the common good, there is a further moral question of the state's respect for freedom of conscience in those cases where refusal to serve rests on a conscientious conviction. Surely the common good requires absolute safeguards for freedom of individual conscience at all times in all circumstances. Subscribing, as I do, to all of that, I am still intrigued by the notion of national service.

The Constitution of the United States offers protection against involuntary servitude to all its citizens. Would compulsory national service, military or otherwise, violate Constitutional rights in this regard? Probably not, but that would be a matter for the Supreme Court to decide. I say "probably not" because I presume there would be provision not only for total objection in conscience to compulsory national service in any form but for selective conscientious objection to a particular form of service. Within a full range of national service opportunities, each addressed to needs touching directly upon the common good, there would be, presumably, an array of options open to the citizen. Posed this way, the question is worth considering.

Comprehensive national service would include health, education, social welfare, conservation, and other types of service in addition to the military. If sufficiently attractive financial rewards were associated with all these services, there would be no need for the state to compel its citizens to render them. Hence, the moral consideration of this complicated issue must not ignore the question of the state's willingness and ability to pay a sufficiently high price for these services and thus render compulsion unnecessary. (I am prescinding here from any consideration of the compulsion that money itself exerts and the related moral responsibility of the one who proffers it.)

Just as it is morally inexcusable to use force to take money unjustly, it would be morally wrong to substitute force for the payment of the money it would take to purchase necessary services when such payment can be reasonably made. The presumption stands on the side of the state's inability to pay for all the services it needs at rates prevailing in private labor markets. Apparently, the all-volunteer army experiment of recent decades in the United States has not been consistently successful in meeting military requirements, although it has worked reasonably well. But this arrangement seems to have shifted the burden of service to the poor, whose enlistment may be freely made but whose job satisfaction is often low, a function probably of both insufficient pay and challenge.

If the widely-held presumption of the state's inability to pay prevailing market rates for all the services it really needs is incorrect, two questions emerge. Are higher taxes needed to support higher spending for national service (assuming a multiple-option national service program to be desirable)? Or, must some spending cease so that available revenues can be applied more generously to higher-priority service needs? This is a form of the guns-and-butter debate. A growing appetite for both guns and butter has inflationary consequences on the economy. When expenditure trade-offs are considered within the government sector only, "soft" items like food stamps and social services appear to be much more vulnerable than military hardware and the personnel needed to tend it.

There are issues here of justice and prudence that can easily be lost in the emotion of national security debates. It is precisely in the national security context that the questions of military and other forms of national service arise.

The case for compulsory national service depends almost entirely on the strength of the argument at any given time that the common good requires it. I think the argument can be made that the United States finds itself now in a condition of national emergency. I do not, however, define that emergency in terms of the presence of an external enemy. The crisis, as I see it, lies within the nation. Specifically, it lies with the youth of the nation. It is a crisis of purposelessness. The temptation is great to say the problem weighs most heavily on the nation's economically and educationally disadvantaged youth, but I do not believe this to be the case. The problem of purposelessness is evident in the suburbs and the ghettos, in the protected environment of college campuses as well as on the sandlots and in the slums.

If this purposelessness, with its derivative frustration, non-participation, vandalism, violence, and destructive dependencies is in fact a national emergency, then the common good would urge appropriate action by the state.

If the state were to compel its youth, both the purposeless and the purposeful, to devote two years of their young adulthood to meeting basic human needs at home and abroad, needs left unattended by the operations of the private labor markets, might the purposeless find direction for their lives and the purposeful gain further maturity without intolerable delay or deflection from their intended goals? Some delay and inconveniences for the purposeful would be justified by a national emergency of widespread purposelessness.

If the state cannot pay attractive wages for services required by the common good, deferred payment in the form of educational and other benefits would be both fair and in the national interest.

If, in addition to the purposelessness crisis within, the state is confronted with a military emergency, the conscripted citizens, with all due allowance for conscientious objection, might fairly be called upon to bear equal shares of the risk and danger associated with the national defense. The underlying assumption, of course, is that the military emergency would satisfy the moral criteria for a just war.

It should be noted that I am not locating a national emergency in terms of national security, or unmet social welfare needs, or decay of the cities, neglect of the elderly, inadequate child care, needs for conservation and environmental protection, inadequate health care, or deteriorating educational services for the poor. My point is that widespread purposelessness among our youth is a fact, and it constitutes a national emergency. Enlisting the young to meet national needs like the ones listed above may or may not be our best way of coming to grips with the real national emergency.

Understandably, we like to have evidence to support assertions of the presence of a national emergency. Such evidence usually presents itself in crisis form. "Remember Pearl Harbor!" was the rallying cry that generated in 1941 a national consensus strong enough to support the mobilization of troops and the alteration of civilian lifestyles. In the face of the evidence, the response seemed quite reasonable.

The nation's present emergency has no focused rallying point. Perhaps Chicago '68 and Woodstock '69 sent up the first signals. Or was the "first shot" the one at Kent State in 1970? Jonestown in 1979 fired both shots and shocks that unsettled a nation not yet sufficiently unified to face an as yet unrecognized crisis. Drug-related deaths of famous young athletes and entertainers are etched into the national memory.

Lesser known events — personal tragedies stunting the development or ending the span of precious young lives — have found their way into countless family histories. But those families have not yet come to a consensus on the presence of a crisis that I define as purposelessness, episodically evident in bursts of violence, organized outrage, individual and communal withdrawal, self denigration, or self destruction. An analysis of the crisis reveals a generally well-educated but undisciplined young, most quite healthy, many affluent, virtually all "unnecessary," even redundant from the perspective of production economics, although quite active and "necessary" for the vitality of the consumption side of the economy.

When goals are unclear, anxieties abound. Our young are more than just uneasy about their future.

In looking toward the possibility of compulsory national service, I am not suggesting that the poor, the sick, the elderly, the ill-housed, and the unemployed at home or overseas be "used" in an exploitative program designed to enable our young to find themselves. I am suggesting that our young can help with the complex task of meeting these basic human needs. A relatively

257

short two-year engagement of this kind would confront and at least reduce our problem of purposelessness. Some needs of the nation's poor and marginated would be served; some significant social problems would be significantly reduced. The conscripted providers of national service would have more than an opportunity to mature and find their way. With actual work experience, they might also develop personal motivation sufficient to influence their subsequent educational decisions and career choices. In all probability some would make career decisions to commit themselves to longer-term engagements with the problems than the two-year service obligation would allow.

The possibility of a two-year service obligation followed by a new or more mature sense of purpose, coupled with an educational benefit, suggests that the common good might be served through compulsory national service. The morality of the compulsion looks first to the seriousness of the national need. It next examines the appropriateness of the means, or avenues of service, employed to meet the need.

I do not now see a military need sufficient to justify conscription. Nor do I assess the seriousness of any single social, environmental, educational, or physical-resource need to be great enough to justify conscription. All these needs in combination do, however, present a formidable national challenge. The Federal financial ability simply is not there to pay market rates for the services required to meet all these needs. Add to this a condition of national purposelessness that has reached crisis proportions (my claim, subject to the affirmation of a national consensus) and you have within a single although complicated framework the question for moral consideration of compulsory national service in the United States today.

A reasonable state will use force on its citizens only with the greatest care. Otherwise, the rule of reason falls into jeopardy. The consequent harm is likely to be greater than the envisioned good which prompted the use of compulsion. Only widespread agreement on the good to be achieved will reduce the risk of a defeat for reason in a situation where service is compelled. That widespread agreement is not present in the United States today.

There remains the question of registration for national service in the absence of a clear condition of national emergency. This, it seems to me, is a matter of prudential judgment. Given the availability of computers and zip codes, together with the prevailing practice of registration by the young for Social Security numbers, I am not persuaded by the argument that peacetime registration is needed to guarantee readiness for a draft in some future military emergency. Neither, however, do I see any great danger of state infringement on individual rights by means of peacetime registration. I see the issue more in terms of a technical judgment concerning the time required to register the young, and a political judgment relating to the possibility of the executive branch of government inducting and mobilizing the registered for combat without enactment, by the legislative branch, of a declaration of war.

Unfortunately for the poor, sick, unemployed, hungry, and homeless of this nation and elsewhere, we are not accustomed, in our national Congress, to declaring war on the enemies that afflict these very needy people. Nor do we have a psycho-social index calibrated to measure the purposelessness of our young whom we view more wishfully than wisely as the future of our nation. Both wisdom and realism — essential elements in any sound moral judgment — would suggest that voluntary national service on a comprehensive scale should be attempted now, and that plans be laid for development of a consensus-building mechanism for compulsory national service, should the common good clearly require it.

I really don't know whether or not this would work. I do know that when I first thought about becoming a Jesuit, I had to think as well about the military draft. It was the fall of 1944, my senior year in high school. I was quite uncertain about what I wanted to do in life. My situation was not exactly one of purposelessness, but I was not clear, in those late teenage years, about which of several purposes I wanted to pursue. The immediate decision was made for me by the military draft. It put me into uniform, opened up an interesting range of developmental experiences, sent me overseas to Germany, and returned me home in 1946 just a little older, considerably more mature, and anxious to take advantage of the educational benefits included in the G.I. Bill of Rights.

After three years of college, I had a much clearer sense of purpose. Subject then to neither drift nor draft, I decided to join the Jesuits. It was a free choice, a mature choice, made after careful consideration of the alternatives. I had a sense of purpose strong enough to overcome the doubts and ambiguities that surround any serious human choice into an unknown future.

As one who benefited from a service opportunity at age 18 and received a free college education as a result, I look at today's young and wonder whether they and their nation would not be better off if we had a new idea of national service. If it is going to work, it will exact opportunity costs from the better educated, better motivated young, and financial outlays from the Treasury. On the benefit side, I would expect to see a significant strengthening of personal and national purpose, along with a measurable reduction of some vexing social needs. Isn't that what good public policy is expected to deliver?

25 Paying for College

The prospect of unmanageable debt is discouraging some young people from beginning college. Mounting indebtedness is frightening those already there. It forces some of them out of the higher-priced independent colleges into the public sector, or, from either sector, out of higher education altogether. And for those who stay, the burden of debt complicates life unnecessarily for millions in their young adulthood. It deflects their career choices toward higher anticipated income streams and away from undercompensated human service work. The debt burden also weighs in heavily, and negatively, on the financial foundations of many new marriages. The situation calls for a courageous and creative policy response.

Somewhere between the familiar notions of loan and grant lies the possibility of a new way to provide Federal assistance to students and families in the important matter of financing higher education. As enabler and facilitator, the Federal government should permit a "working-your-way-through-college" principle to come into play. Only the sequence would be reversed — college first, work later. More on that in a moment.

Enabling and facilitating is the proper role for government. Access and choice in approaching higher-education opportunities that correspond to native ability are appropriate expectations for students and their families in our democratic society.

Parental ability to pay, plus the student's willingness to work, should in every case combine to meet the price of the higher education the student wants to purchase. In some cases parents will, unassisted, be able and willing to pay full price; student work would then be confined to non-market academic activity. No part-time jobs would be necessary to earn tuition money. No tuition loans would be taken out. Relatively speaking, this happy situation is available only to a favored few families and students in the United States today. In most cases, students and their families will share the burden of paying for higher education. In fewer, but by no means an insignificant number of cases, students will have no assistance from their families in financing college expenses. They should, however, and can, if Federal policy permits, have manageable and workable financial assistance from their Federal government, meaningful assistance that provides them with both access and choice.

The new ground that should open up to students whose families cannot or will not pay their entire higher education expenses relates to work — post-graduation, full-time employment. The "working-your-way-through-college" principle need not be restricted to part-time employment during the collegiate years. Indeed it should not be, because part-time employment often interferes with the more important academic demands at the heart of the collegiate experience. New Federal policy options should build on the time-honored conservative principle of "working-your-way-through-college" and transform it to permit a full-time application to study first, and a long-time, even lifetime, repayment responsibility related to earnings from post-collegiate employment. A Federally-capitalized revolving fund would provide the wherewithal to meet college expenses; repayments to the fund during a graduate's working lifetime would make the same form of assistance available to subsequent generations of students.

In my opinion, the present system of financial aid to students should undergo radical change. The change I have in mind would result in neither a loan nor a grant program. It is something in between. It is a revolving fund which would provide an advance (as distinguished from an outright expenditure). The recipient of the advance incurs an obligation to replenish the revolving fund. The amount of the advance would meet all or part (let the Congress decide) of the cost-justified price the college or university sets on its educational services. The advance should also extend to auxiliary services (room and board). It should cover cost-of-education (as opposed to cost-of-attendance) expenses only. This would restrict it to tuition, fees, books, room and board; it would not cover travel and recreational "spending money." Moreover, the advance could, if the Congress so decides, be "capped" at, say, 85 percent of the cost-of-education expenses. Or, an absolute limit could be set on the annual dollar amount available to any participant.

Replenishment of the fund (i.e., a return of the advance) would occur by means of a withholding tax on gross earnings whenever the student works before or after graduation. The sum to be returned via the withholding mechanism could, if the Federal enabling legislation so specified, carry a surcharge that would cover the "cost-of-money" expense or "opportunity cost" to the Federal government for choosing to use its capital this way. (Nothing, however, in reason or law, requires government to maximize returns on its money.) The income-contingent payback, together with the surcharge, would guarantee the replenishment of the capital and the "perpetual motion" of a fund designed to finance the intellectual development, at the costly higher education level, of the nation's young.

Those who earn high salaries shortly after graduation would meet their replenishment obligation in a relatively few working years. Those who choose low-paying professions or occupations might never repay fully, even over the course of a long working lifetime. Beneficiaries of this system who die during college or shortly after graduation would, of course, never repay. All participants should, I think, be required to carry very low premium life-insurance policies during their collegiate years — or some form of limited-pay life policy — with the fund as the sole beneficiary. (Just as the post-World War II experience with the G.I. Bill lends supporting evidence to the claim that this proposal makes educational sense for the nation, so the G.I. life-insurance experience will point to a low-cost, high-yield source of contributions to fund replenishment.) A point worth emphasizing in the present proposal is that no one other than the student — no parent, no survivor — would be responsible for repayment. And the repayment would be both automatic and passive — therefore, no defaults, no collection agencies.

Should children of the wealthy be permitted to participate? Congress may want to designate levels of family income and assets which would bar dependent children from drawing the advance. Presumably, they would have access, by virtue of those assets and income, to higher education without Federal assistance. Would a national revolving fund work without participation of a substantial number of higher -income families? This is an actuarial question which, when asked, should not presume that low-income students will never become high-income earners (the G.I. Bill experience after World War II suggests just the opposite). And when answered, this question should allow for the possibility of capital contributions to the revolving fund, when needed, in order to supplement the income-contingent return-payment stream. Insurance benefits, if a fund-as-beneficiary plan is adopted, would also contribute toward replenishment of capital.

When Boston University President John Silber advocated elements of this idea in print ("The Tuition Dilemma: A New Way to Pay the Bills," *The Atlantic*, July, 1978) and in public at various meetings of national educational associations in the late 1970s, his proposal generated anxiety among educators over the possible problems associated with the introduction of the Internal Revenue Service into Federal student aid and thus into the internal operations of the colleges and universities. In my view, this need not be a problem, and even if it were, it would be a much more manageable problem than the one now faced by tuition-dependent institutions. The academic administrators would, as I envision it, notify IRS of the identity (by name and Social Security number) and the amounts advanced, semester by semester, to enrolled participants. The draw would be from the fund to the institution on the signature of the enrolled participant, the authorizing campus official, and the appropriate Federal authority. (An advance to cover payment for room, board, and books not sold by the institution would be made directly to the student, possibly through a system of stamps or vouchers convertible to cash when presented, with proper verification, by the off-campus vendors.) From then on, the repayment schedule is the business of the IRS, the employer, and the individual taxpayer, whenever the beneficiary of the advance is meeting his or her Federal income-tax obligations. How to define income; how to handle the self-employed; how to deal with spouses who might find here an incentive to combine income; how to monitor those who avoid wage income in favor of increased assets — all of these are definitional and procedural questions to be dealt with conceptually by experts and translated into practice with the powerful assistance of the computer technology now at the service of the Federal tax collectors.

Not to be ignored or underrated, of course, is the bureaucratic burden this repayment procedure will place on the IRS, which is already plagued, according to current estimates, by a $100 billion tax-compliance gap. We have at hand, nonetheless, the new technologies which make the necessary and quite complicated programming practicable in order to recover whatever payments are due the revolving fund, regardless of whether the repayment is collected on a withholding or direct-payment basis.

The big problem in all of this, however, is the injection of sufficient capital into the revolving fund. How much would be needed? How long would it take for a typical advance to be repaid? What, in a word, is the arithmetic of the Federal role in a radically restructured student aid program?

To the best of my knowledge, this revolving-loan-fund form of Federal aid to students who would have to repay by means of an income-contingent withholding mechanism first entered the policy debate in a serious way in 1967 (although seeds of the idea were planted by Milton Friedman in 1945) with a Federal advisory panel headed by Professor Jerrold Zacharias of the Massachusetts Institute of Technology (*Educational Opportunity Bank — A Report of the Panel on Education Innovation to the U.S. Commissioner of Education, Director of the National Science Foundation, and Special Assistant to the President for Science and Technology,* Washington, D.C.: U.S. Government Printing Office, August, 1967). The "Zacharias Plan" called for establishment of an Education Opportunity Bank (EOB) which would lend money for higher-educational expenses to students who would agree to repay a fixed percentage of their personal incomes once they went to work.

A decade later John Silber recast the EOB idea into TAF — the Tuition Advance Fund. Silber's TAF would be available to students only after successful completion of the freshman year. The payback obligation would equal the amount "advanced" plus a 50 percent surcharge. The withholding rate was set at 2 percent of gross income.

I would favor freshman eligibility, a lower surcharge, and a higher withholding rate. I would also like to see explored the possibility of including in the plan a mandatory life-insurance policy for all participants with the fund/bank designated as sole beneficiary.

In January 1969, Wilbur Cohen, the then-Secretary of the Department of Health, Education, and Welfare submitted a Report to the President under title of "Toward a Long-Range Plan for Federal Financial Support for Higher Education" (U.S. Department of Health, Education, and Welfare, Office of the Assistant Secretary for Planning and Evaluation). That report expressed an openness to and interest in the Zacharias Plan. This plan deserves attention again today.

Some observers suspect that the managers of our higher-education institutions are ready to run up their prices just as soon as students have access to an income-contingent payback plan for meeting college expenses. I doubt that will happen, even in the face of pressures to raise compensation levels. No college will want to price itself out of the diversified student market made possible by the income-contingent payback program I have outlined here.

Why income-contingent? What rationale supports the income-contingency feature over other alternatives? First, income-contingency makes repayment manageable. Annual repayment as a fixed percentage of gross income lifts the repayment obligation to a priority level, of course, but does so by definition without imposing a burden that would tax the payer beyond his or her means. Introduction of the IRS device into the collection process eliminates, for all practical purposes, the possibility of default; the one tracking agency follows the graduate as he or she moves from job to job, place to place. The advance is not a loan. This is really an equity-finance plan which structures the payback to a return on invested effort (study) as well as borrowed capital (the Federal advance). But it is more than this. The invested effort carries over from study into work-for-pay at higher levels of skill and productivity than might otherwise be expected. And the return to Treasury is not simply a return of funds advanced, but also a higher personal income-tax payment, assuming higher pay as a function of higher education.

The participating student's future orientation toward service and/or income related to his or her higher education represents a confidence level at least sufficient to support the risk of meeting the "opportunity cost" of attending college — foregone earnings. The government's willingness to forego full return in cases of death or other reasons for withdrawal from tax-paying status, or from low earnings over a working lifetime, or insufficient compensation to government for the full cost of funds applied to this purpose, represents a willingness to wait — as only government can afford to wait — for a return on its investment with an implied acknowledgment that a better educated, more productive nation is worth the wait.

The fixed-percentage feature of the payback provision is regressive but necessary to keep the plan workable. Unlike Social Security, these fixed-percentage payments would not be made by virtually all taxpayers, only by those who chose to finance their higher education this way.

This is not to say the cost of the program will fall only on the shoulders of the beneficiaries. Front-end costs, especially start-up capital, will be a broader societal burden. Subsidies and periodic injections of Federal capital will represent costs spread over a wider spectrum of taxpayers than those who received the educational benefits. Both society and the individual who receives higher education this way benefit from the plan. Both should pay.

I think it is time for the nation to consider adopting the "work-your-way-through-college" principle — but to reverse the sequence by permitting college first and work later. Consistent with that policy would be a requirement to insure the borrower, not the loan, if that device would lower the surcharge without complicating the administration of the plan.

In any case, the obligation to pay would rest with the student, not the parent, once a student decides to participate in the plan. At that point, his or her Social Security number and the amount and date of the "advance" would be registered with IRS. The debt would be collected by means of a schedule of income-contingent and, wherever possible, automatically withheld paybacks. With the Federal government functioning as facilitator and enabler, any student would be free to enroll in the school of his or her choice — subject only to that institution's admissions standards — and thus "bet" on his or her ability to succeed during collegiate years and then, in his or her post-collegiate years, be able to meet whatever financial obligations have been incurred through his or her own earning power.

Our Federal lawmakers and those who assist them in drafting legislation, along with those who shape policy in the Executive Branch of government, have a great opportunity now to refine this idea, define its costs, and present it as a policy option.

How much will it cost? In the short run, a lot; over time it will pay for itself through repayments of the advance and higher tax payments related to higher lifetime earnings resulting from advanced education.

Assuming, as my CUA colleague and economist John J. Murphy has done in preparing these estimates, that four million students drew an average of $5,000 a year and that repayment begins after four years, and assuming further that the average income in the fifth year is $20,000 with a five-percent annual pay increase each year thereafter, a repayment rate of nine percent on gross income would pay off the obligation in 20 years. If the repayment rate were five percent on gross income, it would take 35 years to satisfy the obligation.

If, in order to establish the fund, the government borrowed, at a nine-percent interest rate, the money needed to support $20 billion in annual advances (the above examples), the fund would become self-sustaining after 14 years; if the government pays no interest on the money it advances, the self-sustaining point is reached after 11 years. (These figures assume a payback based on nine percent of the beneficiary's gross income; if the payback were calculated on a lower percentage of gross, it would take longer to strike the point of self-sufficiency.) Multiply $20 billion by 11 or 14 and you have a cumulative total of grand proportions. You also have a solution to a mammoth national problem.

It would be a serious mistake to dismiss this idea by pointing to the deficit and saying, "We don't have the resources." We do have the resources. The point at issue is the place of higher education on our ladder of priorities. The resources are there. We continue to misapply them because we forget that an educated citizenry is, in fact, our first line of defense and our only hope for increased economic productivity.

We also seem to be forgetting that the coexistence of access and choice, for those who have sufficient talent and interest to avail themselves of higher educational opportunities, is at stake here. Without an income-contingent payback plan, choice will diminish even if access remains. Pluralism in America would correspondingly diminish. It need not and should not happen.

President Ronald Reagan's Education Secretary, William J. Bennett, once proposed a misnamed Income Contingent Loan program (ICL) which is not what I am proposing here. The Reagan-Bennett ICL program would be income-sensitive, not income-contingent. Low incomes would qualify borrowers for extended payback periods with longer, and thus greater, interest obligations. True income-contingency means the possibility of less than full repayment related to lower lifetime earnings. In choosing to permit paybacks to be truly income-contingent, Federal student-aid policy would, in some measure, be subsidizing those who carry their high-quality, high-cost, higher education into low-paying occupations like social work and teaching. Still, I view that as a perfectly appropriate use of subsidy, a way of distributing incentives by an enabling and facilitating government which respects individual freedom and promotes the common good.

Would such a plan create, as some critics allege, a new class of "indentured students?" Not at all. It would enlarge our national set of well-trained minds available to work wherever freedom of occupational choice directs. Occupational choice would not be influenced by any undue anxiety about "paying off my loan," as is now so often the case.

There would, of course, be a payback responsibility, but more manageable and less burdensome probably than home-, car- and other credit-repayment obligations. By virtue of its fixed-percentage-on-gross-income feature, this plan would put education on a higher rung on the ladder of personal finance priorities than it now occupies in our society. But we tend to undervalue higher education and undercompensate the professionals who provide it, so this reordering of priorities seems long overdue. And it should be noted that free choice generated the personal income-contingent payback commitment in the first place.

Whether Federal grants or loan subsidies, as we now know

them, would remain available is a separate question. The availability of scholarship and loan assistance from non-governmental sources would presumably not change. In any case, the "indentured student" argument is not persuasive when the financial device in question is not a loan but a manageable, income-contingent repayment of an advance made from the national treasury in the national interest.

Nor would this proposal add administrative costs, risk-assessment responsibilities, or loan-collection functions to any college or university. This is not a campus-based program. After due notification and certification, tuition payments would move from Federal treasury to college treasurer. Repayments would be an income-tax consideration between private citizen and Federal government.

Resistance to the radical changes I am proposing will come from several quarters. Private higher education is wary of excessive government intrusion; IRS involvement, even though such involvement will be primarily with the student and not the institution, is resisted. Public higher education might, if this proposed policy were in place, lose some students to the higher-priced independent institutions. Those students can, of course, count. They will realize that choice of the lower-price public higher education will mean a much lighter and shorter repayment obligation.

If the economic calculus determines choice in any given case, it simply reinforces one of the traditional reasons for the existence of government-subsidized, state-, county- or city-provided higher education, namely, to guarantee the availability of low- or no-price educational alternatives. The private banks, naturally, like the Guaranteed Student Loan (GSL) program now in place (and costing the Federal treasury about fifty cents on every commercial bank dollar loaned). So do the secondary marketers of GSLs, the various bond counsels, guarantors, and loan servicing agencies. Much of this business would be lost if the plan I envision were adopted. Some legislators who have labored not only to construct our present complicated system of

Federal student aid, but also to keep it in place, will be understandably reluctant to dismantle it for an unproven alternative.

Yet most would admit that the way to go, if we were beginning anew to fashion a program of Federal assistance to students and their families in the important matter of higher education, is precisely along the main lines of the present proposal. Rather than beginning a reconsideration of student aid with our sights limited by the horizons of what we have, I would hope that we could begin at the conceptual level with this new idea. I would hope we can design the best possible vehicle to carry the most enlightened and workable student-aid policy we are capable of creating. That is what the nation wants and needs.

26 What Might the Church Have to Say to U.S. Educators?

I speak of, but not for, the Roman Catholic Church when I suggest that the Church has something important to say to American education. The extent of the Church's investment in education is well known. Why make that investment in the first place? An answer to that question will reveal a lot in common between Church and national purpose in providing education. The Church has been at it a long time; it has something to say on the subject which other educators might want to consider.

I would like to offer a set of assertions — measured phrases, if you will — framing principles that apply to any education characterized by quality and completeness. Those two character-istics — quality and completeness — are not to be misunder-stood. By quality I do not mean elitism, although I do mean excellence, which I take to be a relative term. By a complete education, I do not infer a closed end; I do not mean to suggest that learning stops with graduation.

In my view, a school is an organized environment for graded learning under the supervision of teachers who can motivate, guide, and measure progress along the path of inquiry. Learn-ing, I would argue, is self-propelled activity, but activity that needs both motivation and guidance.

By education I mean something more than schooling. Education involves the development of human potential. An education can be formal or informal. If formal, it is defined in terms of goals, it is directed by professionals who have mastered those goals, and it is measured in segments and degrees of graded progress toward those goals. Not all that constitutes a formal education takes place in school. What does take place in school, however, is certain either to stimulate or stunt out-of-school learning that should be part of a formal education — and may well be the most effective part for guaranteeing the continuation of learn- ing when formal education ends.

Intellectual development, as opposed to social, emotional, and physical adjustment, is the primary business of the school and the general goal of formal education. Hence the development of reason and the encouragement of creativity are central to the educational enterprise.

With all of this by way of introduction, I would now like to offer my set of assertions. There are twelve of them. They are all part, I believe, of what the Church has to say to education in America. They are not ranked in an order of priority. Some of them may sound quite secular. No one of them, nor the whole set taken together, is intended to offer the last word on this important question. It would please me immensely if the deficiencies of this list would serve to stimulate others to attempt a better articulation of what the Church might have to say to American education, and still others to reply with thoughts from secular education to those responsible for the Church's involvement in this enterprise.

1. The world moves on words and numbers. Since "God loved the world so much that he gave his only Son" to redeem it (John 3:16), it is not surprising that the Church Christ established on earth should also love the world and want to see it develop. And since centuries of experience in the world demonstrate the power of words and numbers in contributing to human progress, the Church would urge education at every level in America to take words and numbers seriously.

Words and numbers together are the languages of quality and quantity in human affairs. Well-chosen words communicate great ideas in poetry and politics. Well-managed numbers unlock the secrets of nature and drive the great technologies.

The Church, if it is to be faithful to its Founder and itself, would say: treat words and numbers with competence and care; let no developing mind be unchallenged by the demand to master them.

2. Faith and reason are compatible. It is not unreasonable to believe the data of revelation; faith is a form of knowledge. Based as it is on God's own word, faith is a higher form of knowledge than that grounded only on human testimony or natural evidence.

Moreover, it is eminently reasonable to apply human reason to the data of revelation. This is the work of theology. Without theology, without an intellectual opening to a personal transcendent God, a God who acts in human history, education at any level will be incomplete.

It should be added as a corollary to this assertion that the Church would impose no limit on the exercise of reason other than the limits of truth, prudence, and disciplined inquiry, allowing for the Church itself a role in the recognition and articulation of revealed truth.

This raises the further suggestion that disciplined learning is important. A discipline is a mode of inquiry. The canons of a discipline are set by the best minds at work within the discipline itself. Ethical norms applicable to investigation within a discipline are available to human reason and reinforced by divine revelation. Be true to the ethics and the methods of the discipline, the Church would say, and let the disciplined inquiry proceed.

3. A completely secular education is an incomplete education. Without a vital, independent, Church-related sector at all levels of American education, there will be a "flattening out" in American ideas, values, and culture; there will be a loss of pluralism in America. This point was made in chapter 1.

The Church recognizes and has no difficulty at all in accepting the fact that the "non-establishment" clause of the First Amendment of the United States Constitution bars the establishment of a state religion in America. But the Church also recognizes and, at great expense, sponsors schools that help this nation implement the "free exercise" clause of the same First Amendment. Rights not exercised can easily be lost. By action, organization, construction, and programs of service, the churches in America implement and thus preserve the Constitutional guarantee of every citizen's right to religious freedom.

No small part of that implementation is achieved through religiously-oriented, faith-committed schools, colleges and universities. Without such institutions there would be no place in American education for academic instruction, reflection, research, and communication of revealed truth; there would be no place for the integration of religious practice in an academic community. There would thus be no academic protection of a core value in the American heritage — freedom of religion.

Academic instruction and, on the higher level, intellectual investigations without an opening to the transcendent and without a provision for a faith dimension, fall short of realizing the full potential of the human mind. To put it another way, a completely secular education is an incomplete education.

The very existence of church-related schools, colleges, and universities in our day needs fuller notice and wider appreciation. Their present existence, if recognized and appreciated for what it contributes to the preservation of freedom and pluralism in America will, of itself, make a very strong case for their continued existence. The preeminent contribution to be made by Church-related schools to the welfare of America at any time is a strong emphasis on moral values.

4. The human is the locus of divine activity. The Church of Christ takes a fundamentally incarnational view of the world. When God became man, all things human assumed a new worth, a deeper dignity. This is not to say they had no worth, no dignity, before the Christ event. It is merely to say that after Christ there is a faith-driven motive to show a reverence for the human by understanding it more fully.

The Church would therefore insist on the preservation and advancement of the humanities at a time when educators of no theological motivation and of shorter historical memory as well, might look expectantly but unreflectively only to the future. Since those educators, or at least their schools, would not normally and systematically direct the students' attention to God as Creator of the universe, as the ultimate source of our being and term of our quest, and as the Person who holds each human destiny in His hands, there is a danger that the well-trained but unreflective human mind may choose a future which God never intended for us. In the context of modern science and technology, such fateful choices could indeed be irreversible. Hence the Church, for love of all things human, would caution American education not to lose touch with the best thought of the best minds in the human experience.

And without retreating at all from its educational emphasis on words and numbers, the Church would remind American education of the importance of non-verbal imagery, of art and music and dance. By imparting the principles of aethetics, the schools prepare the developing person for life-long appreciation of the literary and non-verbal arts while encouraging some to follow the impulse — God given, in every instance — for creative expression in a particular art form. There is meaning to be discovered in all good art. There is meaning in some persons that will find expression only through good art. Education in an age of meaninglessness cannot afford to ignore the arts. The arts are important for the development of human potential and quite useful for containing the restlessness of the young. Both parents and educators know that art provides a convenient way for the young to run away without ever leaving home.

5. Education should encourage students to go beyond the Golden Rule. The Church of Christ, incarnational in vision, is quite literally founded on a New Commandment. The Old Commandment — "love your neighbor as you love yourself"

(Matthew 19:19) — is insufficient. The Christian is called to love others as he or she has been loved by Christ. Under the New Commandment, love of neighbor involves a willingness to lay down one's life for that person. And who is my neighbor? The parable of the Samaritan provides the answer. The Good Samaritan (a type of Christ) reaches out to a Jew, to a foreign national, to a person not of his own community. The "neighbor" is precisely the distant other, the foreigner, the stranger.

The Church would therefore look for a service orientation in all of its own students (in response to the New Commandment) and might expect all schools to encourage a service orientation in their students regardless of religious belief because the Church has a trans-national and cross-cultural notion of "neighbor." Global education, foreign-language study, intercultural understanding, service orientation, and an emphasis on the use of one's own education for the benefit of others, especially those in need, these are but several of the educational implications of the mandate under which the Church has always lived to go beyond the Golden Rule.

6. Good education will alter a student's attitude toward television, making it more tool than toy, converting it from a mirror on self to a window on the world. Television is often blamed for most of the shortcomings of contemporary education. Television is a given in the educational environment, particularly the out-of-school educational environment. In-school instructional television is useful for several reasons that lie unarticulated in the minds of the young. TV is a congenial medium of communication. It focuses the attention of the viewer. It commands respect, because to be "on TV" implies a special existence of unqualified importance and unassailable authority, a characteristic Walker Percy's "Moviegoer" calls "certification." All of this belonged without question, in an earlier age, to the classroom teacher!

But I am speaking here of out-of-school, recreational televiewing. To see someone you know "on TV" is more exciting than seeing that person in the flesh. To see someone known only "on

TV" in person usually serves as a curious verification process of that person's more authentic television existence. The TV screen has more than a little potential for value reversal!

Televiewing, particularly through the adolescent eye, invites both escape through the screen into fantasy, and inspection on the screen-functioning-as-mirror of one's magnified physical excesses or deficiencies. Prescinding from the question of who sets the norm, let it simply be noted that there is an exclusive emphasis on the physical. Thomas Wolfe caught the essential element of the problem in his pre-television comment about young women whose laughter "asked only the earth to notice them."

When held up as mirror, the TV screen exercises a tyranny on the young. Good education will free them of this tyranny. It will make them more secure, self-confident, and possessed of reference points that run deeper than glib advertising copy. It will equip them with sufficiently sound and critical judgment to ask, in the words of John C. Haughey, S.J., not "what does this ad invite me to buy?" but "what does this ad expect me to be?"

Converting TV from mirror-on-the-wall to window-on-the-world is an immediate question of program selection and a longer-range issue of program production. The schools are educating both the producers and consumers of tomorrow's television programming. Good schools will want to address themselves to this challenge today.

7. The student, not the material to be learned, is the subject in quality education. Schools, too often and too easily, treat students as objects and lesson content as subjects. Church-related schools have done this, although the Church would have it the other way around. The Church would remind the schools that boys are boys and girls are girls. They are not miniature adults. They are developing persons whose stages of development — physical, emotional, and moral — must be respected if the schools are going to make their proper contribution to the release of the full human potential that resides in each of these developing persons. The Church sees each person, in every stage of development, as unique. Each person, at every stage of development, is endowed with rights, dignity, and inestimable value. The patience of teachers will always be taxed, but the Church would require forbearance on the part of every teacher commensurate with the unique worth of each student-person.

Teaching methods should acknowledge that the lesson content as well as the various instructional media are for the student and not the other way around.

Economic pressures sometimes produce quantity education where students are objects and efficiency ratios measure everything. But depersonalization results and little learning takes place. Dependency and passivity are the immediate symptoms of an alienation soon to follow.

Economic forces must shift in the opposite direction to enlarge rather than constrict teacher effectiveness, to encourage rather than render impossible the individual attention the subject-student deserves.

8. Excellence is, in every instance, a relative term. To excel is to move or stand apart from a well-defined starting point. The pursuit of excellence begins with an accurate estimate of where one is in the educational process and a fair appraisal of what one proposes to do. A good school will take the students that it has, as they are. It will have a respect for the varying capacities of its students. It should include no one in its student body who does not have the capacity to carry the academic program it offers. If it offers no academic program, it can hardly be called a school, although it may well be a training center where the same idea of excellence would apply.

Given the baseline of academic admissibility, academic excellence is measured in terms of the development of academic potential, respecting in every case the unique characteristics and varying capacities of the students. There is no one in any school who cannot excel, because there is no one who cannot move forward from the position he or she has taken at the starting line. A simple assertion that "this is an excellent school," or "that is an excellent student body," or "there is an excellent faculty" is

280

meaningless rhetoric unless measured against a well-defined starting point and a clearly established goal. The educational process is dynamic. The excelling student body, the excelling faculty, the excelling school are attainable and desirable expressions of the idea that excellence is, in every instance, a relative term. In an excelling environment, there is no place for shoddy work although there is always room for improvement.

9. Schools are often expected to do too much. Parents are educators. So are grandparents, and coaches, and counselors, and librarians, and journalists, and physicians, and pastors, and those patient adults who provide after-school or vacation-time employment to the young. Skills — not only manual, but literary and scientific as well — can be learned through out-of-school relationships with significant adults.

It is worth asking, therefore, why we seem to assume in America today that the schools must do so much. It is at least worth a moment or two to reconstruct the school day in layers of importance, in terms of what the school is best able to do. This brings us back to words and numbers as the core of the in-school educational enterprise. It also invites a return to a secondary but not insignificant category of after-school, extra-curricular activities. Let matters of lesser but not unrelated value (band, sports, dramatics, debating, publications, clubs) not compete with the more important business of the school day. And on a spectrum ranging from prime-time academics to after-school entertainments, it would be a useful exercise to position, for purposes of discussion in these days of budgetary constraint, those courses that deal more with social, emotional, and physical adjustment than intellectual development. The Church would assign positions of priority to strict academic pursuits handled with academic rigor.

The question might be asked, "Whatever became of homework?," as personnel are assigned to supervise study halls during time periods that could be devoted to instruction.

Parents themselves are part of this problem. So are the teachers. I am not saying "culpably a part of the problem." Parents face great economic pressures. So do teachers. Limits hem them in. They can only do so much.

If teachers cannot supervise or moderate the after-school extra-curriculars, why not use volunteers or part-time employees? Must school-bus schedules control educational decisions? Is there no way to involve working parents in the in-school, after-school, or around-school educational process?

Those who expect too much of the schools are often parents who are unwilling to give more of themselves to the education of the young.

10. Education is expensive. Although the out-of-pocket expense for attendance at publicly supported schools is quite low, the cost of providing public education is high. Tax-paying Church members assist in meeting that cost. Although the price of independent church-related education is relatively high, the cost of providing that education is often low relative to costs in the public sector. Church members, some through dedicated and undercompensated service, others through voluntary contributions, keep that cost, high as it is, relatively low.

The Church, I suspect, would want to remind the American public — parents, teachers, elected officials, all citizens — that education is costly. Whether state-supported or privately financed, education is costly — valuable and costly.

Aware of both the burden and the benefit the First Amendment presents to church-related schooling in America, the Church asks for a fair solution to a very serious economic problem. Its schools help to preserve pluralism, safeguard freedom, and deepen values in America through an educational service marked by quality and completeness. Such service is costly. The Church, through its taxpaying members, helps to make the provision of costly public education possible. As a supporter of public education, the Church feels justified in calling upon policy makers and all who are interested in the preservation of freedom and pluralism through education, to find ways of easing the financial burden for church-related schools, thus activating the "free exercise" clause without violating the "non-establishment" clause.

Tuition tax credits are one possibility. Another is the educational voucher idea. Still another, to be discussed in chapter 30, would be what Neil Gilbert in *Capitalism and the Welfare State* (Yale, 1983) has called a "social credit." Any homemaker who elects to forego employment in order to devote full time to care of children from birth to age 17 would thereby earn a "social credit" for each of up to three children and the credit would be redeemable in the form of payment for the child's higher education. Under this proposal, instead of "working to put the kids through college," a parent could provide for their higher education by devoting full time to their care during the earlier stages of development.

If good education enhances the productivity of the American economy, I wonder why a case could not be made for granting "teacher tax credits" to those who provide that education in the same way that "investment tax credits" are offered as incentives to those who create jobs and enlarge the nation's productive capacity. I try to make that case in Chapter 29. A teacher tax credit would attract and retain good people in the classroom while easing the pressure for higher pay for teachers from their schools' (private and public) already strained funding sources.

Other ideas, practices, and policies are waiting to be tried. The Church would simply ask that they be examined and tested without prejudice. A viable church-related sector in American education is no threat to public schools. Without a viable church-related sector, the quality and completeness of education in America will be seriously diminished.

11. You do not have to be ill in order to get better. Education in America is not without problems to solve and challenges to meet. It is not, however, terminally ill; not even seriously ill. The Church, which organizes a community of believers into a people of hope, would look to the future of its own schools and to the future of all schools in America and say, "Let's get better together."

The Church would want to encourage development of a national consensus on the meaning of both education and schooling in America. The Church would make common cause with any group in America interested in the preservation of academic rigor and the protection of academic standards in American education. The Church would also recognize its share of the national responsibility to provide alternate training or remedial education for those who are unwilling or unable to make progress on a well-defined academic track. Based on its own experience in the classroom, however, the Church would not concede that the number of "unteachables" is unmanageably high.

Moreover, the Church would call upon parents to assume a fuller and more systematic share of the motivating-guiding-organizing-supervising responsibility that is part of teaching. The education of children is primarily a parental responsibility. Both church and state are on the record and in agreement on that important point.

Homework will be assigned if parents demand it. Homework will be done if parents require that it be done and check to see that it is. Study space (part of the organization of the learning environment) will be available at home if parents think the provision of such space is important.

Values, which are first communicated at home, will be communicated in school if persons of principle — persons of both competence and conscience — are in teaching positions in the nation's schools. The Church is willing to continue its work of attracting and educating talented professionals for service in the schools. In its own schools, the Church will encourage reflection on values, not only in light of a Natural Law ethic, but also in light of a tradition of systematic reflection on revealed truth.

To get better education in America without carrying values forward would represent a cultural reversal as well as a loss in both quality and completeness. Hence, if we are serious about getting better in American education, the Church would say we must get better together, because without the church-related sector, education in America will not be able to reflect upon and communicate a systematic understanding of the religious values which are part of the American heritage.

12. Central to the educational enterprise is the encouragement of sound reasoning. The cultivation of thought processes, the development of reasoning powers, and the provision of something worth thinking about are all central to the work of the schools. The Church has a long history of experience in dealing with these challenges. A contemporary expression of the problem the Church has been attempting to address through its universities and schools over the centuries is, as I have noted earlier in this book, Robert Bolt's insightful comment: "Both socially and individually it is with us as it is with our cities — an accelerating flight to the periphery, leaving a center which is empty when the hours of business are over."

It is certainly not an unreasonable expectation to look to the schools to begin filling what might otherwise remain an empty center in the developing human person. If filling up the center, which is the task of human development, is not seen by both teacher and student as the task of good education, real education will not happen. This is not to suggest that there is content waiting to be poured by dutiful teachers and passively received by compliant students. It does suggest that properly directed reasoning processes can enable the developing person to fill his or her empty center with knowledge and assimilated experience of lasting value.

It can be argued that the university is an invention of the Church. It is certainly true that the Church has encouraged structured learning and disciplined reasoning for many centuries. Twelve assertions add up to far less than the Church, in its realism and idealism, its wisdom and long experience, has to say to American education. Not all of what it might say is narrowly self-interested, and even when it speaks from self interest the Church is asserting a right to teach and thus assuring a place in American education for freedom, diversity, and pluralism.

The Church can speak to all the schools — elementary, high, and higher. It can speak to professional educators and to the many others who contribute to the development of human potential but do not think of themselves as educators. At every level and to all who will listen, the Church would warn that neglect of the life of the mind can only weaken America. It would be tragic irony indeed if efforts to revitalize education in America failed to assign highest priority to cultivation of the life of the mind. The Church, with its unparalleled involvement in education at every level, and with its own larger and central mission, can be forgiven for insisting to itself and the rest of American education that the work of education is uncommonly important. Education touches the potential for greatest growth in the human person and it reaches right into eternity.

27 New Partnerships

"If you think education is expensive," commented one harried educator to inflation-weary parents, "try ignorance!" The high social cost of illiteracy and the permanent economic disadvantages of inadequate schooling are obvious. Even more obvious is the fact that education at all levels is costly. Few would argue, however, that education costs are not worth meeting.

It is important to distinguish price and cost in any discussion of education. In public education, the price is low but the costs are high. In private education, the price is high but the actual costs are often lower than the real costs of public education. In each sector, a costly service is being provided. In neither sector does price cover cost. Subsidies are required in each instance — from taxpayers for public education, from financial contributors (and from teachers willing to work for lower pay) in independent schools and colleges. It is simply incorrect to say that private schools "cost more" than public schools. They are indeed higher priced and those who choose private schools, for religious or other reasons, must pay the higher price. This is a major concern and formidable challenge facing Catholic families in the United States today.

In American private education there is a strong and significant Catholic presence at all levels. The question facing Catholics today is how to maintain that presence. Their schools serve both

Church and nation. They deserve, and need, support from both. The Church is doing its part. The nation, particularly its government at all levels, should be doing more. And still more will have to be done both by committed Catholics and by various dispensations and devices available to a sympathetic government.

I know a Catholic parish in Kentucky which runs a tuition-free elementary school ("Why charge our parents at a time in their lives when they are least able to pay?" asks the pastor) by applying 60 percent (on the way down to 50 percent as parish giving increases) of parish income to school support. And this by general consent of the parish community.

In suburban Philadelphia, a tuition-charging parish school received in a recent year tuition revenue of $220,000 but faced costs of $670,000 despite very low teachers' salaries. I suggested to the pastor the possibility of finding eight wealthy parishioners each willing to endow a "chair" for a teacher in his parish elementary school. This would ease the strain on parish revenues, make higher salaries possible, and provide memorial opportunities for grateful parishioners who could afford six-figure gifts that would assure the continuation of Catholic education in the parish. Endowed chairs for elementary school teachers could be established by bequests of $100,000. The number of elderly parishioners capable of making such a provision is not to be underestimated. Neither is the size of the bequest. Where there is a *will*, there is a very effective way of establishing such chairs. We can no longer afford to defer questions about deferred giving to support parochial schools.

There are Catholic schools everywhere which operate openly under something of a Robin Hood ethic — charge full fare to those who can pay, give discounts and even free rides to those who cannot. The rich subsidize the poor. This should continue; it is simply a question of degree. How much is enough?

Catholic colleges, like independent colleges everywhere, look to alumni and friends for help in warding off deficits. Catholic secondary schools are doing the same. Catholic elementary schools can no longer afford to ignore their alumni, nor can they rely on raffles and candy sales for the delivery of needed supplemental revenue.

Catholics are generous and uncomplaining in their support of Catholic schools, but they deserve more relief than they are now getting as they struggle to keep Catholic education alive and well in this country. Here are some ideas which, if embodied in public policy, could ease the burden:

1) Educational Savings Accounts, with the same tax advantages as Individual Retirement Accounts, could encourage and reward savings for education.

2) IRAs themselves could be modified by law to permit early spending, without penalty, for the education of the IRA holder's dependent child. The price to be paid, of course, would be the loss of retirement income; the intent of the original savings plan would be frustrated. It should be noted that the new IRA — i.e., the post-April 15, 1987, product of the Tax Reform Act of 1986 — is both less deductible and considerably more complicated. Most of the revisions brought about by changes in the law are aimed at converting the IRA from being primarily a tax shelter to becoming a true retirement vehicle.

3) Education vouchers have been much discussed; they deserve a try. Proponents of voucher plans usually find the acoustics on Capitol Hill very poor. Why? Public school lobbyists have no enthusiasm for the idea.

4) Tuition tax credits are particularly attractive for elementary and secondary school parents, but they have not been successful in organizing the political will needed to make them a reality.

5) Another policy proposal, ill-timed perhaps in an era of yawning deficits in the Federal budget and reluctant tax reformers in city, state, and Federal legislative bodies, is the "double deductibility" idea. Parents with children in private schools complain of "double taxation," insofar as their taxes support public schools and their tuition payments support private schools. Is it fantasy to suggest that their tax-deductible donations to private schools (not tuition payments, just gifts) be given double deductibility? This would mean that a $100 gift could be listed as a $200 deduction.

New ideas are needed to answer the troubling question of how to pay for Catholic education at all levels. Parents, in exercising their rights as citizens, will have to convince the policymakers of the merit of their new ideas. As stewards of wealth, affluent Catholics will have to stretch a bit to endow Catholic educational efforts. Meanwhile, the religious communities and their dedicated lay colleagues will have to recommit themselves to, and recruit others for, the undercompensated but indispensable work of staffing the Catholic educational enterprise at all levels. Everyone in the Catholic community will have to subsidize the effort in one way or another. Without the subsidy, the enterprise will not survive.

There is, it seems to me, a present need for a new educational partnership between government and families in the U.S. I understand a partnership to be an arrangement where there is reciprocal influence and mutual dependency. The educational partnership I have in mind acknowledges that government depends on parents for education to happen, and families depend on government if their educational responsibilities are going to be met. Moreover, both government and families are each going to have to remain open to the influence (not the control, but the influence) of the other, if a workable educational partnership is to be maintained.

Catholic parents should influence their government's education policies; if they do not, they are not meeting satisfactorily their duties as citizens. Government policies should exert a positive influence on Catholic citizen-parents intent on exercising their parental right to educate and their citizens' right to assistance from government. Without such assistance, they cannot meet adequately their educational responsibilities toward their children (who, of course, are also citizens).

Many families fail on their side of the partnership equation because they make no effort to influence government. They have yet to learn the lesson contained in the Second Vatican Council's Declaration on Religious Freedom that "in matters religious no one is to be forced to act in a manner contrary to his own beliefs.

Nor is anyone to be restrained from activity in accordance with his own beliefs, whether privately or publicly, whether alone or in association with others, within due limits" (No. 2). The Council did not spell out those "due limits." They are there, of course. Religious freedom does not apply in an unrestricted way to religious practice, or to claims on government for subsidy in the area of religious education. It should be noted, however, that the issue of religious freedom arises in the political order, which is the order of human rights. Families should be active in the political order because it is precisely in and through that order that they find protection for their human rights, including the right of a parent to provide for the education of a child. Catholics will never discover the "due limits" on religious freedom in this regard unless families become more active in the policy arena pursuing workable forms of government assistance for Catholic education. As Archbishop Rembert Weakland put it in a February 5, 1987, address to the Wisconsin Assembly (the state legislature), although "no church should align itself with a political party," still "religious bodies do ask for the freedom to be themselves and to take part fully in the life of society without being discriminated against by legislation that would seem to exclude them."

Some educational legislation should exclude them, of course. There are "due limits" on what government can do. Moreover, the state may have a right to put a limit on religious practice on some occasions in the name of public order, of health, and safety. On the other hand, the state may have a right, well within limits set by First Amendment restrictions, to intervene positively in the name of the common good. Such positive interventions might take the form of policies that could ease the financial burden on families intent on providing a complete education for their children in a setting that is not completely secular.

Both "public order" and "common good" might be invoked to rally government support for parents who in turn want to support an educational effort which fits the following statistical portrait assembled by Dr. Alfred J. Lightfoot, professor of education at Loyola-Marymount University:

> 97% average daily attendance at Catholic schools as compared to 67% average daily attendance at public schools.

> 80% of Catholic school graduates go on to higher education while the drop-out rates in public schools such as Los Angeles fluctuate between 40-65% with a system average of 43%.

> 78% of Catholic schools provide basic in-service training on a yearly basis for its teachers as compared to the public schools average of 60%.

> 99% of Catholic schools and less than 10% of the public schools have a written statement of standards for student behavior which is given to each student and parent.

> 99% of Catholic schools have rules about student dress, prohibiting students from leaving the school grounds during class hours, and prohibiting smoking in or around school. In public schools, enforcement of any of these rules is virtually impossible.

These statistics both cheer the hearts and whet the appetite for government help on the part of families now sacrificing to preserve Catholic schools. But how do we know these percentages are precise? The fact is we really don't know very much, statistically speaking, about the relative merits of Catholic and public education in this very large country of ours. In 1867, then-representative, later president, James A. Garfield persuaded Congress to mandate the executive branch of our national government to report regularly to the citizens of our country on "the condition and progress of education in the several states and territories." In the spirit of partnership — reciprocal influence and mutual dependency — families should be calling on the Federal government, the only entity capable of the measurement task, to generate the data. Diane Ravitch argued well for this in the *Washington Post* on September 4, 1986, in an article deploring Federal neglect of "the collection of data, the conduct of research, and the dissemination of reliable information" about education in America.

Only the federal government has both the means and the capacity to determine how much and how well our children are learning; whether they have achieved the level of literacy necessary to function effectively in society; whether they are learning history and geography, science and mathematics, and how they compare with their age-mates in other industrialized nations. Only the federal government can sponsor national research to tell us about trends in the teaching force: How many teachers possess what kinds of backgrounds and qualifications? How many are teaching subjects they themselves have studied? How many teachers will be needed in the next decade?

Comparisons with schooling in other nations is always instructive. Such comparisons can generate agenda for two-way discussion between families and governments about education. The Soviets, for example, seem to be more serious than we are about science in the schools. All Soviet secondary school students take two years of calculus. The Soviet school year is longer than ours. And so many more Soviet students study English than U.S. students study Russian that mere mention of comparative data is an embarrassment in this country.

Behind all of this is rigid governmental policy enforcement on the Soviet side and parental unconcern on the American side. Our non-police state, democratic policy-formation process awaits the stimulus of widespread parental concern for more rigor in the classroom; more mathematics, science, and foreign language in the curriculum; and, indeed, more homework demands imposed on children by their schoolmasters (not a bad word to resurrect for our present purposes!).

Japanese schooling shows itself to be much more open to and dependent upon parental involvement than we might suspect, based on the relatively passive role for parents we have come to take for granted here in America. One important Japanese cultural consideration is enlightening in this regard. A recent U.S. Department of Education study, "Japanese Education Today," notes that in Japan, "the community's perception of a woman's success as a mother depends in large part on how well her children do in school." The negative, even destructive effects of too much parental pressure are obvious and to be avoided. But the positive benefits of reinforcement at home of the work going on, day by day, in school, are not sufficiently appreciated in the American family.

"The cultural environment is the significant factor in Japanese education," writes Dr. Merry White in *The Japanese Educational Challenge* (The Free Press). "If we want to borrow anything from the Japanese," she comments, "it is, paradoxically, the attention they devote to their own paramount cultural priority: the improvement of children."

In Japan, the mother serves as an auxiliary teacher, for all practical purposes. We might be amused to discover that the most popular home-study desk in Japanese households has both a built-in calculator and a buzzer to summon the child's mother for help and snacks! (See "Lessons the U.S. Could Learn" and "Why the Cultural Element is Key" in a special section on "Japanese Education," *The Christian Science Monitor*, February 8, 1987.)

There is indeed a need in America for a new partnership between families and government for the advancement of all education. Each side should be more open to influence from the other, otherwise no true partnership will emerge. Catholic families need not only to overcome some political reticence, but they, together with all other Americans, must raise education to a much higher rung on their ladder of political priorities. In Japan, adults (not just parents of school-age children) rank education very close to the top of their political concerns. As a consequence, average salaries for teachers in Japan compare favorably to those of private-sector professionals.

Despite all our rhetorical protests about the importance of schooling, both Catholic and public, in America, we seem unwilling to pay the price that good schooling requires. This brings us back to the point where the present discussion began. Catholic families need help from government to finance the Catholic education of their young. No one should presume that some such help is constitutionally or politically out of the question.

But Catholic families are also going to have to demand more from themselves — more of their own money, deductible or not, for their schools; and more of their own time in systematic, intensive, at-home involvement of parents with their children to reinforce, for more lasting results, the daily work being done in the Catholic schools.

All of this is applicable, of course, to the schools sponsored by other faith communities, to parents of all denominations who think church-sponsored education is important for their children. They enjoy First Amendment protection of the free exercise of their religious convictions. They should not timidly withdraw from engagement with their government on these issues simply because a misapplied metaphor (the "wall" of separation), which appears nowhere in the Constitution, has been used to deny them support that would be good not only for their children, but also for the entire nation. Secular forces, inimical to religion in American life, would disagree with that. This is no reason to concede, or to let those forces continue to carry the day.

New partnerships between parents and their representatives in government are needed to assure the economic viability of the education parents want their children to have. New working partnerships are also needed between parents and their learning offspring if the education available is to realize its full beneficial potential in the young. The stage is set for a challenging, but as yet unspecified "quid pro quo." More government help to parents; more parental involvement in the education of their youngsters. Both are necessary for better education in America.

28 Taxing Books for Better Libraries

Policy ideas inevitably stimulate discussion; policy ideas involving proposals to levy taxes can propel ordinary discussion into heated debate. I offered a policy idea on the op-ed page of the *Washington Post* in 1983 which generated immediate opposition from the publishing industry. It also failed to catch fire in the library community where "Slow Fires" is the title the Council on Library Resources, the Library of Congress, and the National Endowment for the Humanities have given their jointly-produced film documentary on the "brittle books" phenomenon, the crisis we face in preserving the written word. "What worries me," says Vartan Gregorian, then president of the New York Public Library, "is the *deliberate* indifference that exists toward this problem." The problem, as a promotional brochure for the film puts it, relates to the "deterioration and destruction of our world's intellectual heritage. Millions of pages of paper in books, pamphlets, photographs, drawings, and maps are disintegrating and turning to dust. The high acid content of most paper produced since the mid-nineteenth century has left us with a chronicle that, if not safeguarded, will soon disappear."

Not everything has to be preserved. It will be important to decide what must be preserved in page and printed form and where those portions of the human record should be held. But there is a lot more to it than preservation. Research libraries need funds to fit themselves out with the new technology in order to support productive and efficient scholarly research.

As a nation, we tend to forget to read the minutes of the last meeting.We value credit cards over library cards. Broadly speaking, we do not attach a whole lot of importance to libraries. Hence a proposal to put more of the people's money into preservation of holdings and reinstrumentation and modernization of libraries can expect to meet with indifference, deliberate or otherwise.

There was a highway bill, enacted during the first Reagan Administration, which added a levy of five cents a gallon on gasoline purchases in order to have more public money to spend on roads, bridges, and mass transit. Why not a nickel-a-book for research libraries, I wondered.

By imposing a five-cent tax on every gallon of gasoline sold, the Federal government expected to generate $5.5 billion annually for road repairs. The motorists would pay for better highways. Predictably, the trucking industry was unhappy, but all users, heavy and light, would benefit, and hundreds of thousands of repair-related jobs would be filled. Relaxed size and weight restrictions on trucks eased passage of the bill. Nickel-a-gallon became the law of the land.

Why muse over the possibility of a nickel-a-book for research libraries? There is no Federal library system to speak of. Such a tax would, some will certainly argue, pose a threat to freedom of the press (although the telephone excise tax seems not to impair freedom of speech). Others will ask, "What is a book?" Are pamphlets exempt? Will magazines be next? Isn't the tax regressive? Why raise the issue at all?

Our research libraries are in need of repair. Retrofitting for the new library technology is an even greater need. New equipment is necessary for the new information systems. Roofs, pipes, wiring, shelving, walls, and climate control require attention in most old libraries, of course. Construction and reconstruction jobs are waiting to be done; jobs would be generated.

But even if all our libraries were in perfect repair, a major unmet, and often unnoticed, capital need would remain. Scholarly periodicals can now be published electronically. Scholarly output will be stored in computer banks, not exclusively in printed journals. Users will often access the journal and the article by going to a terminal, not a shelf. Front-end capital costs of electronic journal depositories for scholarly output will be great. So will costs of placing terminals and display screens within reach of readers and researchers across the nation. The print-on-paper record will not disappear. Indeed, it presents the preservation challenge which must be met at great expense if the "slow fires" are to be brought under control. Preserving the old printed records of our civilization and implementing the new library technologies raise financial feasibility questions of mammoth proportions.

Publishers, already uneasy at the prospect of electronic journals, cannot be expected to hail the possibility of a nickel-a-book excise tax any more than the truckers welcomed the nickel-a-gallon on gasoline. The vast majority of book buyers, however, will follow the drivers in accepting the levy without protest. Revenues produced by this tax, if spent wisely on the improvement of research libraries, will guarantee that readers, researchers, and writers will have better resources in the decades ahead.

A Federal initiative toward the improvement of research libraries would be a welcome signal that Uncle Sam expects the nation to tip its hat, instead of tapping its head, in the direction of those who dedicate themselves to scholarly research.

The revenue raised should, in my view, be funneled to a capital-projects fund administered by a division of the National Endowment for the Humanities to be created for that purpose. Dollars in the capital-projects fund would not be part of the annual NEH appropriation; they would flow from the book tax although they could, if the Congress so decides, be supplemented by direct appropriations. The capital grants would, as I envision it, be awarded by NEH to competing research libraries. Definition of a research library would be the responsibility of NEH, as would the resolution of questions regarding eligibility of special-purpose research libraries.

Libraries are important for America's future. So is research. New ways are needed to meet the needs of library-based research. Laboratory-based research enjoys a higher priority with Americans and attracts far more public- and private-sector support. More voices need to be heard on behalf of libraries. More dollars — private and public — must be directed to meet this need. "Nickel-a-book" is one suggestion for getting the necessary dollar-flow going.

29 Teacher Tax Credits for Better Schools

Teacher tax credits represent a new idea for financially troubled U.S. education at all levels in both the independent and public sectors. Not tuition tax credits (an old idea without widespread political appeal), but teacher tax credits, designed to attract and retain good teachers in elementary, secondary, and higher education, public and private.

Education enlarges a nation's economic productivity even more effectively than investment in new plant and equipment. If the Federal government has noticed the possibility of encouraging enlargement of productive capacity by granting an income-tax credit to those who invest in plant and equipment, why should it not acknowledge the link between education and economic productivity by granting an income-tax credit to those whose classroom services transform students into more capable producers of goods and services?

Who would qualify for the credit? Any teacher, at any level, in any subject area, who had demonstrated his or her competence by completing five years of supervised and certified teaching service. The credit would be taken every year thereafter.

Although the idea looks directly to the Federal income tax obligation, it could also apply in those state and local jurisdictions which impose a tax on personal income.

The cost to government would depend, of course, on the value of the credit and the number of teachers at work in the nation's classrooms. By any count, the cost would be much less than that associated with tax credits to parents of children in school. The return to government would be measured by the conventional calculations of tax income generated by increased economic productivity.

Teachers who opposed tuition tax credits for parents of children in private schools are not likely to oppose tax credits for teachers. Public-sector teachers stand to gain, so do private-school teachers. And so do the schools themselves — private and public. They all need relief from the understandable pressure placed on their already strained funding sources by demands for higher teacher pay.

As the policy debate continues over merit pay, mediocrity, and educational outcomes, the world's best-educated nation should consider giving credits where credit is long overdue.

The teacher-tax-credit idea has the potential to become a political issue capable of gaining support from all educational interests in the U.S. As a new initiative, it could spark fresh cooperation between and among all the schools — lower, middle, high, and higher.

It is time to look for issues which will unite, not divide, the private and public sectors at all levels of education. Caught as it is on a rising tide of criticism, education in America is waiting for all the educators to come to some consensus on the purposes and goals of education itself. But instead of talking about education, they argue endlessly over money.

Alternatives to internecine feuds over funding in the academy must be found. Tax credits for teachers are not proposed as alternatives to existing forms of aid. They offer a remedy to an unappreciated and undercompensated profession as new and increased aid to that profession's clients, the students, is also on the public policy agenda. Also in the policy conversation will be the question of finding funds for educational facilities. But the faculty function is central to the success of the whole educational enterprise. So policy options designed to strengthen the economic security of the teachers deserve careful and sympathetic consideration.

Education is an investment, not a consumption expenditure. Those who provide education are not vendors (whose high volume sales net of expenses would be taxable income); nor are they fee-for-service professionals (whose high incomes net of expenses and protected by all available shelters yield high tax payments to Treasury). Those who provide education — the teachers — are low-salaried professionals who create the environment for investment in education to take place. They nurture its growth and guide it to maturity. Except for psychic income — the satisfaction derived from seeing youthful talent develop under one's tutelage — the teacher receives no return on the investment. The dollars invested (the costs of education) are not his or her personal outlays; hence the teacher has no claim on the appreciated value. The higher lifetime income earned by the educated person (the "finished product" or "mature asset" to emerge from the educational process) does not return to the teacher. All he or she has claim to is the agreed-upon payment for classroom work. That work can be described as fostering the growth of an income-producing asset — an asset to the national economy, an addition to the national stock of brainpower, an enhancement of the national supply of skill, and an enlargement of the national potential for productivity. The teacher does much more, but no more need be said to make the point that an enormous national investment takes place and appreciates because of what a teacher does, and yet no financial return on that investment accrues to the teacher who makes the investment possible.

The educated person receives a return in the form of higher lifetime earnings. The government shares in the return through higher tax revenues derived from higher earnings which are a function of more and better education.

The teacher-tax-credit idea provides a simple device to put a return to the teacher at the front end of the process. Without the teacher the process will not happen. The process is, in fact, now in trouble. It is experiencing difficulty in attracting and retaining superior teachers. Other nations with other systems pay their teachers better than we do in the U.S. We need not change our system — economic or educational — to strengthen our teaching ranks. We need only use our familiar, workable, and much-maligned tax-and-transfer system to reward teachers, at the front-end of the educational investment process, for the indispensble work they do.

30 An Idea in Search of a Policy

Parents in the United States have no economic incentive to care for their children at home. If that strikes no one as strange, it is only because our nation takes it for granted that economic incentives belong in the market place and other motives explain behavior at home. And so full-time care for a "priceless" child by that child's natural parent in a supportive home environment is unrewarded economically.

Those who know the price of everything and the value of nothing are, as Oscar Wilde so well said, cynics. What can be said of a nation that regards its children as priceless, but attaches no economic value to child care by the person best qualified to provide it? " Shortsighted" is the term we might use for the moment. Further reflection might prompt us to label as both unwise and dangerous the absence of national support for parents who want to be full-time homemakers.

The issue is complicated.

Children are our nation's greatest treasure, our most precious resource. In the vast majority of cases, children develop best in a stable family unit, in an environment of love — love of parents for each other, of both for the child.

Children need to experience parental love expressed in the form of presence. An attentive, affirming presence seems to work best.

And yet we know that parents are often left without partners. We also know that economic necessity frequently drives both parents into the labor market. Sometimes, a desire to give full stretch to one's talents encourages mothers for whom employment is not an economic necessity to step into the job market. (Our cultural presumption that fathers can enjoy that same full stretch only in employment other than homemaking remains unchallenged, even unexamined.) And then there are those mothers who go to work only for the sake of their offspring: to supplement the family income so that the youngsters can have more — more material things, more and better education, more developmental opportunities, but less parental presence.

Unfortunately, presence — or absence, depending on your point of view — is the coin in which the parent-child relationship pays the price for two-paycheck marriages, or for one-parent households where the parent is employed outside the home.

Well then, should homemakers be paid for their services? Not housekeepers, babysitters, day care providers, but homemakers — parents who choose to devote full time to the task of rearing children.

On November 24, 1983, The Vatican published a "Charter on the Rights of the Family." It is the product of worldwide consultation and a formal process of reflection and research that began in 1980. The charter speaks principally to governments. Article 10 declares:

> Families have a right to social and economic order in which the organization of work permits the members to live together and does not hinder the unity, well-being, health, and the stability of the family, while offering also the possibility of wholesome recreation.
>
> a) Remuneration for work must be sufficient for establishing and maintaining a family with dignity, either through a suitable salary, called a "family wage," or through other social measures such as family allowances or the remuneration of the work in the home of one of the parents; it should be such that mothers will not be obliged to work outside the home to the

detriment of family life and especially of the education of the children.

b) The work of the mother in the home must be recognized and respected because of its value for the family and for society.

Those "other social measures" lie, for the most part, undesigned and hidden in the imaginations of academics and social theorists. Government should be encouraging their development. Although the Vatican statement targets no specific purse from which homemakers' pay would be drawn, the only likely source is government.

Neil Gilbert's *Capitalism and the Welfare State* (Yale, 1983) proposes that the full-time homemaker receive a "social credit" for each year spent at home with children who are under 17 years of age. According to this plan, accumulated credits would either pay for higher education or entitle the homemaker to preferred hiring status in the Civil Service once the youngsters are raised and the parent is ready to enter or re-enter the labor market. Gilbert specifies the Federal government as the provider of this benefit which, like a veteran's benefit, would compensate the homemaker for time spent out of the work force but in service to the nation. In Gilbert's scheme, each unit of social credit (one per child per year of full-time care) could be exchanged for either "(a) tuition for four units of undergraduate academic training, (b) tuition for three units of technical school training, (c) tuition for two units of graduate education, or (d) an award of 1/4 of a preference point on federal civil service examinations." The parent is the implied beneficiary of the tuition grant in this G.I. Bill type scenario. The policy would surely be more attractive and effective if an option to designate the homemaker's child as the educational beneficiary were made explicit.

The "social credit" idea bars no parent, male or female, from opting for paid employment or professional activity outside the home. It doesn't even discourage outside work. It simply provides an incentive to parents who might prefer homemaking to labor market activity. It also answers the need of those parents who bring home the second paycheck just "to put the kids through college." Under this plan, they would stay home, accumulate the social credits, and eventually redeem them in tuition payments.

When the legislative imagination takes up this idea, as I hope will be the case before long, some constraints will have to be set. The first would be an appropriate family-income limit above which neither parent would be eligible. Those who do qualify could, if the policy so directs, be required to treat as taxable income the cash value of the credits exchanged for tuition. By keeping the benefit tax free, however, legislators would preserve for the beneficiary freedom of choice between independent and state-supported higher education. Spending the credits for tuition at the higher priced independent colleges would mean a higher cash value and thus more taxable income. Better to keep the benefit tax free.

It is conceivable that the eligible person who decides to be a full-time homemaking parent would soon become economically active at home. "Worksteading" is the new word for this. With the arrival of the "information economy" and the installation of computers and word processors in the home, the probability of more at-home paid employment rises sharply. Protection for the integrity of the social credit program could come from the Internal Revenue Service and would have to be written into the law. It would be easy to come up with an IRS device that would decertify from social-credit eligibility the homemaker who reports earnings above a relatively low limit specified in the law. Again, the economic incentive. In this case, the threatened loss of the credit would serve as encouragement to hold firm on the homemaking commitment in the face of attractive, remunerative at-home business opportunities.

The credits would, of course, be non-transferable from family to family. Some might argue for a limit on the number of credits one homemaker could earn (Gilbert suggests a three-child maximum), but sensitivity to parental freedom with respect to family size would be an important consideration in any public policy relating to the family.

The program would be more flexible, and thus more practical and attractive, if parents could alternate on the full-time homemaker responsibility. In effect, the parents would commit themselves, as a couple, to the provision of one full-time homemaker's services each year from the birth of a child until that child reaches his or her 17th birthday. This would open up the possibility for a mother (more often than not the mother will be the parent with full-time homemaking responsibilities) to work outside the home. There would be no loss of credit so long as the father personally provides the child care. It is worth noting that a shared responsibility for earning social credits through homemaking could promote cooperation over career competition between spouses in the modern marriage.

The value of the credit would best be expressed as a percentage of the cost of higher education — 100 percent of the cost of tuition, fees, books, room and board, regardless of the college chosen. The inclusion of other expenses that complete the so-called "cost of attending" (transportation, spending money) would be a matter of legislative choice. The point of specifying the percentage rather than an absolute sum is to relieve the parent of anxiety concerning the erosion of the credit by inflation and the consequent inability — 17 years later — to convert the credits into payment for tuition, fees, and books. It seems to me that one year's credit should be worth one-seventeenth of the price, at the point of consumption, of tuition, fees, books, room and board. The total "costs of education," as distinguished from "cost of attendance," would be completely covered in those cases where a child received full-time parental home care for the first 17 years of life.

The proposal is clearly intended to reinforce the nuclear family unit by rewarding a parent for remaining at home. As a policy idea, it will go nowhere unless there is widespread conviction that society needs the services of full-time homemakers.

Such persons need not be confined to quarters all day long. They would be free — free to be with their youngsters in a variety of at-home and out-of-home ways not possible at times for the busy parent burdened with a work schedule. The homemaker's schedule would focus on the child. It would promote parental presence — to the child. When one considers how such time might be spent, expressions like "creative leisure," and "shared learning" come to mind, as do thoughts of joint participation in arts, crafts, games, museum visits, sight-seeing "voyages of discovery" and similar engagements. School plays and athletic contests would attract more spectators. The schools themselves would be able to draw on a larger supply of volunteer service. As the nation deplores the condition of its schools, it should notice the promise this policy holds for the promotion of the life of the mind *at home,* a development which would be nothing but good for the schools.

This policy proposal is open to the criticism that it envisions a middle-class program that would be unavailable to the working poor who, credits or not, could not afford not to work. The criticism is quite fair. This proposal would not meet the needs of those who absolutely have to work. They demonstrate the power of economic incentives; many — by no means all, but many — would prefer to be homemakers. But to meet their needs (and to assist others who are less pressed for funds but most eager to combine careers and parental responsibilities) it is important to consider for inclusion in a national family policy measures that would encourage flexible work schedules, make daycare facilities more widely available, and childcare expenses more readily deductible.

In the following paragraph, Neil Gilbert speaks to an issue that will certainly be raised by many voices in this policy debate:

> For women who want a balanced family life and a full-time career, a family credit scheme would open a successive route along which both are possible. Because this route encompasses a 25-to-30-year period of employment, it may close off a few career options which require early training and many years of preparation. There must be some price for enjoying the choice of two callings in life. This is a different path from the continuous paid career line that men typically follow. It may be better.

I have tested the social credit idea in the op-ed forum and in conversations with friends. The strongest negative reaction chides me for trying to "bribe" people into childcare, "to shoehorn women back into the kitchen and/or the nursery."

The mother of two disabled sons applauds the idea: "The need for social reform to strengthen the family is so great that one would imagine that America as a nation and as a culture depends on the policy you advocate. It is indeed puzzling how an issue that is so fundamental — and so simply obvious — could have been overlooked for so long." The policy, by the way, might well allow for extra credits for homemakers serving handicapped children.

Endorsement of the idea also came from a middle-age male who describes himself as a "well-traveled parent who longs for more time in the home."

A public affairs director in a Federal agency offers a reflective comment which touches upon the crucial question of who will guide the formation of values in one's children.

> As a career woman who has been on both sides of the fence (I stayed home until the children were 10 and 14, and then joined the work force 10 years ago), I think your plan has merit. It seems to me that I have been extremely lucky — I was able to start a career later in life because of extremely hard work and fortunate circumstances. Not everyone is so positioned. I would not have wanted someone else "raising" my children and giving them different views on morality and philosophy from my own. Each parent wants to pass on his basic beliefs to his children, and it is impossible for young women today to do that if they see their child for one or two hectic hours a day.

R. Sargent Shriver, Democratic candidate for Vice President in 1972, called my attention to a speech he gave on "The Family" during that campaign. He repeated the maxim: What is good for families is good for nations; what hurts families, hurts nations. And he remarked that "the institution that has served human beings best and disappointed them least is the family."

A retired obstetrician, himself a father of eight, found the proposal to be "on target." In his medical practice, he said, he "was always well aware of the importance of a mother or parent in a home at all times with growing children; there can be no substitute."

Recently I talked with a 36-year old man whose educational credentials include a doctorate and a law degree. He has worked as a college professor, also as a lawyer. His *curriculum vitae* notes his full-time service as a "homemaker" for the past three years. His wife, also a lawyer, has been in the labor market while he cares for two young children at home. Another child was expected soon. With the birth of their third child, the lawyer-mother planned to remain at home as the professor-lawyer-father returns to paid employment in the market economy. Easy enough for well-educated professionals. But it only happens when parents regard it as important that their children have the full-time attention of one or the other throughout childhood.

Less well-educated parents are no less concerned about child development, just less able, for economic reasons, to consider full-time homemaking as a real option. If the option were available, it would be just that — an option, not an enforced condition. People would be free to take it or leave it, as their values and preferences direct.

We have no such option in the United States today because of the presence of economic pressure and the absence of a national family policy. The social credit idea addresses a policy vacuum. It surely deserves some discussion and debate.

31 Of Camps and Classrooms

"Rochester Asks Teachers for 'Extra Mile,'" according to a February 18, 1988, *New York Times* headline. The story reports the failure of the upstate New York community of 240,000 to educate poor inner-city children, and its plan to provide financial incentives that will "push the student-teacher relationship beyond the classroom, into the community." Essentially, the plan invites teachers "to accept increased accountability and responsibility." They will have a "personal responsibility" for a group of approximately 20 students for several years — this, of course, in addition to normal teaching duties. The newspaper account provides a statistical picture of the problem: "In a system with 33,000 students, 68 percent from minority groups, one in three does not finish high school. Twenty percent are absent at least one day a week. Among girls 15 to 19 years old, one in eight becomes pregnant each year, or almost 1,400 a year."

On January 25, 1988, the *Washington Post* headlined an experiment "Where the 3 Rs Stand for Rowdy, Rebellious — and Redeemable." The acronymn is PAUSE (Providing an Alternative Unique School Environment). The school, created by the school board of the District of Columbia in the wake of a widely publicized series of high-school drug raids in 1986, has had a difficult beginning and has met with less than modest success. It is, according to the *Post*, "filled entirely by students who have been nabbed carrying weapons, attacking other children, selling drugs, assaulting teachers, or simply disobeying virtually every rule of decent comportment."

Experiments like these are not to be dismissed lightly. But, in my view, they miss the point. They do not go far enough. They should eliminate the pretense that the classroom is the place for disconnected, disruptive youngsters whose development needs could be better served by a temporary relocation to a camp-like environment. The D.C. school building dedicated to the PAUSE program could be redesignated as a "camp." Sedentary moments would be rare in the camp environment. Supervised activity in creative urban experiences would be the daily routine. Individual achievement in camp-style, not classroom, activities would be the goal. The hope, of course, would be to generate achievements, one on top of the other, which would literally raise the sights of the achiever to a clearer view of the need for *academic* achievement in literacy and numeracy. Once this perception is clear — namely, that literacy and numeracy are the twin roots of achievement in a better and exciting world that need not remain closed to the camp-based achiever — then the youngster will be motivated to return to the classroom.

Curiously, the efforts of educators to prevent dropouts from school might become more effective if they encouraged, even mandated, dropping into a camp-like setting for awhile. This would eventually and effectively lower the dropout rate by substituting a stopout experience designed to build motivation to return to school. The hoped-for return mechanism would be a positive peer-pressure among the out-of-school "campers" to get back in the classroom in order to acquire the skills necessary for higher and more satisfying achievements. If academic achievers and non-achievers are forced to coexist in chaotic classrooms, the peer-pressure, sad to say, works in a negative direction. The achievers tend to pull back; overall classroom performance declines. Teachers quite literally run for cover.

The U.S. Department of Education's Office of Educational Research and Improvement published in 1987 *Dealing with Drop-*

outs: The Urban Superintendents' Call to Action. It represents the collective experience and reflection of the superintendents of 32 major urban public school districts with a combined enrollment of 4.6 million students. Six drop-out prevention strategies are offered: (1) Intervene early; (2) Create a positive school climate; (3) Set high expectations; (4) Select and develop strong teachers; (5) Provide a broad range of instructional programs; (6) Initiate collaborative efforts. There is virtually no room in these recommendations for a break-away strategy that would take the students out of the school setting altogether in the hope of building non-academic achievement while heightening motivation to return to school.

There is an obvious need for sensitivity to the needs of different age groups as break-away strategies are planned. Intensive "resuscitation" efforts in an in-school environment would clearly be preferred for younger children. But, whatever the strategy, both the effort and the environment should respect the feelings expressed by one dropout quoted in the Department of Education pamphlet: "I didn't like [the school]. I hated it there. It felt like a dummy zoo."

The urban school superintendents agree that parental involvement is crucial to keeping students in school. "Parents who encourage their children to succeed in school beginning in the early years exert a powerful influence over who stays and who leaves. Unfortunately, the bond between school and home is characteristically weak for potential dropouts." Camp has been used to reinforce the home for generations of children in America. It might be helpful in filling an obvious gap where the dropout problem is most pronounced.

Each year I am invited to a dinner in Washington honoring the 40 finalists in the Westinghouse Science Talent Search, an evening of recognition and reward for the nations's most gifted high-school science students. Each year I note the preponderance of Asian-American youngsters in the top ten. There are normally 40 tables in the hotel ballroom where this recognition-of-talent dinner takes place. One of the 40 winners sits at each table surrounded by adults from universities, foundations, the Federal science agencies, and similar organizations. Several years ago it was interesting to me to hear the reply of a bright and vivacious Floridian, not in the top ten, to a table-talk inquiry about what, if anything, she might have learned from the group of Asian-American youngsters (all ten gathered in front of the head table receiving handsome college scholarship awards) with whom she had spent those several days in Washington. "Wow," she said, "you wouldn't believe how hard their parents make them work!"

What if there are no parents to "make" their children work in school? What if there is no parental support for in-school disciplinary requirements? What if there is no parental reinforcement against peer-pressure to disrupt, to drop out? The U.S. Department of Education recommends heroic efforts on the part of teachers, counselors, and principals to contain the problem in school. I applaud those efforts, but I also have a feeling that this kind of containment policy will not work. All of us who are fortunate enough to have had a camp experience in our younger days would do well to reflect on the applicability of that experience to the challenge of conditioning our young people to want to remain in or return to school.

Mention "camp" to kids in school, and watch the surge of enthusiastic expectation. Mention "school" to kids at camp, and brace yourself for a deluge of disappointment.

Both reactions are quite likely to be stored in the memory of childhood experience of those who now set the policy for our nation's schools. Reflection on that experience suggests a policy alternative to our present system of schooling the young for personal fulfillment and productive citizenship.

Camp is a confidence-building experience. Most kids come to love it because they find there some competitive exercise in which they can excel, a craft or skill through which they can produce a measurable, portable, displayable result, and some victory over fear (going off the high-diving board, walking alone through the woods at night). Every camper returns home knowing more and feeling better — in ways that have nothing to do with fresh air, exercise, milk, or cookies. School, on the other hand, is viewed by children as more cage than camp. School need not be, but often is, a lead-pencil laboratory for the discovery of failure. Everyone is "marked," but not all are encouraged and, failure of failures, not everyone learns.

Children of white parents with higher incomes tend to score better on the Scholastic Aptitude Test (SAT), the exam that each year establishes a college-entrance credential for about a million high school seniors (the achievement-oriented, mostly from the eastern U.S.).Those are the same youngsters most likely to have enjoyed repeated summer camp experience in their earlier years. The low-income, minority students who may have had a poverty program, week-in-the-woods escape from the ghetto as a summer alternative to fire-hydrant surfing on city streets, are, with few exceptions, at the bottom of the SAT scorecard.

To what extent does the lower half of the SAT profile make the top half possible? That is a serious question of social justice requiring attention of both scholars and policy makers. To what extent are low-income, minority students, who could run a good academic race, being held back by the presence in school of other kids who ought to be in camp? There's another one for the policy makers, who really do not need the scholars to tell them that students will learn more under the direction of teachers not doubling as prison guards, and in the company of other students who are eager to learn.

Could it be that state laws mandating school attendance to a specified age are hurting the schools and the youngsters who want to learn? I think they are. Am I suggesting that the schools should clear the classrooms of unwilling and uncooperative learners and dump their problems on the streets? Clear the classrooms, yes; turn them loose on the streets, no. Simply send them to camp.

This could be the salvation of the public schools, particularly those large urban public high schools which, in many cases, have become warehouses of defeat and social malaise.

316

Residential camp? Day camp? Rural environment? Urban setting? Let the policy-makers work it out. Public education available to all who seek it, and accredited education for everyone up to a certain age, would remain a matter of public policy. The style of education would change for some, but only for a while in most cases. The camp experience should develop in the young a sense of worth, together with an internalization of a sense of entitlement to academic development. Thus motivated, they can return to school. The classroom door will be open always, and only, to those who want to learn.

In many school districts close to urban centers where the quality of public education is eroding fastest, teachers are facing layoffs and school buildings are being retired from service because of demographic declines. Why not re-employ both these resources, the human and the plant, in this alternate delivery of care and cultivation of young persons (the sort of thing the camps have been doing for generations)? Some teachers will need retraining, a nice alternative to unemployment. Other professionals — counselors, social workers, coaches — will find expanded employment opportunities in the camps. So will persons skilled in arts and crafts, and those prepared to manage not-for-profit organizations.

Will the camps reinforce racial segregation? No more than the schools do now. Will they have the effect of foreclosing academic advancement for minority youngsters? Transfer from school to camp could mean the end of academic training for some; but for those same youngsters it could mean the beginning of real, but non-academic, education. Others — most I would hope — would return to the schools after a confidence-building and maturing camp experience, even if that experience in alternate education took several years. That might mean graduating from an academic program a few years later than the expected age today. But a high school diploma that means something at age 19 or 22 is better than functional illiteracy through a long, unhappy, and unproductive life.

Finally, and typically in a discussion of this nature, the question will be asked: Can the nation afford both camps and schools? Of course it can. All we need is the political will.

Somewhere, and I would hope sometime soon, a courageous school board will bite the pencil. It will decide that its classrooms are open only to those who want to learn. The need for camps will then become apparent. The school board dedicated to the educational needs of all its young will find a way of providing alternate education, to those who need it, outside the classroom walls.

32 On Winning Games And Losing Perspective

The high school I attended provided a first-rate college preparatory experience. It required of all its students three hours of homework each night. Parents policed this requirement five nights a week; students grudgingly accepted it at home and boasted about it in weekend contacts with friends enrolled in less-demanding schools.

Our six-class-hour school days (we had no in-school study periods) added up to a 30-hour instructional workweek. Three hours of homework five nights a week gave us a minimum class-hour to study-hour ratio of two-to-one.

In my college experience, class hours decreased and the expected out-of-class study burden increased. This was spelled out during Freshman Orientation and printed in the *Student Handbook*. The normal ratio was the reverse of high school, two hours of study for each hour of class. Assuming an eight-semester minimum of 120 credits to meet degree requirements, the average college semester would have to contain at least 15 class hours. Add 30 hours of private study and you get an expected minimum study-time commitment of 45 hours per five-day workweek for those who were taking their academic responsibilities seriously.

As a Dean of Arts and Sciences many years later, I voiced the same expectation — two hours of study for each hour of class — whenever I counseled students or interviewed faculty.

My orientation talks to freshmen usually endorsed the "study budget" idea. Take a blank sheet of paper, draw lines to make seven vertical columns (one for each day of the week) and 24 horizontal slots (one for each hour of the day). Blacken those blocks (15 on the average) representing class time. Black out another 56 for sleep (eight hours a night). Take out another 14 (two a day) for meals and personal care. Give yourself at least two hours a day for recreation and you will have "spent" 99 hours a week before any of the remaining 69 hours (shown by the large areas of white space, particularly in the weekend columns) have been committed to out-of-class study, part-time jobs, non-athletic extracurriculars, or practice time associated with a varsity sport. Sixty-nine hours waiting to be budgeted.

As they look at their unspent weekly "wealth" of 69 hours, students have to be reminded of an important distinction between a spending-money budget and a study budget. Money not spent this day, this week or next, is there to be spent sometime thereafter. Study time not "spent" today or tomorrow simply isn't there to be spent in the future. Hence the cramming phenomenon so familiar to every student procrastinator.

As a dean and classroom teacher, I always advised students to commit themselves in advance to study hours, specific as to time and place, Monday through Friday, and marked in red on a study budget. Blocking out appropriate weekend reading and study time was also highly recommended as a safeguard against the recurring temptation to drop everything and run, at a moment's notice, because "I don't have class," or, "I'm free; I don't have anything to do."

This is all, of course, highly idealistic. But it is also quite instructive in providing perspective for a look at the proper ratio of study time to practice time for the student athlete.

Officials at most colleges and universities have a ready reply to inquiries about institution-wide student-faculty ratios. They can quote it by school, division, and even smaller academic units. Few could provide, and most would be embarrassed if they knew, the practice-hour to class-hour ratio for students participating in varsity sports.

99 to 1would be an unusual student-faculty ratio, to say the least. It would raise proper questions about educational quality (accompanied by admiring estimates of the institution's economic well-being). 1 to 1 would be equally unusual. It would echo President James A. Garfield's description of the ideal college as one with "Mark Hopkins on one end of a log and a student on the other." But the ratio would also signal impending economic disaster for the institution.

If Malcolm Gladwell is anywhere near the mark in reporting that "the typical college football player spends 49 hours a week during the season preparing for, participating in, and recovering from football games," it may well be time for presidents, deans, and other academic administrators to begin examining practice-time to class-hour ratios for their student athletes.

I am assuming reasonable adherence to a normal class schedule on the part of the student athlete. I am also assuming a curriculum sufficiently rigorous to justify its classification as higher education. Although 15 class-hours a week would be considered normal, I see nothing wrong with a reduced fall class schedule for football players if compensatory class hours have been successfully completed during the previous summer session. I have made no survey of the current situation but I am aware of one major football program which permitted players to take six hours in the summer followed by nine in the fall and 15 in the spring semester. That still seems reasonable to me, much more so than what I would regard as an unacceptable alternative of a compensatory fifth year of academic enrollment after the four years of playing eligibility have been spent. Reasonable adjustments for other major sports are also conceivable.

In any case, I want now to return to the 15 class-hour base for construction of a class-hour to study-hour ratio. Recall that two hours of study for each hour of class produced a 45-hour academic work week; the base is 15 hours of class a week. After allocating eight hours daily for sleep, two for meals, and two for relaxation, the five-day academic workweek can provide to the student-athlete exactly three hours a day or 15 hours weekly for practice. This 1 to 1 ratio, class-hours to practice-hours, is a Monday-through-Friday guideline. Weekends, of course, provide time for more practice, or more study, or both; not to mention time spent in weekend competition or weekend travel to and from the games.

It is not really necessary, for my present purpose, to try to separate out training time from practice time. Nor is it really important to distinguish time spent reviewing game films from time spent on the field preparing for the next game. The point is to take a look at total time devoted to an intercollegiate sport during a five-day academic workweek, and compare that with time spent in class and in class-related study. Those responsible for maintaining a balance between academics and athletics on their campuses might find ratio analysis useful.

This is not a matter for National Collegiate Athletic Association (NCAA) regulation. It is an issue of concern to administrators; not just academic administrators, but also for those administrators more immediately concerned with the supervision of athletes. Just as anyone serving anywhere in a college or university administrative staff might be expected to have a reasonably precise reply to an inquiry about the institution's student-faculty ratio (it appears in most recruiting brochures), so administrators might be expected to become familiar with the class-hour to practice-hour ratio on campus for the sport in season.

As I indicated earlier, 99 to 1 or 1 to 1 would be extreme and untenable guidelines for the quantitative relationship between students and faculty. No outside agency legislates or regulates an appropriate ratio in this regard. But any accrediting group and every academic planner has a sense for what is an educationally healthy and economically sound student-faculty ratio. That "sense" produces a workable guideline for a given institution.

The on-campus managers of higher education in America must fashion a similar guideline for the right relationship between practice time and class time. Special circumstances and special cases will always justify some deviation from what most would regard as normal. But no circumstance can justify a disregard of this important relationship. And no coach or academic administrator can pretend to be serving student-athletes and yet remain ignorant of, or indifferent to, the proper balance between classroom time and practice time during the five-day workweek within which the traditional teaching-learning transaction is expected to take place. "One-to-one" might be a useful opening quotation to begin both discussion and analysis.

But where will such discussion take place? All of the foregoing calculations emerged from "doodles" on my pad during a semi-annual meeting of the 44-member Presidents Commission of the NCAA. Organized in 1983, this body of 11 chief executive officers from Division III institutions, 11 from Division II, and 22 from Division I, has the simply-stated but difficult-to-achieve mission of regaining control of intercollegiate athletics from the coaches and athletic directors. It has proved to be a formidable task. Efforts on the part of the Presidents Commission to reduce the commercial and raise the academic interests associated with intercollegiate sports have encountered strong resistance within the policy-making arena known as the NCAA Convention. The presidents support no unified or comprehensive reform agenda. Nor do they have the political mechanism in place to move reform proposals to enactment in the full NCAA Convention. Forty-four presidents constitute a commission. Only a handful of them participate in the far larger convention debates and votes. Very few college and university presidents engage themselves at all in the process of NCAA policy formation.

During the January, 1988, convention, the *New York Times* headlined the news of a "Split in N.C.A.A. on Grades: Smaller Schools Vote Standards." The story concerned academic eligibility standards for Division I competitors. The Division I delegates voted to raise them, only to rescind the vote later in the day. Had the earlier vote prevailed, freshman athletes would need a year-end grade-point-average of 1.6; sophomores a 1.8; and juniors would have to present a 2.0 to be eligible for senior-year competition. Editorializing on the failed proposal, the *Washington Post*, under the headline "NCAA: Greed Wins Out," said, "the fact of the matter is that greed won out. Higher academic standards might mean that many star athletes would be ineligible to compete. That would mean fewer victories and smaller revenues."

There is big money in big-time collegiate sports, specifically in Division I football and basketball. The biggest program I know of, one that serves 600 varsity athletes, had a 1987-88 operating budget of $18 million. The average in Division I schools, with football programs, would be $9 million. Turnstiles and television receipts deliver large revenues. But those sources tend to desert the losers. Hence the widespread criticism, as the *Post* editorial put it, that the big schools "care only about two things — winning and money." Strange, though, that the sports pages remain largely uninfluenced by that editorial judgment.

How will the situation change? Can academics and athletics be held in balance at all levels of competition, in all sports? Permit me to suggest one possible change, a return to simpler days, that would represent a step in the right direction.

What if academic football ended its season each year on Thanksgiving weekend? "Academic football"? That's my label for the fall sport which is neither professional nor commercial; it is presumed to be part of the educational experience available to participants and observers under the auspices of accredited academic institutions. If academic football ceased at the end of November, student-athletes and student-fans would have more time for study — a consummation devoutly to be wished by those whose primary concern is the academic welfare of an entire student body.

In college, the fall semester typically ends in mid-December or just a few days beyond. Preparation for semester exams would not have to compete with practice, games, or travel, if the season ended in November. Student athletes would thus have better chances of maintaining the "satisfactory progress" toward graduation as encouraged by the NCAA rulebook. Other students would have institutional encouragement to put football in perspective and to express their own enthusiasm more in classrooms than grandstands as November yields to December.

Ending competition in November would return football to the status of a one-semester sport. For the sport to maintain single-semester status, of course, spring football practice would have to go. Strike another blow for "satisfactory progress," the academic advance the college is presumably there to promote. But let the season extend into January, and sound the call for practice every spring, and you will guarantee an uphill route for satisfactory academic progress.

Why does play continue long after the Thanksgiving turkey is gone? Championships. Commercial football has convinced us that it is not enough to come out on top of one's own conference, or league, or division. That achievement must be improved upon by post-season game after game until only a very few voices, without fear of contradiction, can proclaim: "We're Number One!" The commercial football culture has penetrated the collegiate ranks. As a result, academic football goes into overtime and academic progress suffers an inexcusable delay of the game.

To its credit, the NCAA Presidents Commission went on record in October, 1987, as opposing the idea of a Division I-A football playoff to determine a national champion. Not all of the coaches and athletic directors at the football-power schools agree with the presidents, but a floor vote at the January, 1988, convention set the proposal aside indefinitely. The convention is not yet ready for the question.

Bowl games and all-star contests will continue to keep some football heroes out of libraries and labs long after the fall foliage has disappeared. Only when "satisfactory progress" in the classroom outpoints post-season celebrity on the value scale of the campus community will academic football be back where it belongs — a fall sport capable of enriching a larger and higher educational purpose. Otherwise it will become an endzone in itself, trapping youngsters whose fumbled educational opportunities can never be recovered.

I think basketball should be just a one-semester sport. September, October, and November for football; January, February, and March for basketball. No basketball practice until after first semester exams in December. Outrageous? Only if athletics has priority over academics. Unlikely? Of course it is, and will remain so until the educators have control of all the programs on their campuses, including those which attract grandstand crowds and television audiences. Meanwhile, student athletes will remain caught — quite willingly and happily, I know — in a cultural contradiction that accepts games won and classtime lost as a fair exchange in what continues to pass for sport that is both amateur and academic. Neither is really the case in much of intercollegiate sport, where student-athletes are clearly exploited and educational opportunities are not.

Origins

Chapter 1 began in conversations in the late 1970s with members of the Policy Planning Commission of the National Association of Independent Colleges and Universities (NAICU). There was need, all agreed, for a "case statement" — something that would "make the case" for independent higher education to legislators, donors, parents, and prospective students. This chapter originated as a discussion paper for NAICU, evolved into "Pluralism in Higher Education," *America*, Vol. 153, No. 2 (July 20-27, 1985), and served as a text for a lecture given at Thomas More College, May 2, 1985. The need to "make the case" remains an urgent one today.

Chapter 2 echoes voices heard in every rank-and-tenure review on college campuses. These thoughts on the relationship between research and teaching were written for this book but pre-published in *Envoy*, an alumni magazine of The Catholic University of America, in Winter, 1987.

Chapter 3 originated in a convocation address delivered at the inauguration of the presidency of Daniel G. Gambet, O.S.F.S, at Allentown College of St. Francis de Sales; it appeared shortly thereafter as "Catholic Colleges: Why We Stay in There," *AGB Reports*, Vol. 21, No. 3 (May/June, 1979). Further reflection on the theme of Catholic identity in many conversations and several lectures evolved into the present chapter which first appeared as "The Religious Purpose of Catholic Higher Education" in *The New Catholic World*, Vol. 231, No. 1385 (September/October, 1988).

Chapter 4 is the 1989 Delta Epsilon Sigma Distinguished Scholars Lecture delivered at the annual meeting of the Association of Catholic Colleges and Universities, Hyatt Regency Hotel, Washington, D.C., February 1, 1989.

Chapter 5 was originally written to provide an interpretative framework for interested readers of late summer, 1986, news reports on the controversy involving Vatican officials and the Reverend Charles E. Curran, professor of moral theology at The Catholic University of America. It appeared as "Credentialed, Commissioned, and Free," *America*, Vol. 155, No. 4 (August 23, 1986), and was updated for presentation here.

Chapter 6 originated as an address which I, as dean, delivered to the faculty of the College of Arts and Sciences of Loyola University in New Orleans, at the beginning of the 1973 academic year. It was printed as "A Need for 'Principled Judgment,'" a Point-of-View essay in *The Chronicle of Higher Education*, Vol. VIII, No. 13 (December 17, 1973), reprinted in *The Congressional Record* (January 28, 1974), and both updated and revised for inclusion in this volume.

Chapter 7 began with a question from a group of honors students at the University of Seattle. Before arriving there to give the Lemieux Lecture in November, 1984, I received a request to meet with the student group on the morning after the public lecture to offer in a seminar setting my reply to their question: "What do you see as the most pressing issue our generation will have to confront over the course of our collective lifetime?" My back-of-the-envelope jottings in Seattle developed into commencement addresses in 1985 at Walsh College, Canton, Ohio; Fu-Jen University in Taipei, Taiwan; and College Misericordia, Dallas, Pennsylvania. Fuller development of my response became "Christian Values and Critical Issues," *The Journal of Contemporary Health Law and Policy*, Vol. 3 (Spring, 1987); a revised version constitutes the present chapter.

Chapter 8 is a paper, revised with the benefit of participant discussion, first delivered at a conference of student-life administrators from Catholic colleges and universities who met at Barry University in Miami on January 4, 1989.

Chapter 9 was published as "Structure, Programs, and Persons: Old Designs for Renewed Campus Ministry," in P. Bernard Shaw, O.S.A. (Ed.), *Empowered by the Spirit: Campus Ministry Faces the Future, A Commentary* (Merrimack College Press, 1986). Many of the ideas in this chapter were sharpened from question-and-answer sessions following presentations I made to meetings of campus ministers in Stroudsburg, Pennsylvania, and in Madison, Wisconsin.

Chapter 10 contains reflections developed for and with many groups in numerous seminars and lectures. This version is a revision of my Rightor Lecture at the Law School, Loyola University of New Orleans; it was published as "Ideas and Images of Justice," *Loyola Law Review*, Vol. XXVI, No. 3 (Summer, 1980).

Chapter 11 originated in a presentation I made to religious educators of the Tampa-Clearwater-St. Petersburg, Florida, area in 1974. It developed into "Education, Reconciliation, and Social Justice," *Religious Education*, Vol. LXXII, No. 3 (May-June, 1977), "Education for Social Justice — A Christian Perspective," *Occasional Papers on Catholic Higher Education*, Vol. IV, No. 2 (Winter, 1978), and other essays and lectures up to the present chapter.

Chapter 12 comes out of my long involvement with Bread for the World, a Washington-based Christian citizens' lobby focused on the problem of world hunger. I first connected "bread and blackboards" in a presentation made at Villanova University in 1978; this chapter is a paper I delivered as a keynote address at a conference on Issues in International Food Security at Colgate University in June of 1988.

Chapter 13 contains elements of an essay written at the invitation of David M. Johnson for inclusion in the book he edited for Orbis, *Justice and Peace Education: Models for College and University Faculty* (1986).The chapter was shaped by many discussions and question-and-answer periods following lectures I delivered in many academic settings.

Chapter 14 is rooted in remarks I offered at undergraduate honors convocations at the University of Dayton and Cabrini College. It was published as "Liberal Learning and the Future of Families," *America*, Vol. 142, No. 23 (June 14, 1980) and reprinted under title of "Preparing Youth for Marriage," *USA Today*, Vol. 113, No. 2478 (March, 1985).

Chapter 15 has roots that run deep to my experience as Dean of Arts and Sciences at Loyola of New Orleans. Some of the ideas outlined here were presented by me to the Academic Senate of the University of Scranton during my presidency there. The chapter, however, was written for this book and pre-published in *CUA Magazine* (January, 1989).

Chapter 16 originated in a paper delivered at Santa Clara University in 1983 on the occasion of the dedication of the Leavey School of Business.

Chapter 17 draws from talks given to high school parents and teachers groups. With reaction from teachers and parents factored in, an earlier version of this chapter was published in the journal of the National Catholic Education Association, *Momentum*, "Reconnecting Teenagers with Their Parents," Vol. XVIII, No. 3 (September, 1987).

Chapter 18 stems from a talk I gave to the Washington, D.C., chapter of the National Association of Accountants (October 17, 1984); in abbreviated form it appeared as "Four Funds for the Future" in Peat-Marwick's newsletter *Management Issues* (March, 1986).

Chapter 19 was first a lecture to the faculty of Mary Baldwin College, later a planning background paper for faculty of The Catholic University of America, and appeared as "Needed: Good Managers in Academic Divisions" in *Change*, Vol. 16, No. 7 (October, 1984).

Chapter 20 began as a response to an invitation to address a meeting of Catholic health-care providers in 1981 on "Catholicity and Creativity in the Collective Bargaining Process." The Catholic Health Association was concerned about questionable practices emerging across the country to discourage unionization in hospitals. My experience with collective bargaining at the University of Scranton first started me thinking about the generation of options for improved faculty compensation. Much of this chapter appeared as "Collective Bargaining in Catholic Institutions," *America*, Vol. 146, No. 4 (January 30, 1982).

Chapter 21 originated as an honors convocation address at Wheeling College in 1974. Subsequent experience and reflection shaped my thinking on this perennial problem on the way to my statement of the question in its present form.

Chapter 22 is a revision of "The Purpose and Nature of Leadership," *New Catholic World*, Vol. 223, No. 1337 (September-October, 1980). Thoughts about this topic, coupled with the continuing tension between management responsibilities and leadership opportunities, are on the minds of most academic executives most of the time.

Chapter 23 expresses a long-held personal conviction that no one who is well educated will also be involuntarily poor. Ideas in this chapter were first organized for a lecture at Fairfield University in 1986 and later published as "Poverty and Power: Schooling Can Spell the Difference," *America*, Vol. 154, No. 14 (April 12, 1986).

Chapter 24 deals with a policy issue I first thought about as a beneficiary of the G.I. Bill after World War II. Subsequent thoughts on this topic found their way into print as "Morality, Necessity, and the Common Good: An Ethical Reflection on Compulsory National Service," *Current Issues in Catholic Higher Education*, Vol. 1, No. 1 (Summer, 1980). The same basic ideas found alternate expression in "To Give Our Youth Purpose: National Service," *The Philadelphia Inquirer*, December 7, 1980, and "Of Drift and the Draft," *The Scranton Journal*, Vol. II, No. 3 (Winter, 1981). Much of the same thinking was offered by me as testimony before a Congressional Committee in 1983. Because then Massachusetts Senator Paul Tsongas was proposing National Service legislation in 1982, I took that topic for the commencement address I delivered at Anna Maria College in that state in that year.

Chapter 25 began in a casual conversation with Charles L. Schultze, President Carter's chief economic adviser, who pointed me in the direction of the recommendations concerning student financial aid made more than a decade earlier by the Zacharias Commission. The present chapter evolved through many more conversations, several seminars, and a project organized by Lawrence E. Gladieux, Executive Director of the Washington office of the College Board, who included my essay, "Neither Grant nor Loan: New Ground for Federal Student Aid Policy" in a College Board book he edited, *Radical Reform or Incremental Change* (1989).

Chapter 26 is an amended version of my Seton-Neumann Lecture, sponsored by the United States Catholic Conference, December 5, 1983. It was published in *The Living Light*, Vol. 20, No. 4 (June, 1984) and reprinted in the magazine *USA Today*, Vol. 114, No. 2482 (July, 1985).

Chapter 27 is a response to an invitation to address the 1987 annual convention of the National Catholic Educational Association in New Orleans. Program planners asked me to address the need for "A New Educational Partnership Between Government and Families." The paper appeared under that title in *America*, Vol. 156, No. 22 (June 6, 1987).

Chapter 28 stirred up some anxiety among Washington lobbyists for book publishers when it appeared in summary form on the op-ed page of the *Washington Post* (February 3, 1983) under the title "A Nickel-a-Book Tax?" The anxieties were not allayed when the essay was reprinted two weeks later in the Congressional Record. Nothing much has happened since, even though the problems of research libraries have grown worse.

Chapter 29 entered the policy debate through the op-ed page of *The Philadelphia Inquirer* on January 17, 1984. The idea of teacher tax credits is a simple, direct, and affordable way to help both public and independent schools attract and retain quality teachers.

Chapter 30 began as a *New York Times* op-ed essay, "Reward Parents at Home," January 5, 1985; expanded into "Paid Homemaking: An Idea In Search of a Policy," it appeared in *USA Today*, Vol. 113, No. 2470 (July, 1984), and has generated much discussion but no action on the firing lines of public policy.

Chapter 31 outlines an uncomfortable idea which began in a conversation with a lawyer friend about the origin of laws requiring compulsory school attendance up to a specified age. I first tested the notion of separating problem students not simply from public classrooms but also from public schools in "Send the Nonperformers to Camp," *The Philadelphia Inquirer*, January 17, 1984.

Chapter 32 comes out of my experience since 1984 as a member of the Presidents Commission of the National Collegiate Athletic Association (NCAA). Organized with the hope of regaining control of intercollegiate athletics from the coaches and athletic directors, the Presidents Commission has an understandable interest in maintaining a balance between academics and athletics. This chapter expands my article "Athletes Need Help in Managing Time," *The NCAA News*, Vol. 23, No. 42 (November 24, 1986). It also draws on "End College Football in November," *The Philadelphia Inquirer*, November 11, 1987.